D0900167

# Do Justice and Let the Sky Fall

## Elizabeth F. Loftus and Her Contributions to Science, Law, and Academic Freedom

# Do Justice and Let the Sky Fall

## Elizabeth F. Loftus and Her Contributions to Science, Law, and Academic Freedom

*Edited by*

**Maryanne Garry**
*Victoria University of Wellington*

**Harlene Hayne**
*University of Otago*

LAWRENCE ERLBAUM ASSOCIATES, PUBLISHERS
2007 MAHWAH, NEW JERSEY LONDON

Lawrence Erlbaum Associates, Inc., Publishers
10 Industrial Avenue
Mahwah, New Jersey 07430
www.erlbaum.com

Cover design by Tomai Maridou

*Front cover photo*: Members of the Institute for Mathematical Studies in the Social Sciences at Stanford in 1967. *First row*: Lester Hyman, Richard Atkinson, Ed Crothers, William Estes, Gordon Bower, Harley Bernbach. *Second row*: Unknown, Richard Shiffrin, Unknown, Steve Link, Elizabeth Loftus, George Wolford. *Third row*: Gordon Allen, Unknown, Unknown, Unknown, David Rumelhart. *Fourth row*: Ken Wexler, Rich Freund, John Brelsford, Leo Keller. *Fifth row*: Mike Clark, David Wessel, Peter Shaw, Don Horst, Dewey Rundus. Members not pictured include Pat Suppes, Guy Groen, Bob Bjork, Dave Wessel, Gary Olson, Bill Batchelder, Hal Taylor, Joe Young and Jim Townsend.

**Library of Congress Cataloging-in-Publication Data**

Elizabeth F. Loftus : contributions, to science, law, and academic freedom / edited by Maryanne Garry, Harlene Hayne.
p. cm.
Includes bibliographical references and index.
ISBN 0-8058-5232-8 (cloth : alk. paper)
1. Loftus, Elizabeth F., 1944-2. Psychologists—United States—Biography. 3. Memory. I. Garry, Maryanne. II. Hayne, Harlene.
BF109.L64E452006
150.92—dc22 2006013766
CIP

Books published by Lawrence Erlbaum Associates are printed on acid-free paper, and their bindings are chosen for strength and durability.

Printed in the United States of America
10 9 8 7 6 5 4 3 2 1

*Dedication*

*For Devon, and for all the ducklings (MG)*

*For Mike, Marea, and Sara (HH)*

# Contents

Preface ix

Contributors xiii

1 Memory Distortions: Problems Solved and Unsolved 1
*Elizabeth F. Loftus*

2 Tracking the Birth of a Star 15
*Gordon H. Bower*

3 Elizabeth F. Loftus: The Early Years 27
*Geoffrey R. Loftus*

4 Misinformation Effects and the Suggestibility of Eyewitness Memory 35
*Maria S. Zaragoza, Robert F. Belli, and Kristie E. Payment*

5 Loftus's Lineage in Developmental Forensic Research: Six Scientific Misconceptions About Children's Suggestibility 65
*Stephen J. Ceci and Maggie Bruck*

**6** Verbal Recall of Preverbal Memories: Implications for the Clinic and the Courtoom 79
*Harlene Hayne*

**7** Illusory Recollection in Older Adults: Testing Mark Twain's Conjecture 105
*Henry L. Roediger III and Mark A. McDaniel*

**8** False Memories 137
*Deryn Strange, Seema Clifasefi, and Maryanne Garry*

**9** Incorporating Elizabeth Loftus's Research on Memory Into Reforms to Protect the Innocent 171
*Jaqueline McMurtrie*

**10** Elizabeth F. Loftus: Warrior Scientist 193
*Mahzarin R. Banaji*

**11** The Cost of Courage 199
*Carol Tavris*

Author Index 215

Subject Index 225

# Preface

This is a book about a scientist who turned her little corner of science upside down. Usually this is the part of that book where we would explain her One Big Idea, show you how it runs through all the chapters, introduce you to the variety of research that flows from the One Big Idea, and—ultimately—ask you to think about how that body of research can make the world a better place. As scientists, students, or professionals in allied disciplines, we would all be happy to have a book like that about us, our most significant contributions, our Big Idea.

But this is a book about Elizabeth Loftus, someone who seems to have had One Big Idea after another. For more than 30 years, Beth has walked around kicking the props out from under some of the sturdiest platforms in science, law, and academia.

In January, 2005, many scientists and students gathered here in New Zealand for a celebration of Beth's career. The all-day celebration was not a festschrift, at least not in the traditional sense, because Beth is not retiring. She would also be the first to tell you that festschrifts mean that you're old, and she's not old. Instead, that event—the "Bethschrift"—was really a way to honor someone who has done so much and sometimes paid so high a price.

So this book, then, is not that kind of festschrift book. Beth herself was adamant that this book not be one of those "boring books, with essays that nobody ever reads, sitting on your shelf gathering spider webs." It is, we hope, a working text, something that challenges, intrigues, and inspires established scientists, emerging scientists, graduate students, lawyers, and health professionals. This is a multipurpose volume. It is a collection of state-of-the-art research in theoretical and applied areas of human memory, an overview of the application of memory research to legal problems, an introduction to the costs of doing controversial research, and a chance to get to know one of the most important psychological scientists a little better as a person.

Beth gives us a sketch of her career in her own chapter (chap. 1), and from the excerpts of interviews with her, which are woven throughout the book. The remaining chapters color in that sketch.

In chapter 2, Gordon Bower tells us that right from the beginning, Beth rejected the popular topics of the day. She had no desire to work on abstract problems, preferring instead to tackle real-world ones. According to Bower, even in her earliest scientific endeavors Beth relied on "creative experimental methods to investigate novel, important questions in naturalistic field settings," especially when other scientists seemed not to have any good ideas about how to approach those same problems. Soon, says Gordon, Beth's creativity "opened the door for the stampede of other experimenters...following her innovations."

And a stampede there was. To hear Geoff Loftus tell it (chap. 3), studies poured forth from Beth's lab "one after another like waves on a beach," showing that memories go awry in systematic and predictable ways. He also tells us that Beth was not satisfied with stirring up a revolution in psychology; she began messing with the conventional wisdom in the field of law, too.

In chapter 4, Maria Zaragoza, Robert Belli and Kristie Payment review one of Beth's earliest contributions: the misinformation effect. The misinformation effect, which they describe as "one of the best-known and most influential findings in psychology" is the finding that feeding people inaccurate information about an event they witnessed can lead them to say they saw things they did not. Zaragoza et al. also make the often overlooked point that work on the misinformation effect is important in understanding the more recent issue of false autobiographical memories, a topic covered in depth in chapter 9.

Although Beth's research has been almost exclusively on adults, it has had tremendous influence in the field of children's memory. We learn about that influence in chapters 5 and 6.

In chapter 5, Stephen Ceci and Maggie Bruck review research on child suggestibility, with an eye to disabusing readers of the notion that we have identified the problems and fixed them. Ceci and Bruck show how Beth's paradigms have been launching pads for developmental researchers trying to understand issues of special significance for children in the courtroom.

Chapter 6 is the bridge between childhood and adulthood, at least when it comes to memory. Harlene Hayne, who specializes in memory development, recalls how she was influenced by one of Beth's landmark papers, "The Reality of Repressed Memories," from a 1993 issue of the *American Psychologist*. Hayne identifies a fundmental assumption among proponents of recovered memory therapy: that if we really can recover our very earliest memories, then at some point we must be able to translate our preverbal memories into verbal ones. Her review of the research shows that infants and very young children can remember their experiencces, even after over long delays. However, as they get older and acquire language, they do not seem to be able to convert those preverbal memories into a verbal report.

Reporting research on the other end of the human lifespan, Roddy Roediger and Mark McDaniel (chap. 7) discuss memory distortions in older adults. Some of that research adopts Beth's methods, while other research fits squarely alongside the body of work Beth has accumulated. They show that compared to young adults, older adults are less likely to remember past events, but are more likely to remember events that never happened. Roediger and McDaniel also examine whether various neuropsychological tests can identify differences that are related to these memory distortions.

In chapter 8, Jackie McMurtrie—a law professor and Director of the Innocence Project Northwest—shows how Beth's work has helped to identify one of the leading causes of wrongful convictions: errors in human memory. The idea that DNA evidence will safeguard us from wrongful convictions based on these errors is only partly true. DNA testing never would have done much to help the 43 adults from Wenatchee, who were arrested on 29,726 charges of child sexual abuse involving over 60 children.

Deryn Strange, Seema Clifasefi and Maryanne Garry (chap. 9) review one of the most contentious psychological issues in recent times: repressed and recovered memories. Beth's professional introduction to the topic came when she testified in the George Franklin case. Franklin stood trial in California, accused by his grown daughter of murdering her best friend dozens of years earlier when they were both children—a memory she claims to have repressed and only recently recovered. Despite Beth's testimony about there being no scientific evidence for the notion of repression, the jury convicted Franklin anyway. And Beth began working in earnest, trying to understand what might be going on when people claim to have recovered a memory for a horrible, long-ago event. She pioneered a line of research that, in less than a decade, helped to slow the seemingly endless parade of civil lawsuits, unravelling families, and dangerous therapists.

The last two chapters are decidedly more personal, and put a human face on a person who is portrayed by her enemies as being something close to the Devil's offspring. The first of these chapters (chap. 10) is Mahzarin Banaji's heartfelt tribute to her mentor. It captures Beth—the many faces of Beth—better than anything ever has: Warrior, scientist, rockstar, mentor, friend. Students, find a mentor like the one you read about in this chapter....but maybe one who can cook. In the second of these chapters (chap. 11), Carol Tavris shows us what can happen when scientists find a wrong and try to right it. Or even write about it. Academics often talk about the need for academic freedom and the importance of having essential protections in place for those who do unpopular research that annoys others. But how many scientists take that right—that *gift*—and study something that really shakes people up? And how many scientists would respond to nasty letters, phone calls, emails, lawsuits, illegal investigations and so on by keeping on doing the very thing that shakes people up? Too few of us, sadly. Yet Tavris reminds us that Beth's fights are our fights, too. As the Romans said, *do justice and let the sky fall.* Do what is right, regardless of the personal and professional consequences.

This book would still be sitting in a file drawer in a "Cool ideas" folder if it were not for people at Erlbaum like Lori Stone, Nicole Buchmann and, of course, Larry Erlbaum. We are indebted to Sophie Parker, our local assistant editor and project manager, for helping to chase the cornflakes around in the bowl, to Matt Gerrie and Vicki Lea for creating the indices, to Deryn Strange and Julien Gross for being our fresh eyes on new drafts, and to Elizabeth Connell for her prodigious editing skills. And of course, we are grateful to Beth Loftus for giving us her time, her photo albums, her wine, and most of all for having the kind of life that we could turn into a book.

*—Maryanne Garry*
*—Harlene Hayne*

# Contributors

**Mahzarin R. Banaji**
Department of Psychology
Harvard University
Cambridge, MA USA

**Robert F. Belli**
Department of Psychology
University of Nebraska–Lincoln
Lincoln, NE USA

**Gordon H. Bower**
Department of Psychology
Stanford University
Stanford, CA USA

**Maggie Bruck**
The Department of Psychology
and Behavioral Sciences
Johns Hopkins Hospital of Medicine
Baltimore, MD USA

**Stephen J. Ceci**
Department of Human Development
and Family Studies
Cornell University
Ithaca, NY USA

**Seema Clifasefi**
Addictive Behaviors Research Center University
of Washington
Seattle, WA USA

**Maryanne Garry**
School of Psychology
Victoria University of Wellington
Wellington, New Zealand

**Harlene Hayne**
Department of Psychology
University of Otago
Dunedin, New Zealand

**Elizabeth F. Loftus**
Psychology & Social Behavior
University of California, Irvine
Irvine, CA USA

**Geoffrey R. Loftus**
Department of Psychology
University of Washington
Seattle, WA USA

**Mark A. McDaniel**
Department of Psychology
Washington University
St Louis, MO USA

**Jaqueline McMurtrie**
School of Law
University of Washington
Seattle, WA USA

**Kristie E. Payment**
Department of Psychology
Kent State University
Kent, OH USA

**Henry L. Roediger III**
Department of Psychology
Washington University
St Louis, MO USA

**Deryn Strange**
School of Psychology
Victoria University of Wellington
Wellington, New Zealand

**Carol Tavris**
Los Angeles, CA USA

**Maria S. Zaragoza**
Department of Psychology
Kent State University
Kent, OH USA

*Q:* So, what did you want to be when you grew up?

*Beth:* Oh, gosh, I don't really remember. . . . I mean it was later I sort of thought I might want to be a stockbroker or a private detective, you know, briefly maybe an astronaut. See, my model was my mother really, who had been a librarian and was now a housewife. So I thought, really, most of the time I thought I was going to just have a normal family and be somebody's wife. For a while I thought maybe I would marry some important man and make the dinner parties.

I do remember that I was always very good at handwriting. When I'm just sloppy on the credit card or whatever, it's awful, but I can have perfect handwriting. You know, my third-grade teacher told me that my handwriting was like a dream. So, that was the first thing I really think I excelled in.

CHAPTER

1

# Memory Distortions: Problems Solved and Unsolved

Elizabeth F. Loftus

It never stops feeling strange when I read about myself. I sometimes feel like I'm Beth, reading about some woman I don't know who happens to be named "Elizabeth F. Loftus." It happened again recently when I picked up a book by science writer Morton Hunt titled *The New Know-Nothings* (Hunt, 1999). There she was, that woman, leading off Chapter 9:

> Elizabeth Loftus never supposed, when she tried a little experiment on her students in an undergraduate psychology course many years ago, that it would profoundly change her life, steering her onto a track that would lead her to fame ... and on which she would find herself deluged by hate mail, vilified by fellow professionals, and defamed in the media and on the Internet. (p. 263)

Hunt rightly noted that I was one of a number of contemporary experimental psychologists who uses the scientific method to demonstrate that human memory is malleable. He mentioned the professional success and comfortable lifestyle that accompanied these accomplishments. And he commented repeatedly on the downside. "Loftus has made a host of angry, vindictive, and often aggressive enemies who have tried to discredit her findings, besmirch her reputation, and harass her in an effort to force her to abandon her research ... " (p. 264).

These kinds of things didn't seem to happen to William James, who had intuitions about false memories a century ago. "False memories are by no means rare occurrences in most of us," he said in *Principles of Psychology* (James, 1890, pp. 373–374). "The most frequent source of false memory is the accounts we give to others of our experiences. Such accounts we almost always make both more simple and more interesting than the truth" (pp. 373–374). James had intuited a basic truth about memory, but it was a truth that not everyone wanted to hear.

## A LIFE IN MEMORY

For more than three decades, I've been soaked in the study of human memory. Growing up, I never for a moment thought I would be a scientist studying the fickle creature of memory. Mostly I thought I would stay at home raising a family, just as my mother had done when she gave up working as a librarian after marrying my father, a workaholic physician. Before settling on psychology, I considered the possibility of becoming a mathematics teacher and briefly flirted with the idea of being a private detective or a stockbroker. I was almost through graduate school before I had an inkling that memory would be the field for me. It was even later that the specific problem of the malleability of memory would take center stage.

## FINDING A PROBLEM TO SOLVE

I first delved into the malleability of memory back in the early 1970s, at least a couple of years after receiving my PhD. Until then I had done research in graduate school on a totally different topic (computer-assisted instruction) and completed a doctoral thesis titled "An Analysis of the Structural Variables That Determine Problem-Solving Difficulty on a Computer-Based Teletype." It was about how adolescents solve mathematical word problems, which problems are more difficult to solve, and why (Loftus, 1970). I managed to publish the work with my thesis adviser (Loftus & Suppes, 1972), but computer-assisted instruction never captivated me the way memory distortion would.

While working on my thesis, I began another project on semantic memory. I studied how people reach into their long-term memory storage and produce appropriate answers to questions. When asked, "What is the name of an animal that begins with the letter *Z*?" people are extraordinarily fast to find a correct answer, "zebra." When asked for a "fruit that is yellow" they have no problem coming up with "banana" in 2 seconds or so. How do they do it? With thousands and thousands of facts stored in memory, how do they find just the one so quickly? Analyses of the response times to these simple questions revealed a great deal about how human beings organize information into concepts or categories within long-term memory (Collins & Loftus, 1975; Loftus & Freedman, 1972). I was captivated by this problem for a few years.

But studying accurate and fast memory retrieval would give way to a budding, then blossoming, interest in erroneous memory retrieval. It happened serendipitously. I had lunch with my lawyer-cousin Laurie who said, "So, you're an experimental psychologist. Have you made any discoveries?" "Yes, "I proudly said. "I, and my former professor, discovered that people are faster to give you the name of a "fruit that is yellow" than they are to give you a "yellow fruit"—faster by about a quarter of a second." Laurie seemed less than impressed. Her response was sarcastic, something along the lines of, "So how much did we pay for that result?"—a reference to government funding of scientific research.

It was that conversation that got me started thinking that I would really like to study something that had more obvious social relevance. I had always had an interest in legal issues and cases and, with a background in the area of memory, the idea to study the memory of witnesses to legally important events such as crimes and accidents seemed to be a natural fit. As luck would have it, one of my former professors from Stanford had gone to work in Washington, DC, for the U.S. Department of Transportation. "There's money in accidents," he told me. And so I wrote a grant proposal to secure funding for a project studying the memories of witnesses to accidents. Whereas other researchers were studying memory for words or numbers or nonsense syllables or other simple objects, I borrowed 16-mm films from the local traffic safety council and police departments and studied subjects' recollections of filmed traffic accidents. I showed the film, then quizzed the subjects on what they saw, but I altered the wording of the questions slightly from subject to subject. I found that by wording the questions differently, I could transform the subjects' memories of what they saw. For example, when I asked how fast the cars were going when they "smashed into" each other, the subjects consistently remembered higher speeds than when I used the word *hit*. These studies showed that the words you use in a question could affect the answer someone gives you. Moreover, just changing a single word or two in a question can sometimes have a sizable effect on the answer, changing the recollection from one in which a driver behaved legally to one in which the driver exceeded the speed limit.

One day, I stumbled onto a greater effect. The wording of a question could not just have an immediate effect on a witness's memory—it could have long-range effects. The wording of an initial question could affect the answers to questions that were posed later, often much later. Consider what happened to subjects who were asked the "smashed" or "hit" question about the speed of the vehicles in a simulated accident. A week later they were asked whether they saw "broken glass." Those who had been asked the "smashed" question were far more likely to claim they'd seen broken glass, even though none existed (Loftus & Palmer, 1974). This was my earliest indication that the initial leading questions were contaminating memory in a profound way.

I began to see the leading questions that altered my subjects' answers as just one means by which this could happen. Leading questions were a vehicle for communicating information to witnesses, but they were only one vehicle. It could be done by feeding a witness the version of the event as told by another witness, or by exposing witnesses to mistaken news coverage about a previously seen event. In all of these ways, the potential to contaminate a witness's recollection was there.

## PROBLEMS SOLVED

Over the next 20 years, this research area flourished as many innovative researchers joined the collective scientific adventure. Thanks to their efforts (and some of mine), the world now has a sizeable body of published research showing that new, postevent information often becomes incorporated into memory, supplementing and altering a person's recollection. New "information" invades us, like a Trojan horse, precisely because we do not detect its influence. This body of research showing how memory can become skewed when people assimilate new data typically utilizes a simple three-part procedure. Subjects first witness a complex event, such as a simulated crime or accident. Subsequently, half receive new and misleading information about the event. The other half get no misinformation. Finally, all attempt to recall the original event. In virtually every study done using this paradigm, those who had not received the phony misinformation had more accurate memories. Large memory distortions have now been found in hundreds of studies, involving a wide variety of materials. People have recalled nonexistent broken glass and tape recorders, a clean-shaven man as having a mustache, straight hair as curly, and even something as large and conspicuous as a barn in a bucolic scene that contained no buildings at all. In short, misleading postevent information can alter a person's recollection in a powerful, even predictable manner. The phenomenon became known as the "misinformation effect" (Loftus & Hoffman, 1989).

## MEMORY PROBLEMS IN THE REAL WORLD

After having spent a few years doing these laboratory studies, I had a craving to see how they related to real witnesses of real events. I had recently moved to the University of Washington, and one of the few people I knew in the area before moving was the chief trial attorney at the local public defender's office, Phil Ginsberg. He was working at the time on a case of a woman, I'll call her Sally, who shot her boyfriend after a violent argument. She had indeed shot the boyfriend, but she said it was self-defense. In exchange for allowing me to watch the various phases of the case involving the witness testimony, I volunteered to educate Phil about the findings of psychological science that might be relevant or helpful to his case. Sally was ultimately acquitted of murder. I thought Sally's story, and the role of psychology, might make an interesting article, so I wrote one for *Psychology Today* magazine, which titled the article "Reconstructing Memory: The Incredible Eyewitness." I wasn't too crazy about the artwork because it reminded me of *Ripley's Believe It or Not,* but the content of my article was fine. I managed to incorporate a number of my recently published studies, such as the "smashed" versus "hit" results, showing the malleability of memory. The circulation of the magazine was quite large (over a million at the time) and, before writing the article, I was unaware that so many judges and lawyers read the magazine, but would soon learn that they did. After "The Incredible Eyewitness" was published (Loftus, 1974), lawyers began calling to see if I would help them on their upcoming cases. Other lawyers, and then judges, called to see if I would give continuing-education lectures about eyewitness testimony and its implications for the legal system. I began lecturing every summer at the National Judicial College—a program for state-level judges at the University of Nevada.

And thus began a new phase of my professional life—consulting for the legal profession. I became involved in the court cases and the cases became material for my classes; students loved the true-crime connections. Research ideas came whenever a case posed a question that I could not answer. Studies and their publication led to more interest in the psychological aspects of eyewitness testimony. I met some notorious people in the process—Ted Bundy, the Hillside Strangler, the Nightstalker. I also met people about whom I was so convinced of their innocence that it kept me up at night. Steve Titus, accused of rape; Tim Hennis, accused of murder; Clarence Von Williams, accused of rape; Howard Haupt, accused of murder. I told some of these stories in a book called *Witness for the Defense,* coauthored with Katherine Ketcham, who was, for a time, working as a secretary for me. Now she is a very successful nonfiction writer (Loftus & Ketcham, 1991).

## BIGGER MEMORY PROBLEMS

I spent more than a decade trying to unravel the misinformation effect. I had so many questions: Are we all equally susceptible to the misinformation effect or are some of us more susceptible than others? What are the conditions under which people are especially susceptible? When people give a misinformation response and claim it as a memory, do they really believe it is true? And, the trickiest of all, once the misinformation is injected and accepted, what happens to the original memory? Hundreds of experiments involving tens of thousands of human participants helped to provide some answers.

But at some point, to tell the truth, I started getting a little bored with the misinformation effect. Gathering with friends one New Year's Eve, we wrote our resolutions on little slips of paper and put them into a box to be opened the following year. Mine said something like "I want to carve out maybe a third of my time and do something totally different." A year later, when I opened that little slip of paper and read the previous year's resolution I thought, "How sad, I didn't do it." I took the piece of paper, added the phrase "This time I really mean it," and put it back in the box to be opened the following year. And the "something different" serendipitously came to me. My research would take a new turn in the early 1990s and that turn was prompted by an unusual court case that fell into my lap.

I got a call from Doug Horngrad, an attorney in San Francisco, who had a most unusual case. Doug had been a public defender and so had had lots of trial experience. He was now in private practice, where he acquired even more experience, including murder cases. But he'd never had a case quite like the one he was handling. The case involved a man named George Franklin, who was accused of murdering 8-year-old Susie Nason back in 1969. Franklin was accused of raping and murdering Susie 20 years earlier based on the testimony of Franklin's daughter Eileen, who claimed she witnessed the crimes in 1969 and repressed her memory for two decades. I began to search for evidence that the mind could repress years of horrible brutalization because Eileen had also claimed years of sexual abuse committed upon her by her father that was also repressed. I was shocked to find that there was no credible scientific support for this hand-me-down Freudian notion. Despite the lack of support, the jury bought into Eileen's story (bolstered by mental health professionals), and they convicted George Franklin of murder. They were so persuaded that they found him guilty after only a day of deliberations. And Franklin became virtually the first American citizen to be convicted of murder based on nothing other than an allegedly repressed and de-repressed memory (see Loftus & Ketcham, 1994, chap. 6, for a detailed description of the Franklin case).

After the conviction, Eileen Franklin went on television talk shows. She published a popular book about her horrible father. Her story was aired in a made-for-TV movie. Occasionally I was asked to appear on the talk shows to tell "the other side." On one such occasion, I was invited to appear on the Oprah Winfrey show to discuss Eileen's case. I flew to Chicago the day before my birthday, and at 10 p.m. that night I received a call from the producers saying that Eileen and her supporting psychiatrist were refusing to appear if I were allowed on the stage with them. I was given two options—sit in the audience and be able to speak for a minute or two, or go back home. I decided a minute or two was better than nothing to get an important message across. (Oprah did feel bad about this, and after the show offered me the use of her limousine and lunch at a restaurant she owned. A sort of "sorry" and sort of "birthday" peace offering.)

Public appearances on Oprah and elsewhere were almost certainly responsible for my receiving hundreds of letters and phone calls from desperate parents who also found themselves accused of recently "de-repressed" abuse. "One week before my husband died after an 8-month battle against lung cancer," wrote one woman from California, "our youngest daughter (age 38) confronted me with the accusation that he had molested her and I had not protected her. This has broken my heart; it is so utterly untrue." Thousands of people would find themselves facing these sorts of accusations; hundreds if not thousands also faced civil lawsuits against them filed by their alleged victims.

In the midst of trying to help some of these individuals, I would also realize that if I wanted to talk about memory distortion on the same page as a discussion of experiencing years of rapes, at the very least it would be useful to know that one could do more than turn stop signs into yield signs, or make people believe the bad guy had curly hair instead of straight hair. Would it be possible to plant entirely false memories into the mind of someone, making them believe in all their heart that they had seen or done something that never happened. Of course to attempt this experimentally, one had to be very cautious; you couldn't plant memories of sexual abuse by a relative—for ethical reasons. But perhaps we could find something else that would have been at least mildly traumatic if it had happened. But what should it be?

## "LOST IN THE MALL"—A SERENDIPITOUS IDEA

I spent hours over months with graduate students tossing around possible ideas, never quite satisfied with what was on the table. In between these brainstorming sessions, I periodically went off to give a talk at some other university, and on one such occasion it happened to be the University of Georgia. I gave my standard talk on the misinformation effect but let the audience know that I was searching for a new experimental method that would allow me to plant the seed of an entirely false memory and to watch it grow. I wanted it to be traumatic, but not so traumatic that the experiment would be considered unethical. It was on the way back to the airport that the idea came to me, as I have described in *The Myth of Repressed Memory* (Loftus & Ketcham, 1994, p. 93). I got a ride from the cognitive psychologist Denise Park, who brought along her kids Rob and Colleen. "How about getting lost?" Denise asked. "At that moment we happened to be driving past a huge shopping mall, which provided that sudden burst of inspiration—"What about getting lost in a shopping mall?"

I came back to the University of Washington excited to meet my Cognitive Psychology class and present them with their next assignment. I instructed them "to go out and try to create in someone's mind a memory of an event that never happened." I told them they could try to convince a roommate that she had chicken last night instead of hamburger. Or they could try to convince a relative that he owes you money and it's time to pay it back. I had given that same assignment most years, and it was one the students really loved. But this year I included a slight twist. I told them I'd been wondering about the possibility of planting a whole memory for a fictitious event, such as making people believe they got lost in a shopping mall as a child when in fact that had not happened. One student, Jim Coan, was enthralled by the idea, and tried it out on his 14-year-old brother Chris. Through several suggestive interviews, Jim managed to convince Chris that he got lost at the University City shopping mall in Spokane, Washington, and that he was eventually rescued by an elderly man, possibly wearing a flannel shirt, and reunited with the family. Chris eventually came up with a memory for this made-up event. His memory even included a rescuer with a blue flannel shirt, glasses, and a balding head with a ring of gray hair. He remembered crying and his desperate mother saying "Don't you ever do that again!"

Listening to the tapes of Chris talk filled me with amazement. I became convinced that we had an idea here for a formal experiment, and this anecdote showed that it would likely be possible to experimentally plant an entirely false childhood memory. And that such a memory might be very detailed.

The formal "lost-in-the-mall" study used a procedure whereby subjects were given short narratives of childhood experiences ostensibly obtained from their relatives. Over several weeks these people were encouraged to try to remember the events. All but one of the narratives was true; one was a made-up event about being lost for an extended time, at age 5 or 6, in a specific shopping mall or public place, and eventually rescued. In this first study, about a quarter of adults fell sway to the suggestion and adopted the belief. Some went so far as to dramatically embellish their reports (Loftus, Coan, & Pickrell, 1996; Loftus & Pickrell, 1995).

People attacked this study before it was even published. Getting lost is so common, they said. How dare you compare getting lost to being "sodomized by one's father?" (The critics frequently, for some reason, expressed their attacks in such colorful dramatic language.) This prompted other investigators to try to plant false memories of events that would have been far more unusual, bizarre, painful, or even traumatic if they had actually happened. And so over the next few years, experimental subjects all over the world were convinced by various research teams to believe that they had been hospitalized overnight or that they had an accident at a family wedding (Hyman, Husband, & Billings, 1995). They were led to believe that they had nearly drowned and had to be rescued by a lifeguard (Heaps & Nash, 2001). They had the suggestion that they had been victims in vicious animal attacks or serious indoor or outdoor accidents (Porter, Yuille, & Lehman, 1999) planted in their minds. In short, they developed very rich false memories, replete with details and expressed with confidence.

Of course it is a rather strong form of suggestion when you tell someone "We've talked to your mother and she says this happened." Could false beliefs and memories be planted with more subtle suggestion? I and others found that a variety of techniques, such as guided imagination, dream interpretation, exposure to the stories of others, and false feedback, could all lead people to become more confident that they had experiences they almost certainly had not had. People even came to believe that they had experienced events that would have been rather implausible (like witnessing demonic possession) or impossible (like meeting Bugs Bunny at Disneyland). (See Loftus, 1997, 2003a, for descriptions of some of these studies.)

## MORE REPRESSED MEMORIES

Back in the legal world, after thousands of people had been prosecuted or civilly sued by alleged victims, a new type of case cropped up. A number of women began to realize that their memories were false and had been planted by psychotherapists. They sued their former therapists for malpractice. And more than a few accused parents fought back in another way: They sued the therapists for planting false memories in the mind of their now-adult children. One memorable case that I worked on involved accusations against a winery executive, Gary Ramona, whose daughter had sued him after she recovered memories of being raped by her father for a decade, from the ages of 5 to 16. Her memories came out through individual and group therapy, as well as sodium amytal, the supposed "truth serum." After Holly sued her father, he, in a separate action, sued the therapists and the hospital for planting false memories in Holly's mind. He was awarded $500,000 by a California jury, but his life was in ruins. He had lost his family, his house, and his job in the ordeal.

The Ramona story has been told in a fabulous book titled *Spectral Evidence* by an investigative jurnalist Moira Johnston (Johnston, 1997). As the book jacket reveals, it is "the definitive report on the 'recovered memory wars' that have raged through America's families, the courts, and the scientific community for most of the decade." It went on to describe the case as one of a seemingly perfect American family

> destroyed when a daughter's "flashbacks" of incestuous rape by her father turned to accusations and lawsuits—and of the explosive landmark trial in Napa Valley that gave a father, for the first time, the right to strike back legally at the therapists he believed had planted false memories of sexual abuse in his daughter's mind.

Frederick Crews, Professor Emeritus from Berkeley, described the book as "a gripping, masterfully told story" and praised Johnston's "keen insight into both the domestic discontents that form a breeding ground for illusions and the intolerance that can turn a community into a kangaroo court." It was about this time that some insurance companies issued warnings to mental health professionals that they would not be covered if they practiced repressed-memory therapy.

The Ramona case was one of many tragic life stories in which faulty assumptions about memory played a role. It has been a privilege for me to work on these cases, while simultaneously being involved in the wonders of scientific discovery. But life has not always been easy living through the Memory Wars. A woman once recognized me on an airplane and shouted "You're that woman!" while trying to swat me with her newspaper. A prosecutor once called me a whore under his breath in a courtroom hallway. Grown academics tried their hardest to get speaking invitations to me rescinded. Some organizations were threatened with lawsuits. Occasionally, armed guards had to be hired to accompany me at university lectures where I had been invited to speak.

The worst situation I could imagine came after I looked into a bogus case history and attempted to help a mother whom I believed was falsely accused. After the accusing daughter, Jane Doe, lodged a complaint, my former university put me under a dark cloud of investigation and gagged me for several years. Although eventually exonerated of any wrongdoing, I left the university, my friends, and a house with a sweeping view of Lake Washington. And, it might sound odd, but I sadly left the café where I drank morning coffee with friends for more than a decade. I turned down the university's counteroffer, and moved to sunny Southern California for a great job at the University of California–Irvine. At UCI, I found wonderful colleagues, great friends, and a little house in the faculty ghetto surrounded by professors of sociology, dance, and mathematics. And I just found a group that has coffee together every Saturday morning at a local dive. I published the exposé of the case history, hoping to put it to rest (Loftus & Guyer, 2002a, 2002b), and I got back to work. I was feeling pretty lucky to have a life filled with the pursuit of interesting scientific questions. I devised some new studies to show that when a false belief or memory is planted in the mind, it has repercussions for later thought and behavior. When our subjects were led to believe that they got sick eating hard-boiled eggs as children, they don't want to eat eggs so much later on (Bernstein, Laney, Morris & Loftus, 2005). This means that false memories can have long-range consequences.

But the enemies had not forgotten me for a moment. In 2003, Jane Doe filed a lawsuit suing for invasion of privacy and defamation. We had never once revealed her name and yet she sued under her real name, thereby guaranteeing that the world would know who she is. She sued my coauthor, Mel Guyer, and our colleague, psychologist Carol Tavris, whom we had thanked in a footnote for her help with our article. And so we three psychologists join others who have been sued for speaking out about matters of great public controversy (Loftus, 2003b). Harassment of scientists can be a strong impediment to others, who might think twice about publishing legitimate findings on controversial topics. That would be most understandable. The harassment I have suffered has been psychologically painful, and sometimes I can't help but think: Was this all worth it? But the thought is fleeting: I just can't seem to stop lecturing, publishing, or presenting research evidence in lawsuits involving innocent people. Pursuit of truth and knowledge is too important for a democratic society, no matter whether the truth is controversial or just plain ordinary. I've chosen to put up with the costs.

I had a burst of inspiration after a visit one sunny Sunday afternoon to the magnificent Franklin Delano Roosevelt Memorial in Washington, DC. Roosevelt's powerful words call out from the walls of this memorial. It was in the latter years of his presidency, as America was preparing for war, that Roosevelt spelled out his "Four Freedoms," intending to remind citizens of what we must fight for: freedom of speech, freedom of worship, freedom from want, and freedom from fear. Based on my experiences, I believe we need to be reminded that there is a fifth freedom that we cherish in our open society: freedom of advocacy. Although I am primarily a scientist studying the science of memory, that scientific work has occasionally led me to be an advocate, particularly when I think someone is falsely accused. If a political scientist wants to spend weekends at voter registration drives among the poor, or a biologist wants to spend summers working for the Sierra Club, I sincerely hope they will not be subjected to the kind of harassment that I experienced over the last few years.

I'm often asked, "How do you manage to put up with all the harassment heaped on you?" One trick that works for me is to relish those occasional letters and e-mail that come from appreciative people. I save them in a "When Blue file" and return to them often.

Arriving amid the slings and arrows, these messages have meant so much that I am including a few here. Perhaps readers of this chapter will take the time to send something similar to individuals they encounter who are facing difficult challenges as a result of taking a stand on a matter of great controversy.

This one came in 1996, from a woman who spent years believing she had been abused and later retracted:

> ... you have been in my thoughts and prayers. I know you are going through a really tough time. You know you are doing the right thing, but it can still feel pretty crummy anyway! Hang in there. You are making the tough ethical choices that most people only hope they would have the integrity to make when their back is against the wall. Remember, your voice is not the only one out there anymore. Speak up loudly and soon you will give others the courage to also speak up. You are truly a woman of history. I admire you deeply.

This one came in 1999, from a Texas lawyer who has worked on behalf of many falsely accused individuals:

> Hey lady, I came across a quote by Dr. Albert Schwitzer that reminded me of you: "The purpose of life is to serve and show compassion and the will to help others. Only then have we ourselves become true human beings." On behalf of those who appreciate your dedication the most, thanks again.

## WHERE ARE WE TODAY?

In Harry Potter's world, you could make something disappear by casting a Memory Charm by muttering "Obliviate." But, as one science writer has noted, "The wrinkled wizard in your head already does famously well when it comes to distorting memory" (Highfield, 2002, p. 171). In other words, it does not take much to create a memory illusion that does not match what went on in the real world. Research on such memory distortions continues today, and the field is thriving. The evidence is in this volume.

Almost certainly the field will continue developing new ways to create false memories, and to understand the process by which false memories take hold. Speculating about the future, we will continue taking advantage of advances in neuroimaging to help us determine what parts of the brain are similarly or differently activated when a person has a true memory versus a false one. We will explore the role of genetics, intelligence, and other individual differences in the creation of false memories. We will develop more precise recipes for planting false memories, and learn which recipes work best with which people. We might find that very potent recipes involve drugs that we are on the brink of discovering. Already we have "date rape" drugs, apparently abused by bodybuilders, dancers, and teenagers seeking to get high, and by would-be criminals intent on sexual assault. Some of the drugs are colorless, tasteless, and mix easily in drinks. Some cause sedation and even amnesia where a user forgets events that happened while she was under the influence of the drug. That's why some of these drugs are called "sexual assault" drugs. When memory distortion techniques are mastered and take on a pharmaceutical twist, the potential for mind engineering would undoubtedly be enhanced. When we do get the false-memory recipes down pat, we will be left with critical questions: Who controls the technology? What brakes should be imposed on police, lawyers, advertisers, and others who try to manipulate people using these findings? When the memory creation technology becomes readily available, how will society protect itself from misuse? We are going to need brakes to prevent this mind technology from being used in nefarious ways. In debating these societal issues, we will truly come to appreciate an essential message: Memory, like liberty, is a fragile thing.

The research on memory distortion is having an effect on public policy. For example, the FBI Law Enforcement Bulletin published an article on strategies to avoid interview contamination (Sandoval, 2003). The author warned that therapists, in their efforts to find the truth about allegations of possible sexual abuse, face a danger when counseling alleged victims that they may be distorting their memories. He goes on to cite my book with Kathy Ketcham warning about how unintentional suggestions can be planted that can lead to the creation of false memories. By considering the factors that contribute to contamination, the author notes, investigators can minimize these effects and maximize the prospects of conducting a successful interview.

Some of the individuals who got caught in an unfortunate memory net have more or less landed on their feet. George Franklin spent nearly 6 years in prison until a federal court reversed his conviction in 1996 and the prosecutors declined to retry him. He sued his daughter, several governmental officials, and various trial witnesses (including the psychiatrist who had supported Eileen's repressed-memory stories). In 2003, the U.S. District Court for the Northern District of California dismissed the last of George Franklin's claims (*Franklin v. Terr,* 2003).

Gary Ramona found a lovely new lady friend, and began importing excellent wines from Chile. He is still estranged from his family.

Of the thousands of parents whose families fell apart, some have reunited, but many are still estranged. They struggle to find answers. One especially memorable recent example came to my attention when a woman whom I'll call Katy contacted me. She was deeply distressed over accusations from her grown daughter who was now reporting recent recovery of allegedly repressed abuse by parents, an uncle, and a grandmother. Mother and daughter were estranged. I asked Katy if she knew who her daughter's therapist was; perhaps it was someone known to be implicated in other false-accusation cases. Katy said she'd dig around, and eventually she contacted me again with information about her daughter's therapist. She was a female therapist who had been recommended to the daughter by others in the community. As it turns out, that therapist had a colorful history of her own. She had sued her own father after recovering memories of sexual abuse. The therapist's name was Holly Ramona.

## REFERENCES


Bernstein, D. M., Laney, C., Morris, E. K., & Loftus, E. F. (2005). False memories about food can lead to food avoidance. *Social Cognition, 23,* 10–33.

Collins, A. M., & Loftus, E. F. (1975). A spreading activation theory of semantic processing. *Psychological Review, 82,* 407–428.

Franklin v Terr et al. 294 F. Supp. 2d 1145 (N.D. Cal. 2003).

Heaps, C. M., & Nash, M. (2001). Comparing recollective experiences in true and false autobiographical memories. *Journal of Experimental Psychology: Learning, Memory, and Cognition, 27,* 920–930.

Highfield, R. (2002). *The science of Harry Potter.* New York: Penguin.

Hunt, M. (1999). *The new know-nothings: The political foes of the scientific study of human nature.* New Brunswick, NJ: Transaction.

Hyman, I. E., Husband, T. H., & Billings, F. J. (1995). False memories of childhood experiences. *Applied Cognitive Psychology, 9,* 181–197.

James, W. (1890). *Principles of psychology* (Vol. 1). New York: Holt.

Johnston, M. (1997). *Spectral evidence.* Boston: Houghton Mifflin.

Loftus, E. F. (1970). *An analysis of the structural variables that determine problem-solving difficulty on a computer-based teletype.* Unpublished doctoral dissertation, Stanford University, Stanford, CA.

Loftus, E. F. (1974). Reconstructing memory: The incredible eyewitness. *Psychology Today,* 8, 116–119. Loftus, E. F. (1997). Creating false memories. *Scientific American,277*(3), 70–75.

Loftus, E. F. (2003a). Make-believe memories. *American Psychologist, 58,* 864–873.

Loftus, E. F. (2003b, Fall). On science under legal assault. *Daedalus (Journal of the American Academy of Arts & Sciences),* pp. 84–86.

Loftus, E. F., Coan, J. A. & Pickrell, J. E. (1996). Manufacturing false memories using bits of reality. In L. M. Reder (Ed.), *Implicit memory and metacognition* (pp. 195–220). Mahwah, NJ: Lawrence Erlbaum Associates.

Loftus, E. F., & Freedman, J. L. (1972). Effect of category-name frequency on the speed of naming an instance of the category. *Journal of Verbal Learning and Verbal Behavior, 11,* 343–347.

Loftus, E. F. & Guyer, M. (2002a, May/June). Who abused Jane Doe?: The hazards of the single case history. *Skeptical Inquirer.* Part I. *26,* 24–32.

Loftus, E. F. & Guyer, M. J. (2002b, July/August) , Who abused Jane Doe? Part II. *Skeptical Inquirer, 23,* (4), 37–40, 44.

Loftus, E. F., & Hoffman, H. G. (1989). Misinformation and memory: The creation of memory. *Journal of Experimental Psychology: General, 118,* 100–104.

Loftus, E. F., & Ketcham, K. (1991). *Witness for the defense: The accused, the eyewitness, and the expert who puts memory on trial.* New York: St. Martin's Press. Loftus, E. F., & Ketcham, K. (1994). *The myth of repressed memory.* New York: St. Martin's Press.

Loftus, E. F., & Palmer, J. C. (1974). Reconstruction of automobile destruction: An example of the interaction between language and memory. *Journal of Verbal Learning and Verbal Behavior, 13,* 585–589.

Loftus, E. F., & Pickrell, J. E. (1995) The formation of false memories. *Psychiatric Annals, 25,* 720–725.

Loftus, E. F., & Suppes, P. (1972). Structural variables that determine problem-solving difficulty in computer-assisted instruction. *Journal of Educational Psychology, 63,* 531–542.

Porter, S., Yuille, J. C., & Lehman, D. R. (1999). The nature of real, implanted, and fabricated memories for emotional childhood events: Implications for the recovered memory debate. *Law and Human Behavior, 23,* 517–537.

Sandoval, V. A. (2003). Strategies to avoid interview contamination. *FBI Law Enforcement Bulletin, 72,* 1–11.

CHAPTER

2

# Tracking the Birth of a Star

Gordon H. Bower

I first met Beth Loftus (formerly Fishman) when she entered Stanford's PhD psychology program in 1966. She had been admitted as the sole woman in the cohort of young men brought into the mathematical psychology program. Beth fit the criteria as an ideal applicant because she had a joint major in psychology and mathematics from UCLA, a combination eminently suited for our program. Mathematical learning theory was (and probably still is) a field dominated by males—the power players were Bill Estes, Duncan Luce, George Miller, Bob Bush, Pat Suppes, Dick Atkinson, Bennett Murdock, Frank Restle, and Eugene Galanter. Beth was distinctive and unique: Not only was she well trained in higher mathematics, she was also a very motivated, enthusiastic, engaging, and efficient worker. Moreover, overriding the stereotype threat under which she operated, Beth's intellectual skills and competence quickly commanded respect from her peers and professors. Beth's peers in the mathematical psychology program during that period were a formidable group of soon-to-be stars of that field such as Rich Shiffrin, David Rumelhart, Bob Bjork, Jack Yellott, Mike Humphries, and Bill Batchelder.

Beth started with an interest in human learning, a major area of specialization in our program. She was a student in my graduate seminars on human learning. In one of those seminars, I assigned students the exercise of helping me critically read and review a few of the flood of manuscripts I was receiving as a reviewer for several professional journals. Subgroups of students and I would read a given manuscript, meet to analyze it critically, and then they would present the substance of the findings, the theoretical explanation, and their review to the larger seminar group for discussion. Then we would come to a consensus view of the manuscript. I would take intensive notes and then write my final review of each manuscript for the action editor.

Because the students were learning their theory and experimental design principles in the front lines of our science, this exercise proved to be a valuable educational experience. The subgroups took their assignments seriously, and woe befell those who overlooked a flaw in experimental design or theoretical argument that the rest of us might catch. Moreover, their opinions and decisions had real consequences for the quality of work being published in our science. The exercise was clearly more consequential than handing in one more set of hypothetical homework problems. Beth later told me that those weekly exercises were some of the more meaningful and educational tasks for the students.

In those days, most of the students in the program were working with their professors on the popular Markov models for standard laboratory memory tasks like paired-associate learning, free recall, and short-term memory (see, e.g., the topics in our standard textbook by Atkinson, Bower, & Crothers, 1965). The classic paper, held up as the ideal prototype for students' aspirations, presented the model of short-term memory written by Beth's adviser, Richard Atkinson, and her fellow student, Richard Shiffrin (1968). But almost singular in her ways, Beth did not start down that career path. She had little interest in creating another Markov model that might provide a good fit to laboratory data from nonsense syllable learning. Rather, she wanted to work on intellectual puzzles closer to real-world situations.

In Stanford's psychology program at that time, the only available option close to her goal was for Beth to work on the computer-assisted instruction (CAI) projects that Pat Suppes and Dick Atkinson were conducting alongside their primary interest in mathematical learning theories. So Beth signed on to conduct research within CAI, joining the group of mainly Education-school students working with Suppes and Atkinson. This led to her first CAI publication (Fishman, Keller, & Atkinson, 1968) on teaching word spelling to elementary school children in local schools. Her second publication (Suppes, Loftus, & Jerman, 1969) continued in a slightly different line—arithmetic problem solving in fifth-grade children. Her dissertation, done in 1968 (published as Loftus & Suppes, 1972), was part of a larger project investigating mathematical problem solving in the elementary school curriculum. In that investigation, she and Pat Suppes were successful in identifying and measuring the many aspects of math word problems that contributed to the problems' difficulty, such as the length and complexity of sentences describing the problem, the number of steps in the solution path, the number of different operations to be performed, and so on. The collection of factors they measured were successful in predicting problem difficulty, with a multiple correlation of .73 in predicting the percentage of students who would solve the problems.

Although this research was successful in calibrating math and word problems for drill-and-practice exercises for fifth graders, Beth gained little satisfaction from such projects. In *Witness for the Defense* (Loftus & Ketcham, 1991), Beth wrote about her reactions to those projects:

> It was tedious work, no doubt about it. The theoretical model had been set up years earlier by my Ph.D. advisor, and I was just one of several graduate students, each of us plugged into a specific slot, computing our statistical analyses, feeding our results into a common pot. It occurred to me that my particular job was a little like cutting carrots to put in a soup. To the left or the right of me were other students, equally frenzied and meticulous about cutting up their onions, celery, potatoes, chunks of beef, and then tossing them into the same huge pot. And I couldn't help thinking; all I've done is cut up the carrots. (p. 5)

The passage goes on to describe the beginning of her collaborative research with Stanford Psychology Professor, Jonathan Freedman. In that context, she was able, for the first time, to investigate her own research questions and not simply add her efforts to a large project in which she played a small part. Freedman and Beth began their collaborative research on semantic question answering, measuring how rapidly answers could be retrieved to various questions posed to a person's long-term, semantic memory. These results were interpreted as indicating something about the representation, organization, search, and activation of a person's long-term knowledge. They found, for example, that answers to category-then-property questions ("Name a *fruit* that is *purple*") were retrieved 250 milliseconds quicker than with the reverse ordering of the cues—indicating that people's semantic memory is likely organized around object categories rather than properties (Loftus & Freedman, 1970). They published several similar papers on semantic retrieval, which at the time was a very popular topic (Freedman & Loftus, 1971; Loftus & Freedman, 1972).

As she neared completion of her dissertation, Beth began looking for an academic job. She and I recall my telling her that the New School for Social Research in New York City was looking to hire a cognitive psychologist. Because she considered herself a specialist in human learning, she wondered whether she qualified for the job. I told her to apply and if she got the job, to shape it to fit her talents and interests. So she applied and obtained her first job at the New School, starting in fall 1970. That position had several advantages: First, her husband, Geoff Loftus, had received a postdoctoral fellowship with George Sperling at New York University, close by the New School; and second, Beth could continue her collaborative research with Jonathan Freedman, who had recently moved to Columbia University. Her research on semantic retrieval continued along a successful path for the next few years (Loftus, 1972, 1973; Loftus & Cole, 1974).

During this time, she had an encounter with an attorney friend that caused a major change in her attitude and approach to research. She'd been describing to him how her research had demonstrated that "*fruit - P*" retrieved an answer (*plum*) a quarter second faster than the reverse order, "*P - fruit*." The friend asked, "But how important to the human condition is the difference of a quarter second? Why not study some really significant problems such as the reliability of eyewitnesses testifying to crimes?" That and similar challenges caused an epiphany for Beth—as it came to be for many other research psychologists (e.g., Gruneberg, Morris, & Sykes, 1978; Neisser, 1978, 1982). Beth decided deliberately to aim her research increasingly at questions about the operation of memory in applied settings.

But even before that, already in 1971, there were intimations of Beth's interest and creativity in attacking applied questions. One of these was her little known paper on the strength of different cues in jogging people to remember their intentions (Loftus, 1971). This rarely cited paper is remarkable in two respects: First, her subjects were local inhabitants and staff members she encountered in and around the New School buildings and who she'd persuaded to answer a brief opinion survey; and second, it is one of the earliest papers in the nascent research area of "prospective memory." That topic was to mushroom into special prominence in memory research about 15 years later. So already in 1971, Beth was starting to use creative experimental methods to investigate novel, important questions in naturalistic field settings.

The first really applied issue Beth investigated was with John Keating (Keating & Loftus, 1975) on how to increase people's attention to, and their compliance with, public address emergency announcements, such as fire warnings to occupants of high-rise buildings. This research led to a series of collaborative papers published over succeeding years, detailing the efficacy of different forms of disaster announcements and how to reduce panic and instigate efficient responses among members of a threatened crowd (Keating & Loftus, 1977, 1981; Keating, Loftus, & Manber, 1983; Loftus, 1979).

A later applied issue that attracted Beth's curiosity was the framing of questions in survey questionnaires used, for example, in collecting national health statistics or surveys of economic well-being (Feinberg, Loftus, & Tanur, 1985; Loftus, Feinberg, & Tanur, 1985). This was an area ripe for exploration with concepts of cognitive psychology, and especially memory, because so many survey questions ask people to remember how often they've done something. She was able to demonstrate, for example, strong anchoring influences on people's retrospective reports of the frequency of their physical complaints or their taking medications. Thus, after discussing a headache remedy (Anacin), the question "How many headache products would you say you tried—one, two, three?" elicited far lower estimates of headache remedies tried than did the same question but with higher suggested anchors—"one, five, ten?" (Incidentally, this was around the time when she appeared in a long-running television commercial for a headache remedy!) In later work, by checking health records, she and her colleagues were able to discover how impoverished were people's retrospective reports of many of their medical facts and, moreover, how different forms of memory questions led respondents to be more or less accurate. Beth also investigated methods for improving respondents' temporal dating of events from the past (Loftus & Marburger, 1983). Research in this area by Beth and her collaborators has had a substantial influence on the manner in which national survey questions are posed and their results interpreted.

The major shift in Beth's research career took place in 1974, soon after she and Geoff had moved to the University of Washington. She published two articles that were to catapult her onto the national stage as an expert on eyewitness testimony. One was her article with John Palmer titled "Reconstruction of Automobile Destruction" (Loftus & Palmer, 1974); the other was her article "Reconstructing Memory: The Incredible Eyewitness" in *Psychology Today* (Loftus, 1974). Both articles demonstrated how easily eyewitnesses' reports about a car accident could be altered by very subtle changes in the wording of questions. The national response to those articles, and to the subsequent one on leading questions (Loftus, 1975), put Beth on a fast track to prominence as an expert witness in legal court cases. Important to note, Beth had the drive, stamina, and zealous work habits that allowed her to rise to the challenges of this new identity—lecturing throughout the country to many attorney groups, law school forums, police associations, and the entire spectrum of psychology conferences and conventions, writing popular and semipopular books, while continuing her production of a steady stream of basic research articles in the foremost journals of our field. Her productivity is nothing short of amazing.

While writing these remembrances, I asked myself why Beth was able so easily to investigate eyewitness memory for filmed accident or crime scenes when so many other memory researchers had not ventured into that territory, despite its obvious allure. I know the answer in my case, at least, and I suspect it is typical for my generation of memory researchers. For us traditionalists, the "Gold Standard" test of memory was to have participants attempt *full recall* of all the material studied, much as we examined full recall of a list of unrelated words presented to an experimental subject for study. But we simply had no good ideas about how to study full recall of a film's naturalistic events such as accidents or crimes. What would be the "memory units" to be recalled or counted, as our subjects tried to recall a staged event or accident film?

There are many hundreds of bits of information in a film of a naturalistic event, at multiple levels of generality, that one might look for in a person's recall. If we asked subjects to attempt their unaided recall, we had no good ideas on how to score the complex protocols that could result. Just consider that realistic protocols would surely include all manner of generalizations about the filmed events, personal evaluations, stylistic commentaries, paraphrases, inferences of all varieties, fragmentary sentences, combinations of sentences and propositional knowledge, ellipses, compressed summaries of multiple parts, warranted and unwarranted importations added to the story, and so on. In a word, it would be a linguistic morass, and no one (least of all memory researchers) had very good ideas of how to code and score recall protocols from films—simply counting words won't do, even assuming words were spoken in the film. Those coding schemes were to come into the field somewhat later for meaningful texts (e.g., the text-analysis techniques of Kintsch, 1974, 1998; Meyer, 1975; van Dijk & Kintsch, 1983) and very much later still for scoring recall memory for filmed events (e.g., Berger, 1998; Magliano, Dijkstra, & Zwaan, 1996; Magliano, Miller, & Zwaan, 2001; Zacks & Tversky, 2001; Zacks, Tversky, & Iyer, 2001). Even today, most memory researchers view the analysis of full recall of films to be an intractable methodological problem.

It was Beth Loftus's insight to notice that one need not be able to score all of people's full recall of a film to be able to examine interesting questions about their memory of it. Rather, experimenters could confine themselves to asking pointed recognition-memory questions aimed at probing subjects' memory of specific details of the filmed event. In this manner, the experimenter could create films and, say, a confederate's recounting of it in order to see the impact of their joint manipulation on memory for specific details of interest. It was this very slight shift in defining the dependent variable (viz., recognition memory for specific details) that opened the door for the stampede of other experimenters using Beth's method following her innovations. As this view implies, most of Beth's early experiments in this area never reported subjects' recall of the film—in fact, only rarely was there any reporting of subjects' overall recognition accuracy for large number of facts about the filmed event. Those measures were simply not relevant to answering the pointed questions that Beth was considering. Before that, traditionalists would have viewed testing only one or two critical recognition items from a whole mass of studied material as an egregious waste of a possibly rich data source.

The mark of a major advance in psychology is that it becomes "obvious" once it is pointed out; we slap our foreheads and exclaim, "Of course, why didn't I think of that?" Beth's insight in making a small but crucial change in experimental method—selecting only a few specific facts of a film to be varied and then measuring recognition memory for them—was one of those simple methodological innovations that immediately attracted the research community to her paradigm. Moreover, her techniques for inserting misinformation into a person's memory of a filmed event were ingenious—by exposing subjects to the account of another witness, or having an examiner ask preliminary questions containing subtle presuppositions (Loftus, 1975). These methods were so simple but powerful in distorting subjects' memory that everyone could appreciate their significance. The clear implications for applications of the methods were also appealing to laboratory memory researchers.

Furthermore, Beth has always had an engaging, informal style of conveying her findings and she explains them using easily accessible ideas characterized by catchy phrases such as "destructive overwriting" versus "coexistence" of an earlier with a later memory of an event, or the "mentalmorphosis," that is, the "integration" or "blending" of the memories of an original and a subsequent event (e.g., Loftus, 1981).

I recall asking her once about this (I paraphrase): "Isn't your misinformation effect just another example of the old idea of retroactive interference? That is, subjects first see 'INTERSECTION has a STOP sign' (A–B association), then later hear an informant claiming that 'INTERSECTION had a YIELD sign' (A–C), so having learned that A–C association interferes with later retrieval of the original A–B association. In addition, your catchy term 'destructive overwriting' of memories seems to be just the old idea of unlearning from interference theory, wherein learning A–C weakens an earlier A–B association in an absolute sense (e.g., Barnes & Underwood, 1959; Postman, 1971)."

In her inimitable style, Beth thought a moment and produced a most insightful answer (again, I paraphrase): "Technically, you're right. But strategically, for getting people interested in the distortion of eyewitnesses' memories, interference theory with its stable of laboratory experiments has no 'sex appeal.' These findings with these formulations are breathing new life into some old ideas that are once again exciting researchers and reaching a public audience. The misinformation paradigm provides a useful test ground for examining the suggestibility of people's memories."

At the time, I didn't fully appreciate her reply, because I thought that connections to earlier research should always be acknowledged to the world. But to what world? Other researchers? The funding agencies and lay public that supports our research? In retrospect, I think Beth's reply was right on the money (no pun intended). A measure of the pragmatic worth of some ideas is how much they influence the research of others, and how easily they diffuse out into the popular press and the lay audience for general use. After all, it is their taxes that support our laboratory research.

Psychologists appreciate that Beth's findings are fascinating and easy to describe to our nonpsychologist acquaintances and they find such research very worthwhile. The findings are far more engaging than just a few more facts about lab subjects' loss of access to A–B, (in a modified-modified free-recall test) due to learning a second list (A–C) of arbitrary nonsense syllable pairs. Consider a personal example: As a memory researcher, I am sometimes asked to talk about memory research to lay audiences. I can rarely get through such talks without giving special prominence to Beth's findings on eyewitness memory errors, and memory distortions due to misinformation, imagination inflation, and implanting totally false new memories. Those tend to be the more attention-grabbing parts of my popular talks to lay audiences. In this respect, Beth's research has rescued me many times from boring my lay audiences. For that I (and I'm sure other researchers) can be profoundly grateful to her.

Beth's early research on distortions in eyewitness memories ushered her into a deep involvement with legal issues, where she has often provided testimony as an expert witness in court cases. These contacts have been extremely valuable because the legal issues she encountered there led her into more court-related research. This includes her work on clarifying the judge's instructions to a jury, on the impact of discredited information on mock jury decisions, the impact of a witness's recovered memory of an assault (compared to a persistently available memory of it) on the evidential weight mock jurors give to that testimony, the impact of memory testimony elicited under hypnosis, the impact of level of detail versus vagueness in a witness's memory, or people's accuracy in judging whether they had years before remembered or forgotten a given fact. Her research along these lines showcases an excellent use of the "real world" (if criminal court cases can be so considered), bringing these applied issues into controlled laboratory settings to investigate. But important to note, Beth takes the further crucial step of moving her laboratory results back out to the real world in her lecturing and writings for lawyers and judges and her testimony in court cases.

Over the years, Beth and I would frequently meet at psychology conventions or whenever she'd be visiting Stanford, and we enjoyed discussing our respective researches. Over time those conversations (and e-mails) evolved into an informal mentoring relationship that has proved very satisfying to me. We would discuss her concerns about challenges to her findings and approach, her standing in the field, what tenure or career issues she should be considering at a given time, what to do about various job offers that came her way, and so on.

One persisting issue in our conversations that has continued over the past 10 to 15 years is her concern with the many criticisms and occasionally vicious attacks on her and her work by her legal opponents or from those disputing her skepticism about recovery of "repressed memories" of childhood abuse (see, e.g., Loftus & Ketcham, 1994; Tavris, 2002, and this volume). In the early years, these attacks caused her some distress and self-doubt. I could only offer her sympathy and general support in these battles—to "stick to her guns," not to overextend her findings or let herself be pushed into a more extreme position on an issue than she was comfortable with, to look for the concerns motivating her critics, and to try to educate rather than counterattack. Throughout the past decade, she has withstood many such threats, legal suits, and assaults on her expertise, education, character, ancestry, grant support, access to research venues, academic positions, and subconscious motivations. The large "silent majority" of memory researchers who agree with Beth's basic position on most scientific issues greatly admire her steadfast courage in holding her scientific ground while surviving a barrage of attacks from some irate therapists and their clients. She is an outstanding example of a scientist who has the pluck, moral backbone, and scientific certitude to stand up to her critics and emerge from the battles even stronger than when she started.

Another issue that used to vex her was whether her applied, popular research and extensions would be viewed as less valuable to "rigorous" experimental psychologists. That is, should she be aiming to publish more theoretical articles like the famous one she wrote with Allan Collins in the *Psychological Review* (1975)? After all, that's how her esteemed Stanford peers such as Rich Shiffrin, Dave

Rumelhart, Bob Bjork, and John Anderson were earning solid academic reputations. Beth worried that her applied research might prevent her from earning the respect and recognition in her field that brings the accolades that all academics covet—research grants, honorific awards, good job offers, election to distinguished positions in professional organizations, and so on.

I recall advising Beth not to worry about her reputation among academic memory researchers or hard-nosed experimental psychologists, because her applied research and legal consulting were having a major impact in many worlds far beyond academic psychology. If truth be told, many experimental psychologists would be very gratified if their research could have half the real-world impact and international recognition that Beth's work has received.

I recall saying something like this (paraphrased): "This kind of applied research may not get you elected to the National Academy of Sciences, but you shouldn't care about that. What's important is that your heart is in it, you love it, your research is of high quality, and you're having a huge impact inside and outside our field. Better that your contributions be respected and admired by 10,000 applied psychologists, lawyers, and judges than by 10 theoretical psychologists."

But happily, I was terribly wrong in my forecast. Over the past 10 years, worldwide recognition of her research has showered upon her many honors and awards far beyond what most academic researchers ever achieve in their careers. Significant ones were her election to the presidency of the American Psychological Society (APS) and her selection to William James Fellow status in APS ("For significant lifetime contributions to the basic science of psychology"). In 2003, Beth along with Steve Ceci received the coveted award for "Distinguished Scientific Contributions for the Applications of Psychology" from the American Psychological Association.

The capstones to her brilliant career occurred with her election in 2003 to the American Academy of Arts and Sciences and in spring 2004, her election to the august National Academy of Sciences, recognized as the most prestigious scientific honor that can be bestowed on a psychologist. Moreover, her candidacy within the National Academy rose with extraordinary speed, from her nomination to a majority vote within the psychology and social science sections, and thence to the ultimate election by the entire membership of the Academy. (This is a process that ordinarily takes several years of balloting.)

Her election to the National Academy doubtless put the *coup de grâce* to Beth's longing for respectability of her research. In addition, in 2005 she was honored with the famous Grawemeyer Award for Psychology, receiving the $200,000 unrestricted prize for "*her research on memory and how it can be altered. Her work has implications for law and for psychotherapy, particularly methods of probing memory.*"

As frosting on the cake, a recent study was published in the *Review of General Psychology* in which the authors used several objective criteria (e.g., citations, awards, textbook mentions) to evaluate the impact of the scholarly work of thousands of psychologists (Haggbloom et al., 2002). In that assessment, Beth ranked

58th and was the *top-ranked woman* among the 100 most influential psychologists of the 20th century. I think we can all agree that she might now lay aside concerns about the respectability of her research.

From her earliest days at Stanford, Beth Loftus has always shown signs of stardom. Tracking her rising star for the past 40 years has been fascinating to behold. She has made her success in spectacular fashion, and she's done it on her own terms. I am immensely proud to have been associated with her.

## REFERENCES


Atkinson, R. C., Bower, G. H., & Crothers, E. J. (1965). *An introduction to mathematical learning theory*. New York: Wiley.

Atkinson, R. C., & Shiffrin, R. M. (1968). Human memory: A proposed system and its control processes. In K. W. Spence & J. T. Spence (Eds.), *The psychology of learning and motivation* (Vol. 2, pp. 89–195). New York: Academic Press.

Barnes, J. M., & Underwood, N. J. (1959). Fate of first-list associations and transfer theory. *Journal of Experimental Psychology, 58,* 97–105.

Berger, A. A. (1998). *Media analysis techniques* (2nd ed.). Thousand Oaks, CA: Sage.

Collins, A. M., & Loftus, E. F. (1975). A spreading activation theory of semantic processing. *Psychological Review, 82,* 407–428.

Feinberg, S. E., Loftus, E. F., & Tanur, J. M. (1985). Cognitive aspects of health survey methodology. *Millbank Memorial Fund Quarterly, 63,* 547–564.

Fishman (Loftus), E. F., Keller, L., & Atkinson, R. C. (1968). Massed vs. distributed practice in computerized spelling drills. *Journal of Educational Psychology, 59,* 290–296.

Freedman, J. L., & Loftus, E. F. (1971). Retrieval of words from long-term memory. *Journal of Verbal Learning and Verbal Behavior, 10,* 107–115.

Gruneberg, M. M., Morris, P. E., & Sykes, R. N. (Eds.). (1978). *Practical aspects of memory.* London: Academic Press.

Haggbloom, S. J., Warnick, R., Warnick, J. E., Jones, V.K., Yarbrough, G.L., Russell, T.M., et al. (2002). The 100 most eminent psychologists of the 20th century. *Journal of General Psychology, 6,* 139–152.

Keating, J. P., & Loftus, E. F. (1975). People care in fire emergencies—psychological aspects. In *Proceedings of the National Fire Protection Association Meeting.* Boston: Society of Fire Protection Engineers. Technical Report, 75–4. (pp. 1–12).

Keating, J. P., & Loftus, E. F. (1977). Vocal alarm system for high-rise buildings—a case study. *Mass Emergencies, 2,* 25–34.

Keating, J. P., & Loftus, E. F. (1981). The logic of fire escape. *Psychology Today, 15,* 14–19.

Keating, J. P., Loftus, E. F., & Manber, M. (1983). Emergency evaluations during fires: Psychological considerations. In R. F. Kidd & M. J. Saks (Eds.), *Advances in applied social psychology* (Vol. 2, pp. 83–99). Hillsdale, NJ: Lawrence Erlbaum Associates.

Kintsch, W. (1974). *The representation of meaning in memory*. Hillsdale, NJ: Lawrence Erlbaum Associates.

Kintsch, W. (1998). *Comprehension: A paradigm for cognition*. Cambridge, England: Cambridge University Press.

Loftus, E. F. (1971). Memory for intentions. *Psychonomic Science, 23,* 315–316.

Loftus, E. F. (1972). Nouns, adjectives and semantic memory. *Journal of Experimental Psychology, 96,* 213–215.

Loftus, E. F. (1973). Category dominance, instance dominance, and categorization time. *Journal of Experimental Psychology, 97,* 70–74.

Loftus, E. F. (1974). Reconstructing memory: The incredible eyewitness. *Psychology Today, 8,* 116–119.

Loftus, E. F. (1975). Leading questions and the eyewitness report. *Cognitive Psychology, 7,* 560–572.
Loftus E. F. (1979). Words that could save your life. *Psychology Today, 13,* 102–110, 136–137.
Loftus, E. F. (1981). Mentalmorphosis: Alterations in memory produced by the mental bonding of new information to old. In J. B. Long & A. D. Baddeley (Eds.), *Attention and performance IX* (pp. 417–434). Hillsdale, NJ: Lawrence Erlbaum Associates.
Loftus, E. F., & Cole, W. (1974). Retrieving attribute and name information from semantic memory. *Journal of Experimental Psychology, 102,* 1116–1122.
Loftus, E. F., Fienberg, S. E., & Tanur, J. M. (1985). Cognitive psychology meets the national survey. *American Psychologist, 40,* 175–180.
Loftus, E. F., & Freedman, J. L. (1970). On predicting constrained associates from long-term memory. *Psychonomic Science, 19,* 357–358.
Loftus, E. F., & Freedman, J. L. (1972). Effect of category-name frequency on the speed of naming an instance of the category. *Journal of Verbal Learning and Verbal Behavior, 11,* 343–347.
Loftus, E. F., & Ketcham, K. (1991). *Witness for the defense.* New York: St. Martin's Press.
Loftus, E. F., & Ketcham, K. (1994). *The myth of repressed memory.* New York: St. Martin's Press.
Loftus, E. F., & Marburger, W. (1983). Since the eruption of Mt. St. Helens, did anyone beat you up? Improving the accuracy of retrospective reports with landmark events. *Memory &Cognition, 11,* 114–120.
Loftus, E. F., & Palmer, J. C. (1974). Reconstruction of automobile destruction: An example of the interaction between language and memory. *Journal of Verbal Learning and Verbal Behavior, 13,* 585–589.
Loftus, E. F., & Suppes, P. (1972). Structural variables that determine problem-solving difficulty in computer-assisted instruction. *Journal of Educational Psychology, 63,* 531–542.
Magliano, J. P., Dijkstra, K., & Zwaan, R. A. (1996). Generating predictive inferences while viewing a movie. *Discourse Processes, 22*(3), 199–224.
Magliano, J. P., Miller, J., & Zwaan, R. A. (2001) Indexing space and time in film understanding. *Applied Cognitive Psychology, 15*(5), 533–545.
Meyer, B. J. F. (1975). *The organization of prose and its effects on memory.* Amsterdam: North-Holland.
Neisser, U. (1978). Memory: What are the important questions? In M. M. Gruneberg, P. E. Morris, & R. N. Sykes (Eds.), *Practical aspects of memory* (pp. 3–24). London: Academic Press.
Neisser, U. (1982). *Memory observed: Remembering in natural contexts.* San Francisco: Freeman.
Postman, L. (1971). Transfer, interference, and forgetting. In J. W. Kling & L. A. Riggs (Eds.), *Woodworth and Schlosberg's experimental psychology* (3rd ed., pp. 1019–1132). New York: Holt, Rinehart & Winston.
Suppes, P., Loftus, E. F., & Jerman, M. (1969). Problem-solving on a computer-based teletype. *Educational Studies in Mathematics, 2,* 1–15.
Tavris, C. (2002, July/August). The high cost of skepticism. *The Skeptical Inquirer,* pp. 41–44.
Van Dijk, T. A., & Kintsch, W. (1983). *Strategies of discourse comprehension.* New York: Academic Press.
Zacks, J. M., & Tversky, B. (2001). Event structure in perception and conception. *Psychological Bulletin, 127,* 3–21
Zacks, J. M., Tversky, B., & Iyer, G. (2001). Perceiving, remembering, and communicating structure in events. *Journal of Experimental Psychology: General, 130,* 29–58.

CHAPTER
# 3

# Elizabeth F. Loftus: The Early Years

Geoffrey R. Loftus

## 1966–1970: STANFORD, CALIFORNIA

Stanford graduate students in the mid- to late 1960s were roughly divided into two cultural camps. In the traditional scientist-in-training-as-nerd camp dwelt a collection of individuals, almost exclusively male, who wore motley neckties every day, and took their work seriously, 24/7. In stark contrast stood the still small, but nevertheless ascendant, scientist-in-training-as-hippy camp whose members wore tie-dyed shirts and spent weekends going to Dead concerts at the Fillmore, encounter groups in Big Sur, and protest marches in Golden Gate Park.

Elizabeth Jane Fishman arrived on campus in August 1966, not fitting neatly—or at all—into either of these camps or any other. The closest one could come to a nutshell description of her is that she resembled some big-studio Hollywood portrayal of an up-and-coming assistant DA—21 years old, glamorous, with finely chiseled high cheekbones, long dark hair, perfectly tailored business suits, trademark LA sunglasses, and a body to die for. In a seemingly calculated, but actually inadvertent counterpoint to this image, her principal means of transportation was a yellow, three-on-the-handlebars, 1964 Schwinn. She took the Stanford Psychology Department by storm, becoming, without trying, the center of attention wherever she went: making friends with most people, annoying a few others, and generally stirring up controversy. She was endlessly animated, the tip of her nose bobbing up and down slightly as she talked, providing subtle emphasis to whatever point she was making. No one knew quite what to make of her.

Beth quickly found herself placed in Ventura Hall, home of the imtimidatingly named Institute for Mathematical Studies in the Social Sciences, headed by the venerable Patrick Suppes. Every Friday afternoon she, along with other assorted Serious Scientists, was required to attend an Institute seminar in which was soberly discussed the latest developments in mathematical learning theory, or mathematical memory theory, or mathematical judgment theory, or whatever other mathematical flavor was in vogue that week. Having majored in mathematics at UCLA, Beth was no stranger to the abstruse equations that bespeckled the blackboards, but she wasn't all that interested in them either. As others animatedly argued about constraints on, and relations among *d*'s and *q*'s and *x*'s, Beth surreptitiously hemmed her skirts, caught up on her correspondence, and concocted drink recipes for whatever party she anticipated would soon herald the upcoming weekend. In a covert poll taken among her colleagues, she was enthusiastically and unanimously voted least likely to succeed as a psychologist, and an Institute pool sprang up, with contributors placing bets as to when she'd quit and return to Los Angeles to become an advertising executive or something.

By the fall of her second year, Beth had aced all her first-year courses and traded in the Schwinn for a red Alfa-Romeo convertible, but aside from those accomplishments, had made little progress in defining her career goals. One new diversion materialized: She was made a "big sister"—assigned the job of mentoring—one of the incoming first-year students, a black-leather-jacketed Bostonian named Geoff Loftus who had blown in from the East Coast astride a large black BMW. Beth approached the job with typical aplomb: Within 3 months she and her mentee were engaged, and the following June they were married under a chupah in the backyard of her family's Bel-Air home. Although still not very serious about experimental psychology, the radiant bride hedged her bets, spending but 1 day on her honeymoon, followed by 3 months of intense study for the departmental General Exams.

Part of Beth's motivational problem was that she had minimal independence in her research endeavors. Her day job was to be a small cog in the "Pat Suppes machine"—a massive educational juggernaut designed to bring computer-aided instruction to the masses, to diverse elementary schools ranging from waspy Palo Alto to the far reaches of the Indian subcontinent. Beth's role was to write arithmetic problems and hand them off to an eclectic collection of curriculum designers, computer programmers, and educational researchers, who would then stir them into an immense educational stew that, in turn, would issue forth via telephone lines to assorted teletypes around the globe. Although cosmically worthwhile, working for the Suppes machine was not an activity that fostered a great deal of personal satisfaction among its many drones. Beth felt herself to be professionally stifled and, in desperation, even briefly considered becoming a clinician.

In 1969, things changed. Somewhat by chance Beth began working with a social psychologist, Jon Freedman, on the problem of memory organization. Although her PhD dissertation developed out of her still-small role in the Suppes machine, her professional interest had shifted to the structure of semantic memory. Suddenly she blossomed, and on the strength of her groundbreaking work in this area, was offered a position by the New School for Social Research. In the summer of 1970 she moved to Manhattan where, at the epicenter of the New York academalopolis, she thrived.

## THE 1970S: SEATTLE

A traditional conundrum for married professionals is that of trying to find two jobs in the same geographic area. Beth and her husband were not immune to this problem: In 1972, after a year's postdoc at New York University, Geoff joined the faculty at the University of Washington, and a year later, Beth turned down a position at Harvard to follow him there. Her interest in the study of memory organization had peaked at that point—what else can you do after writing an article called "How to Catch a Zebra in Semantic Memory"—and she viewed her new position in Seattle as an opportunity to rummage around in quest of new research attractions. Such an opportunity arrived from an unexpected source, the U.S. Department of Transportation, which had granted Beth a little money to carry out some vaguely defined research involving motor vehicle accidents. One rainy November night, in a seedy St. Louis motel room, she and her husband were sitting around discussing what she might do with these funds. Suddenly, Beth was struck with a burst of inspiration—the eventual far-reaching implications of which were utterly opaque at the time. "I know!" she said. "I'll show people a movie of a car crash. Then I'll ask them, 'Did you see a broken headlight?' or 'Did you see the broken headlight?'" She beamed expectantly at Geoff. "Yeah?" he answered, with his typical enthusiasm for ill-specified research questions. "So what?"

Characteristically undaunted, Beth set forth to actually do that experiment, the results of which demonstrated what lawyers and linguists had known for centuries: that the phrasing of a question affects the answer that you'll get. In this case, people were more apt to "remember" *the* broken headlight than *a* broken headlight. Many Serious Scientists would have taken that result straight to the ivory tower—numerous distinguished careers have been built on considerably less dramatic linguistic phenomena. But Beth was no more interested in esoteric, removed-from-the-real-world research than she had been in the differential equations back at Ventura Hall, and her little *the*-versus-*a* result formed a seed from which would grow a revolution in our understanding of human memory. Before long, articles began to emerge from Beth's lab, one after another like waves on a beach, demonstrating via many elegant experiments that memories for real-life events were often inaccurate—but systematically inaccurate in ways that were entirely predictable on the basis of casual, but relevant information provided after the fact. For instance, just asking a witness to a car crash "How fast were the cars going when they smashed into each other?" triggered witnesses to reconstruct their memories, unconsciously adding false, but "smashed"-relevant details, such as broken glass. Of critical importance was that Beth and her colleagues demonstrated that these reconstructed memories seemed just as real to their owners as did those based on actual perceptual experience. Accordingly, such memories could potentially form bases of highly confidence-invoking-but-dead-wrong reports provided by people in many critical situations such as ... well, such as by an eyewitness testifying in a court of law.

Which led to the reasons that Beth will be remembered by future generations not only as an unusually inspired and insightful scientist, but also as a profoundly influential exponent of social change within a key cultural setting. As she was busily fostering a paradigm shift in our understanding of how memory works, Beth was also assembling the underpinnings of another revolution, this one in the field of law. She had always been a crime buff. From the time she was little, she had immersed herself in crime movies, crime TV shows ("Colombo" was a favorite), crime novels, and accounts of real-life crime. It was partly this interest and partly her emerging understanding of the relevance of her new work to evaluating eyewitness testimony that propelled her to begin hanging out with defense lawyers and drifting into Seattle courtrooms to observe trials.

And so it came to pass that in 1974, she was observing a murder trial, offering suggestions to the defense lawyer, her friend, Phil Ginsberg. At length, she told him, "You know, Phil ... there are eyewitness issues here that are very similar to those that my students and I have studied in the laboratory. Maybe this work could be offered as expert testimony." Phil agreed this would be a great idea but explained that the laws of evidence work according to a perplexing tradition: If some class of evidence had never been presented before, then there's no precedent for it, and if there's no precedent, then it's inadmissible. Beth soon began to understand this dilemma firsthand: She tried to present such testimony several times over the next year or so and sure enough, judges wouldn't allow it in. In light of this frustrating judicial catch-22, it seemed almost a miracle that on June 3, 1975—the day her father died of cancer in his Los Angeles home—Seattle Superior Court Judge Janice Niemi allowed Elizabeth Loftus to provide Washington State's first, and of course precedent-establishing, expert testimony on the topic of eyewitness identification.

## 1975 TO THE PRESENT

This seminal event took place 30 years ago. It is at that juncture in the saga of Beth's life that my part of this story largely ends, and I leave to others the task of filling in the many details of her subsequent pivotal contributions to science and society. But I would like to end my tale with two observations.

First, it's axiomatic that no person, no matter how persuasive and charming she is, can make serious contributions to controversial arenas without acquiring enemies along the way. Beth is no exception. Her original work on behalf of those accused of heinous crimes earned her the bitter animosity of many individuals whose judicial philosophy, contrary to "innocent until proven guilty," appeared to be, "where there's smoke, there's fire." This animosity ramped up dramatically in the 1980s and 1990s when the beneficiaries of Beth's forensic interests morphed from suspects in muggings and convenience-store robberies to individuals who, after having shown up as perpetrators in "repressed but recovered" memories of alleged victims, were accused of having sexually abused their children many years earlier. Beth took a strong position on these issues, which amounted to "repressed memories are often false memories," and for this stand attracted firestorms of criticism that touched every corner of her life. This incessant enmity affected Beth in many ways, none of them pleasant. But of the many and varied forms of harassment devised by Beth's detractors, none devastated her more than a cynical betrayal by her home institution: The University of Washington administration, spearheaded by its powerful human subjects review committee, trumped up—and eventually dropped without comment or apology—charges against her that, for a 2-year period, crippled her ability to carry out research or to publicly present her views. Beth hit back in a 2002 *Skeptical Inquirer* article, but at that point she was fed up with the University of Washington. In 2002—to the dismay of her many departmental colleagues and other supporters there, and despite having built a satisfying and multifaceted life in Seattle during her 29 years of University of Washington service—Beth departed for the sunnier climates of California where she currently teaches at UC–Irvine.

The second observation is more personal. Like many people whose lives are driven by a passionate commitment to a changed world, Beth has been consumed by her work. Alas, this view was not entirely shared by her husband, who was continually lobbying for, for example, a vacation that wasn't tied to a professional convention or a continuing-education seminar. In 1991, unable to reconcile these differences, the couple divorced. However, their fundamental relationship never changed and they have remained close friends. Close enough, indeed, that Beth's ex-husband even gets a kick out of writing book chapters about her.

*So, I had one of those systems—I don't know if you remember them. This was of course way before computers. I had a card system, sort of like a punch card system. On the front of the card you have a reference, and then you can take notes. The cards are big—they're like 4 × 6s or 4 × 7s even, and you can write things on these cards. And then you had to punch holes in the cards. I'd say okay, hole 3 is, you know, is cross-racial identification, and gender differences is hole 4, and so on. So let's say you want to find all the references on cross-racial identification.*

*And you had a big needle, like a knitting needle. Well, you stick the needle through hole 3, and I guess either everything drops through but the ones you want, or just the ones drop through that you want—but you get a picture. You know it's all very clever. Well that's what we had to work with back then, and when I was getting ready to write the eyewitness testimony book, that's what I used.*

*So how the Eyewitness book is arranged—there's acquisition, retention, retrieval—and in acquisition there's cross-racial—that was where my needle stuck in the punch cards that made that book. (Laughs.) You had to organize it that way up front, 'cause it's hard to change. Once you've made your punches, you're stuck with it.*

CHAPTER

# 4

# Misinformation Effects and the Suggestibility of Eyewitness Memory

Maria S. Zaragoza, Robert F. Belli, and Kristie E. Payment

Social scientists and legal practitioners have long suspected that suggestive forensic interview practices are a major cause of inaccuracies in eyewitness testimony. However, it wasn't until Elizabeth Loftus published a highly influential series of studies on eyewitness suggestibility in the 1970s that a systematic body of scientific literature on this topic started to emerge. Since then, hundreds of empirical studies on eyewitness suggestibility have been published, all of them variants of the basic experimental paradigm that Loftus developed.

In the early 1970s, research and theorizing about memory was based almost exclusively on studies of memory for lists of words or sentences (see, e.g., Crowder, 1976). By studying memory for complex, fast-moving, and forensically relevant events (typically depicted in film clips or slide shows), Loftus demonstrated that it was possible to conduct well-controlled experiments that were high in ecological validity (Banaji & Crowder, 1989). Her studies provided clear evidence that suggestive interviews can lead to profound errors in eyewitness testimony, thus raising serious questions about the reliability of memory and eyewitness testimony. Her work established that scientific research on memory and suggestibility can and should inform the courts. In addition, her findings inspired many theoretical debates about the constructive nature of memory, mechanisms of forgetting, and the permanence of memory.

In this chapter, we review the empirical evidence and theoretical proposals that have been put forward to account for the misinformation effect—the finding that exposure to misleading postevent information can lead eyewitnesses to report items and events they never actually saw.

## THE MISINFORMATION EFFECT

In the experimental paradigm introduced by Loftus, participants view a slide sequence depicting a complex and forensically relevant event, such as a traffic accident or theft. Immediately thereafter, participants are questioned about the event they witnessed. The critical manipulation is that the questioning includes leading or misleading information. Finally, participants are tested on their memory for the witnessed event. The dependent variable of interest is the extent to which misled participants incorporate the misleading suggestions into their eyewitness reports (as compared to control participants that were not misled).

Early demonstrations of the effects of leading questions revealed several ways in which eyewitness reports could be influenced. For example, for participants who had seen films of automobile accidents, the question, "About how fast were the cars going when they *smashed* into each other?" elicited higher estimates of speed, and more false claims of having seen broken glass on a later test, than questions that used verbs such as *bumped* or *hit* instead of *smashed* (Loftus & Palmer, 1974). Subsequent studies showed that misleading postevent questions could also cause a variety of other distortions in eyewitness reports. For example, Loftus (1977) had participants view an accident involving a green car and later exposed them to misleading questions that presupposed the car was blue. When later asked to select the color of the witnessed car from a color wheel, misled participants showed a marked tendency to shift their color responses in the direction of the misinformation by selecting a "blue-green" color, a tendency that was not observed in control participants. Thus, most misled participants reported a color that was a blend of the original and postevent information (see also Belli, 1988, for similar evidence of color blends following postevent information). Finally, other studies showed that participants could be led to report entire objects that were not present in the originally witnessed event. In Loftus (1975), participants who were asked, "How fast was the white sports car going when it passed the *barn* while traveling along the country road?" (when, in fact, no barn appeared in the scene) were much more likely to later claim they had seen a barn than were control participants who had not been misled (Loftus, 1975).

It is important to note, this study also showed that misinformation was more likely to influence later testimony when the false information appeared as a presupposition, rather than the direct focus of the question. For example, participants who were directly asked "Did you see a barn in the film?" were much less likely to later claim they had seen a barn than those who'd answered the previous question where the presence of the barn was presupposed (Loftus, 1975).

In 1978, Loftus, Miller, and Burns published a study demonstrating that eyewitness testimony was much more malleable than previously thought. The experimental procedure was nearly identical to that described in the studies reported earlier, with the crucial exception that the misleading postevent information directly contradicted some aspect of the originally witnessed event. In Loftus et al., for example, participants who witnessed an auto–pedestrian accident involving a stop sign were subsequently asked "Did another car pass the red Datsun when it was stopped at the yield sign?" In a later test of their memory for the witnessed events, participants were given a forced choice between the slide depicting the stop sign and a nearly identical slide depicting a yield sign. The finding was that 75% of the control participants (who had not been misled) correctly chose the slide they had seen depicting the stop sign, whereas only 41% of the misled participants did so—a 34% difference in accuracy. Additional studies showed that when participants who selected the misinformation were later asked to give a second guess (e.g., "Was it a 'stop sign' or a 'no parking' sign?"), their likelihood of selecting the original item was not greater than chance. On the basis of these findings, Loftus et al. claimed that misleading postevent information could not only supplement eyewitness memories, it could also transform them.

The "misinformation effect" documented by Loftus et al. (1978) is one of the best-known and most influential findings in psychology. Demonstrations of the surprising ease with which people could be led to report objects and events they had not seen challenged prevailing views about the validity of memory and raised serious concerns about the reliability of eyewitness testimony. Since its publication, countless studies have replicated and extended these findings: Misinformation effects have been demonstrated in participants of all ages (from preschoolers to older adults), for a variety of different types of events (live events, emotional events, naturally occurring events), types of misinformation (about people, places, and things), methods of delivering the misinformation (narratives, questionnaires, and face-to-face interviews), and all manner of methods for assessing memory for the witnessed event (e.g., free recall, cued recall, and recognition).

Early studies of the misinformation effect also identified factors that influence the magnitude of these effects. For example, Loftus et al. (1978) showed that misinformation effects increase as a function of the delay between the witnessed event and exposure to misinformation, presumably because memory for the original event becomes weaker over time. Social factors, such as the credibility of the postevent source, are also an important variable. Whereas participants are easily influenced by misinformation that is provided by a credible source, they will effectively resist suggestion that is provided by a source who lacks credibility or whom they perceive as having intentions to mislead (Dodd &

Bradshaw, 1980; Smith & Ellsworth, 1987; Underwood & Pezdek, 1998). Indeed, even young children are less influenced by suggestion when it is provided by a peer rather than an authoritative adult (Ceci, Ross, & Toglia, 1987; Lampinen & Smith, 1995). A more recent, and related, finding is that the magnitude of the misinformation effect is also influenced by more subtle social cues, such as the perceived power and social attractiveness conveyed by the accent of the person providing the misinformation (Vornik, Sharman, & Garry, 2003). Finally, the extent to which participants detect a discrepancy between their memories of the witnessed event and the postevent account also reduces misinformation effects (Tousignant, Hall, & Loftus, 1986), and in the extreme case where participants are given blatantly contradictory suggestions, they are sometimes not misled at all (Loftus, 1979c). In sum, although studies have identified some of the boundary conditions of the misinformation effect, the high reliability and robustness of these effects is well established.

## WHAT HAPPENS TO MEMORY FOR THE ORIGINALLY SEEN DETAIL FOLLOWING EXPOSURE TO CONTRADICTORY POSTEVENT MISINFORMATION?

One of the most influential aspects of Loftus's work on misinformation phenomena were the bold theoretical proposals that she initially advanced to account for these effects (Loftus, 1979a, 1979b; Loftus & Loftus, 1980; Loftus et al., 1978). Specifically, Loftus proposed a "destructive updating" process whereby contradictory misleading postevent information replaces the original information and, as a consequence, permanently erases the original information from memory. Her claim that misinformation could permanently erase information from memory generated tremendous interest, and many researchers set out to show that the original details were not gone from memory but merely rendered less accessible by the misinformation (e.g., Bekerian & Bowers, 1983; Christiaansen & Ochalek, 1983).

In 1985, McCloskey and Zaragoza published an article in which they argued that the traditional misinformation effects (e.g., Loftus et al., 1978) could not be taken as evidence that misleading postevent information caused impairment of original event details. The arguments advanced by McCloskey and Zaragoza (1985a) began with the observation that in the typical eyewitness suggestibility experiment (as in real-world eyewitness testimony situations) participants' memory for the witnessed event is far from perfect, even before they are exposed to misinformation (as evidenced by the finding that control performance is well below ceiling). Hence, according to McCloskey and Zaragoza, the finding that participants given a choice between stop sign and yield sign report the misleading item (yield sign) does not necessarily imply that the participant once had a memory for a stop sign that was now impaired. Rather, for those participants who fail to remember the stop sign (e.g., because they failed to encode it), the misleading suggestion "yield sign" does not conflict with a stored memory representation, it merely fills a gap in memory. McCloskey and Zaragoza argued further that misled participants who fail to encode the originally seen detail (stop sign) are likely to systematically select the more recently presented misleading detail (yield sign) because "yield sign" is all they remember and they have no reason to distrust the postevent source. In contrast, control participants who fail to encode the original stop sign detail, and were never exposed to misinformation about a yield sign, will have no reason to favor the incorrect misleading response (yield sign) on the test. Rather, they will be forced to guess, thus leading them to select the correct alternative (stop sign) 50% of the time on a two-alternative forced-choice recognition test. McCloskey and Zaragoza concluded that for these reasons, misled participants are likely to perform more poorly than control participants on the stop-sign-versus yield-sign test even when their original memory has not been impaired by the misinformation. Finally, McCloskey and Zaragoza also noted that the demand characteristics of the experiment (where the postevent information is presented by an authoritative experimenter as truth) may lead some misled participants to report the suggested detail on the test even if they can remember the original event detail (see also Lindsay, 1990).

To assess whether contradictory misinformation erases or impairs access to original event details, McCloskey and Zaragoza (1985a) developed a Modified Test procedure in which the misleading detail was not an option. Rather, participants had to choose between the original detail and a new detail. In their experiments, participants who witnessed an office theft involving a handyman holding a hammer were later given the misleading suggestion that he was holding a screwdriver. In contrast to the Standard Test where participants are given a choice between the original and misleading item (hammer vs. screwdriver), on the Modified Test, participants were given a choice between the originally seen item and a new item (hammer vs. wrench).[1] In six experiments using the Modified Test procedure, they found that misled participants selected the original item as often as control participants (grand mean was 72% vs. 75% correct for misled and control conditions, respectively, when collapsing across experiments), thus providing no evidence of memory impairment. In the same six experiments, McCloskey and Zaragoza tested a second group of participants with the standard misinformation test (a choice between the original [e.g., hammer] and misleading [e.g., screwdriver] items) and showed that under these circumstances there were robust misled–control performance differences (collapsing across the six experiments mean performance was 37% vs. 72% for misled and control conditions, respectively, a

[1] In all of these experiments, the materials are completely counterbalanced so that across participants, hammer, screwdriver, and wrench serve as the original, misleading, and new information equally often.

difference of 35%). Collectively, the McCloskey and Zaragoza results showed that, when given the opportunity, misled participants had an overwhelming tendency to select the misleading alternative over the item they originally saw on the final memory test, thus replicating the misinformation effect first demonstrated by Loftus et al. (1978). However, when the misleading alternative was not an option on the test, participants evidenced the ability to remember the original event detail as well as participants who had not been misled. These results support the conclusion that factors other than memory impairment contribute to these dramatic errors in participants' performance.

McCloskey and Zaragoza's (1985a, 1985b) claim that contradictory misinformation does not impair memory for originally seen details was highly controversial and generated considerable debate, a debate in which the authors of this chapter held contrasting points of view (e.g., Belli, 1989; Loftus & Hoffman, 1989; Loftus, Schooler, & Wagenaar, 1985; McCloskey & Zaragoza, 1985b; Metcalfe, 1990; Tversky & Tuchin, 1989; Zaragoza & McCloskey, 1989; see also Ayers & Reder, 1998, for a review). McCloskey and Zaragoza's "no impairment" claim seemed to fly in the face of decades of research on retroactive interference effects, and considerable research was devoted to obtaining unambiguous evidence of memory impairment caused by contradictory misinformation. Although McCloskey and Zaragoza's (1985a) results with the Modified Test have been replicated many times and under a variety of conditions (e.g., Belli, 1993; Bowman & Zaragoza, 1989; Loftus, Donders, Hoffman, & Schooler, 1989) clear evidence that misinformation *can* impair memory for original event details has now been obtained with the Modified Test procedure (Belli, Windschitl, McCarthy, & Winfrey, 1992; Eakin, Schreiber, & Sergent-Marshall, 2003; Schooler, Foster, & Loftus, 1988; Schreiber & Sergent, 1998), though it has been difficult to identify the circumstances under which it consistently does so. Payne, Toglia, and Anastasi (1994) conducted a meta-analysis of 44 published experiments that used modified recognition tests and showed that, individually, only 14 of the 44 experiments yielded significantly poorer misled than control performance. Collectively, however, the overall memory impairment effect across the 44 experiments was statistically significant.

What determines whether memory impairment effects are detected? On studies using the Modified Test, evidence of memory impairment has most consistently been obtained when participants are given an interpolated test that forces them to overtly commit to misinformation (by not providing the correct item as an option) prior to taking the Modified Test (Eakin et al., 2003; Schooler, et al., 1988; Schreiber & Sergeant, 1998) but not when participants freely commit to the misinformation prior to taking the Modified Test (see Belli, 1993, for evidence that freely committing to the misinformation does not lead to such impairment). Presumably, forcing participants to overtly commit to the misinformation further boosts activation of the misleading item, thus inhibiting access to the originally seen details. Another factor that appears related to the detection of memory impairment effects is overall memory performance. Memory impairment effects have more readily been observed when overall memory performance is relatively high as opposed to when it is low (Chandler, 1989; Payne et al.. 1994), and when participants are misled about centrally presented items and tested after a lengthy retention interval (Belli, Windschitl, McCarthy, & Winfrey, 1992; although see Windschitl, 1996, for contradictory evidence regarding the effects of retention interval). There is some evidence that memory impairment effects are more likely to be observed when participants are preschoolers rather than adults (Ceci, Ross, & Toglia, 1987; although see Zaragoza, 1991, and Zaragoza, Dahlgren, & Muench, 1992, for failures to replicate these findings under nearly identical conditions).

Evidence for memory impairment has been more readily observed when the final test requires recall rather than recognition (for evidence of memory impairment with cued-recall tests, see Belli, Lindsay, Gales, & McCarthy, 1994; Lindsay, 1990). An important condition for obtaining impairment effects in recall tests is that the misinformation is permitted as a potential response. When cued-recall tests disallow reporting of the misleading information (e.g., by providing a cue to which the misleading item does not apply), no impairment is observed (Zaragoza, McCloskey, & Jamis, 1987). Whether these impairment effects are at times due to destructive updating of memory traces or solely due to retrieval failure is still not completely resolved (e.g., Belli & Loftus, 1996), but what is clear is that the bulk of the evidence favors a role for the retrieval failure hypothesis in most of the conditions that have been observed so far (for recent treatments of this issue, see Chandler, Gargano, & Holt, 2001; Eakin et al., 2003). In summary, research on the memory impairment issue shows that one potential consequence of exposure to contradictory postevent information is impaired access to the originally seen event.

The paper by McCloskey and Zaragoza (1985a) and those that followed in response (Belli, 1989; Loftus & Hoffman, 1989; McCloskey & Zaragoza, 1985b; Tversky & Tuchin, 1989; Zaragoza & McCloskey, 1989) marked a turning point in the history of research on the misinformation effect. It soon became clear that research on the memory impairment issue—which focuses on the "fate" of the original memory following exposure to suggestion—did not address a fundamental aspect of misinformation phenomena, namely, participants' tendency to incorporate misleading postevent suggestions into their eyewitness reports. Whether or not misinformation impairs memory for originally seen details, the fact remains that participants can be easily led to report misinformation that has only been suggested to them. Hence, a critically important issue of both theoretical and practical concern is understanding the nature and extent of this misleading influence. Does misleading questioning simply influence what participants say, or might such questioning lead to the development of false beliefs about the witnessed event? Alternatively, is it possible that exposure to misinformation might lead participants to create genuine false memories of having witnessed the suggested events? Much of the research that followed was concerned with addressing these issues.

## DO PEOPLE DEVELOP GENUINE FALSE MEMORIES OF HAVING WITNESSED SUGGESTED DETAILS?

From her earliest writings, Loftus was a strong proponent of the view that misleading postevent suggestions led to distortions in eyewitness *memory* rather than simply influencing what eyewitnesses report (see, e.g., Loftus, 1979a, 1979b; Loftus & Loftus, 1980). However, as alluded to in the preceding section, the misinformation effect does not provide definitive evidence for this conclusion. It wasn't until researchers started employing methods that probed participants more extensively about the basis for their eyewitness reports that clearer evidence bearing on the false-memory hypothesis started to emerge. Although Loftus's claim that misleading suggestions can lead to false memories was ultimately proved correct, this research has also shown that misled participants sometimes report misinformation for other reasons.

In the standard eyewitness suggestibility experiment, misinformation is presented to participants as an accurate description of the events they witnessed by an experimenter whom they are likely to view as knowledgeable and credible. As many have noted (see, e.g., Lindsay, 1990) this experimental situation is imbued with substantial demand. Participants may feel pressured to report the suggestion whether or not they believe the suggested information or misremember seeing it in the original event. Hence, to rule out the possibility that participants report misinformation simply because they are playing along, it is necessary to make every effort to eliminate this demand. At a minimum, participants need to be alerted to the possibility that the information provided by the postevent source may not correspond to the events they witnessed.

Although it is a relatively straightforward matter to change the demand characteristics of the experiment, it is somewhat more difficult to discriminate between situations where a participant-witness has developed a *false belief* in the suggested information as opposed to a *false memory* of having witnessed the suggested information. Even a high-confidence endorsement of the suggested details may simply reflect a strong belief that the suggested events transpired. As mentioned previously, in cases where participants have no memory that contradicts the misleading suggestions, they have little reason to distrust the experimenter and may therefore come to believe that the suggested information is true. In an attempt to be helpful, participant-witnesses are likely to report everything they know about the event without regard to whether they specifically recollect witnessing it at the original event or whether they learned it from another source

One method that investigators have used to more directly assess whether participants misremember witnessing the suggested information is to give them a source-monitoring test, which forces them to discriminate between possible sources of information in memory. In the typical study, participants are asked to identify the source of the suggested item by choosing among multiple possible sources (e.g., the witnessed event, the postevent questions, both, or neither). Note that source-monitoring test procedures inform participants prior to the test that the postevent narrative and questions contain information that was not in the witnessed event, thus reducing any perceived demand to go along with the suggested information.

Studies have shown that when misled participants are given a source-monitoring test, rather than a traditional recognition test, their tendency to claim they remember witnessing the suggested items is substantially reduced (Zaragoza & Lane, 1994) and in some cases eliminated (Lindsay & Johnson, 1989; Zaragoza & Koshmider, 1989). Nevertheless, a great deal of evidence supports the conclusion that misled participants do claim to remember witnessing the suggested details, even when given a source-monitoring test (Belli, Lindsay, Gales, & McCarthy, 1994; Lindsay, 1990; Chambers & Zaragoza, 2001; Drivdahl & Zaragoza, 2001; Frost, Ingraham, & Wilson, 2002; Hekkanen & McEvoy, 2002; Lane, Mather, Villa, & Morita, 2001; Mitchell & Zaragoza, 1996, 2001; Zaragoza & Lane, 1994; Zaragoza & Mitchell, 1996; see Zaragoza, Lane, Ackil, & Chambers, 1997, for a review). Moreover, if, in addition to the mild warning provided by the source-monitoring test, participants are told very directly and explicitly that they were misinformed (e.g., by telling them that the misleading source contained inaccuracies [Zaragoza & Lane, 1994] or telling them that the experimenter was trying to trick them [Chambers & Zaragoza, 2001]), they still persist in claiming they remember witnessing the suggested items on the source-monitoring test (see also Lindsay, 1990, for evidence that the very strong warning *not* to report any information from the postevent source on the test does not always eliminate false reports on a cued-recall test).

It might be argued that participants' tendency to claim they remember witnessing the suggested items on the source-monitoring test is a reflection of a false belief that they saw the suggested item rather than a genuine false memory of having witnessed the suggested event. To address this possibility, several studies have also assessed the phenomenological experience that accompanies participants' "memory" of witnessing the suggested item or event (cf. Schooler, Gerhard, & Loftus, 1986). One method that has been used to assess the phenomenological experience of false memories is Tulving's (1985) remember/know procedure, a technique that has been used quite extensively in other domains (see Gardiner & Java, 1993, for a review). Following recall or recognition of a test item, participants are asked to indicate whether they remember seeing it during the original event or they just know it occurred, but cannot actually remember the specific episode (see also Zaragoza & Mitchell, 1996, for a related measure where participants are asked to distinguish between "remembering" and "believing"). The distinction between "remembering" and "knowing" is carefully explained to participants (see, e.g., Gardiner & Java, 1990; Rajaram, 1993) and it is emphasized that one can be quite confident that something happened without being able to recollect the specific experience. The question of interest is whether misled participants given remember/know instructions would indicate they "remember" witnessing suggested details, and several studies have now shown that they do (Drivdahl & Zaragoza, 2001; Frost, 2000; Roediger, Jacoby, & McDermott, 1996; Zaragoza & Mitchell, 1996).

In summary, even when participants are warned about the misinformation and are given a source-monitoring test that forces them to discriminate between different sources of information in memory, they continue to claim they remember witnessing suggested details. Moreover, on measures of their phenomenological experience, participants indicate that they recollect seeing the suggested items, much like they recollect memories derived from perceptual experiences. Collectively, these studies provide clear evidence that participants sometimes develop genuine false memories for items and events that were only suggested to them.

## A THEORETICAL FRAMEWORK

The belief that one remembers witnessing an item that was only suggested is an example of a situation where a memory derived from one source (e.g., misleading suggestions provided by an experimenter) is misattributed to another source (e.g., the witnessed event), an error we refer to as a source misattribution error. Marcia Johnson and colleagues (see Johnson, Hashtroudi, & Lindsay, 1993; Johnson & Raye, 1981; Lindsay, 1994) have developed a general theoretical framework, the source-monitoring framework (SMF), that provides some insight into how such errors come about.

According to the SMF, memory for source is an attribution (see also Jacoby, Kelley, & Dywan, 1989, for a similar approach) that is the product of both conscious and nonconscious judgment processes. From this view, information about the source of a memory is not stored directly, but is based on an evaluation of the characteristics of the memory representation. The SMF assumes that memory representations are records of the processing that occurred at encoding and thus contain features or characteristics that reflect the conditions under which the memory was acquired (where and when each piece of information was acquired, modality of presentation, emotional reactions, records of reflective processes, etc). So, for example, if a memory contains a great deal of visual detail, an individual would likely attribute this memory to an event he or she saw. People can, and often do, accurately attribute the source of their memories because memories from different sources tend to differ on average in the quantity and quality of the characteristics associated with them (e.g., memories of perceived events typically have more vivid perceptual, temporal, and spatial information than memories of imagined events; Johnson, Foley, Suengas, & Raye, 1988). Nevertheless, because there can be overlap in the distributions of the features associated with memories from different sources, errors can occur. For example, imagining words spoken in another person's voice increases people's tendency to confuse what they imagined they heard the person say with what they actually heard the person say, presumably because it increases the overlap between the characteristics of the two sources of information (Johnson, Foley, & Leach, 1988).

In situations where eyewitness suggestibility is a concern, the overlap between the witnessed event and postevent interviews is extensive. First, the two episodes are intimately related because they share a common referent—the witnessed event. Note that the common referent factor is inherent in every eyewitness interrogation because, by definition, the postevent interview is always about the witnessed event (Mitchell & Zaragoza, 2001). As a consequence, with the exception of several misleading details in the postevent interview, the content of the original and postevent episodes is nearly identical. Second, in attempting to answer questions about the witnessed event, participants are likely to actively retrieve and reconstruct the originally witnessed events in their minds. This process of activating the original memory while processing the postevent misinformation likely increases the overlap between the original event and postevent questioning even further. Hence, from the perspective of the SMF, it is not surprising that participants sometimes confuse suggested items for items they witnessed firsthand.

The SMF also assumes that the accuracy of source-monitoring judgments is heavily influenced by the circumstances at the time of retrieval (i.e., the appropriateness and stringency of the decision-making processes and criteria used). A good illustration of this is Lindsay and Johnson's (1989) finding that a suggestibility effect is obtained with a yes–no recognition test but not on a source-monitoring test. They proposed that yes–no recognition tests may encourage participants to use a familiarity criterion when responding on a test of memory for the witnessed event. Because the test list consists primarily of witnessed items interspersed with novel foils, responding on the basis of familiarity will in most cases lead to a correct response. For this reason, participants may slip into a tendency of using high familiarity as the basis for deciding whether or not a test item was seen. Of course, the suggested items are familiar not because they were witnessed but because participants had been exposed to them recently in the context of a postevent narrative. In contrast to the yes–no test, the source-monitoring tests direct participants to retrieve and use source-specifying information, thereby enhancing participants' ability to discriminate between memories of the witnessed event and memories of the postevent narrative.

Just as the criteria for deciding whether something was "seen" might change as a function of test demands, the SMF also posits that the criteria by which people judge a memory as "real" might change over time. Specifically, Johnson et al. (1993) posit that the amount of perceptual detail needed to accept a remembered experience as a real memory (and not imagined or suggested) is much greater for recent events than for events from the distant past (see also Belli & Loftus, 1994). In support of these predictions, Frost (2000) has shown that when misled participants are asked whether the suggested details they report are "remembered" or "known," participants are more likely to claim they "remember" seeing the misinformation on delayed tests than on immediate tests.

An important aspect of the source-monitoring account is that people can mistake the origin of some item in memory even if memory for the item itself is very good. Consistent with this idea, several of the studies reviewed in the following sections show that people can have very strong memories of the content of misleading suggestions yet misattribute their source.

## MECHANISMS OF FALSE-MEMORY DEVELOPMENT

Inspired in part by the SMF, some progress has been made in identifying factors that, in combination with misleading suggestion, influence the creation of false memories for suggested events. We review some of this research in the following subsections. Because our primary concern in this section is false memories, we restrict this review to studies that have used methods that attempt to differentiate between false reports that reflect false memories and false reports that occur for other reasons (e.g., source tests, warnings, measures of phenomenological experience).

### The Role of Processing Resources

When attentional resources are limited, memory for an item's source is more likely to be disrupted than is the familiarity of the memory's contents. This is because the encoding and retrieval of source-relevant information are highly effortful, attention-demanding processes, whereas familiarity is a relatively automatic consequence of exposure to an item (Johnson, Kounios, & Reeder, 1994). Thus, limiting attentional resources can cause a relatively selective impairment of source-specifying information that renders the memory highly susceptible to misattribution (cf. Jacoby, Woloshyn, & Kelley, 1989). A study by Zaragoza and Lane (1998) verified these predictions. In one experiment, participants encountered the misinformation under conditions of either divided or full attention, and in a second experiment participants were either given ample time to make the source judgment or were forced to provide source judgments very quickly. The results showed that a scarcity of attentional resources—either when encoding misinformation or when retrieving misinformation—led to impoverished memory for the suggested information's true source but no impairment in memory for the content of the suggested item. This, in turn, led participants to misremember the suggestion as part of the witnessed event. These results are consistent with the finding that forgetting of source information that occurs over long retention intervals is accompanied by increased suggestibility (see, e.g., Lindsay, 1990; Zaragoza & Mitchell, 1996), although the possibility that other factors related to delay (e.g., weaker memory for the witnessed event over time) might contribute to these latter results cannot be ruled out. In sum, the finding that attentional resources influences suggestibility is highly relevant to assessing and predicting suggestibility in real-world contexts, where multiple environmental and internal stimuli (e.g., distraction due to heightened arousal) compete for attentional resources.

## Repeated Suggestion and False Memory

Whereas the foregoing study shows that poor memory for the suggested item's source increases suggestibility, it is also the case that "source amnesia" is not a precondition for misattribution errors. Paradoxically, there are some variables, such as repetition, that simultaneously increase source misattributions and improve memory for the suggestions' source.

Understanding the cognitive consequences of repeated suggestive interviews has considerable practical, as well as theoretical implications. For example, repeated suggestive questioning is not uncommon in eyewitness interrogation procedures. Moreover, one of the reasons the therapeutic process is thought to be potentially conducive to the formation of false memories is because suggestions encountered in the course of therapy are likely to be repeated over time. Given the current controversy surrounding allegedly false memories induced by therapy (see chap. 8, this volume), the need for scientific evidence on the relationship between repeated suggestion and false memory seems especially acute.

Several studies that have attempted to mimic the complexity of real-world interview situations involving repeated suggestion have demonstrated striking examples of false memory in which participants claim to remember entire fictitious events, such as getting lost in a mall (e.g., Ceci, Huffman, Smith, & Loftus, 1994; Ceci, Loftus, Leichtman, & Bruck, 1994; Hyman & Billings, 1998; Hyman, Husband, & Billings, 1995; Hyman & Pentland, 1996; Loftus & Ketcham, 1994; Porter, Yuille, & Lehman, 1999). However, in the interest of ecological validity, in all of these studies repeated suggestion was confounded with several other variables including the passage of time, experimenter demand, and generation of elaborative details. Hence, the role that repetition alone played in the creation of these memories is difficult to discern.

Zaragoza and Mitchell (1996; see also Mitchell & Zaragoza, 1996) conducted several studies whose goal was to isolate the effects of repeated exposure to suggestion on false-memory creation. Zaragoza and Mitchell found that, relative to a single exposure, repeatedly exposing participants to suggestions increased the incidence of false memories for the suggested items, even when controlling for differences in recognition of the suggested items. Using a variant of the remember/know paradigm, they also showed that repeated suggestions increased participants' claims that they specifically recollected witnessing the suggested item in the video. In a follow-up study, Mitchell and Zaragoza showed that increasing the contextual variability of the repeated exposures (i.e., each repetition occurred in a different modality) further exacerbated the repeated-exposures effect. In both these studies, the deleterious effect of repeated exposures could not be attributed to better memory for the suggested information following repetition, because the repetition effects remained the same when the data were conditionalized on old–new recognition (see Mitchell & Zaragoza, 1996; Zaragoza & Mitchell, 1996). Hence, it is not the case that this false-memory effect is merely a function of the greater familiarity of the repeated suggestion. It was also the case that in both these studies, one consequence of repeated suggestion was an increase in participants' claims that the suggested item came from two sources: both the witnessed event and the postevent questionnaire. Hence, rather than impair participants' memory for the suggestions' actual source (the postevent questionnaire) repeated suggestion had the opposite effect. What became more difficult with repeated suggestion was discriminating between the original and postevent episodes, as evidenced by the increase in "both" responses. Recall that in the typical eyewitness suggestibility situation, simply knowing that some piece of information came from a postevent source is not very diagnostic with regard to its accuracy, because much of the information provided by the postevent source is highly accurate. Hence, the difficulty for participants was discriminating between information that was only in the postevent questionnaire as opposed to both the postevent questionnaire and the originally witnessed event.

How might repeated exposure to suggestion lead participants to misremember witnessing suggested events? In the studies by Zaragoza and Mitchell (1996; Mitchell & Zaragoza, 1996) the misleading suggestions were embedded in questions about the video event that participants were required to answer. They proposed that in answering such questions participants were likely to retrieve and reflect upon the events they had witnessed. When the questions contained misleading suggestions, it is likely that participants implicitly incorporated the suggested information into their imagined reconstructions of the witnessed event. With repetition, these images of suggested events probably became more elaborate and detailed (see Suengas & Johnson, 1988, for evidence that rehearsing imagined events serves to preserve and embellish them), thus increasing their similarity to records of actually witnessed events. In addition, it is likely that repetition increased the speed or fluency with which images of the suggested events could be generated by the subjects, thereby increasing participants' confidence that the memories were real (cf. Kelley & Lindsay, 1993).

A less studied but related issue is the effect of repeatedly reporting suggested information on false-memory creation. Using a cued-recall paradigm, Roediger, Jacoby, and McDermott (1996) induced participants to report misinformation on a first occasion, and assessed whether this would alter participants' performance on a later recall test (relative to a condition with no inducing manipulation). The clear finding was that producing the misinformation on a first test increased the likelihood that participants misrecalled the misinformation on a later test (where they were explicitly warned to ignore the postevent information). Moreover, repeated reporting of suggested details also made participants more likely to claim they "remembered" witnessing the misinformation when instructed to use the remember/know procedure. Hence, Roediger et al. showed that repeated reporting of suggested information, like repeated exposure, increases false memories for suggested information.

## Mentally Elaborating On Suggested Events

Several different lines of evidence have shown that mentally elaborating on suggested events increases false memory for these events. By "mental elaboration" we mean any type of mental processing that embellishes the suggested event with details or other characteristics that render it confusable with a memory for a "real" event.

*Imagery Instructions.* There is considerable evidence that imagery is a catalyst for false-memory formation. For example, there is evidence that both imagery ability (e.g., Dobson & Markham, 1993) and preference for an imagic cognitive style (e.g., Labelle, Laurence, Naden, & Perry, 1990) are related to susceptibility to false-memory creation. In addition, studies have shown that instructing people to imagine fictitious childhood experiences increases their belief that these fictitious events actually occurred (Garry, Manning, Loftus, & Sherman, 1996; Paddock et al., 1998) and can lead to false memories for fictitious childhood events (Hyman & Pentland, 1996). For example, Hyman and Pentland instructed participants to reminisce about a number of events from their childhood, including one that had never actually happened but had only been suggested by the experimenter (e.g., that they had tipped over a punch bowl at a wedding onto the parents of the bride). Those participants who were repeatedly instructed to imagine these events over three sessions were later more likely to claim they remembered them (both fictitious and real) than participants who were repeatedly instructed to merely think about them. Similar findings have been obtained with a somewhat different paradigm where participants are repeatedly instructed to imagine performing simple actions (Goff & Roediger, 1998; Thomas, Bulevich, & Loftus, 2003).

Why might imagery be associated with false-memory creation? It is well documented that discriminating between imagination and reality can be difficult, especially when imagined events contain large numbers of features or characteristics that are typical of actually experienced events (e.g., Johnson, Foley, & Leach, 1988; Johnson & Raye, 1981). In the case of false memories, imagining a fictitious event likely results in a mental representation that closely resembles a real event, because the act of imagination involves creating a specific instantiation of the fictitious event in one's mind. To use an example from a study by Hyman and Pentland (1996), imagining that as a child I once spilled a punch bowl at a wedding probably involves creating a mental version of this incident that specifies such things as who was there, what they looked like, where the wedding took place, how I spilled the punch bowl, what the consequences were, how I felt about it, and so forth. In other words, imagining and visualizing an event (in this example, a fictitious one) involves reflectively elaborating on a hypothetical idea in a variety of ways so as to produce a more concrete, specific, and perceptually and semantically detailed version of the incident in one's mind. At a broader level, imagining a fictitious event likely renders the imagined event more familiar, available, and plausible, thus increasing the likelihood that one would accept the imagined event as a real one (see, e.g., Garry et al., 1996). Thus, there are probably multiple dimensions, both general (e.g., familiarity) and specific (e.g., sensory-perceptual detail), on which imagined events resemble real ones.

*Sensory-Perceptual Elaboration.* Although the association between imagery and false-memory creation is well documented, the mechanisms by which imagery induces false-memory creation are not yet well understood (cf. Thomas et al., 2003). Given that imagining a fictitious event likely involves a great deal of perceptual elaboration (as well as reflective elaboration on other dimensions) Drivdahl and Zaragoza (2001) set out to assess whether leading participants to reflectively elaborate on the perceptual characteristics of misleading suggestions would increase false memory for the suggested events. To this end, they used an eyewitness suggestibility paradigm where participants viewed a videotape depicting a burglary and were later exposed to misleading suggestions (e.g., they were misinformed that the thief stole a ring, when in fact he did not steal any jewelry). The perceptual elaboration manipulation was implemented by asking participants yes-or-no follow-up questions about the perceptual characteristics (e.g., location, physical appearance, etc.) of a previously mentioned item. For example, some participants who had been misinformed that the thief stole a ring were asked the follow-up question, "Did he find the ring in the top drawer?" When a suggestion was repeated, participants answered a different question about the suggested item each time they encountered it (e.g., "Was the ring in a box?" "Did the ring have a gemstone?"). In this way, the follow-up questioning resembled interview situations where witnesses are pressed to provide specific details of fictitious or poorly remembered events. Two days later, participants were given a test of their memory for the source of the suggested items. The results showed that participants who answered questions that encouraged them to elaborate on the perceptual characteristics of the suggested items, such as their location and physical appearance, were much more likely to later claim they "definitely" remembered seeing them than participants in a no-elaboration group, who were exposed to the same suggestions but answered follow-up questions about relatively superficial aspects of the suggested items (e.g., its rhyming characteristics). Drivdahl and Zaragoza proposed that answering perceptual-elaboration questions increased false memory because it induced participants to form a more perceptually detailed, specific, and embellished representation of the suggested events than they would have otherwise done (see Thomas et al., 2003, for the related finding that instructing participants to include sensory details in their imaginings increased source misattributions). Consistent with this proposal, there is considerable evidence that the greater the vividness, clarity, and detail associated with imagined events, the greater the likelihood that they will be confused for actually experienced events (see Johnson et al., 1993, for a review). Note that one important way in which the Drivdahl and Zaragoza study differs from previous imagination studies is that participants were not explicitly instructed to imagine the suggested events, but were asked follow-up questions that encouraged the implicit generation of visualized detailed images of the suggested events.

*Semantic Elaboration.* Although the foregoing results show that the sensory-perceptual characteristics of imagined suggested events contribute to false-memory creation, it is also possible that the effects of imagery are also due in part to the meaningful elaborative processing that imaging entails. Note that attempts to imagine fictitious items/events are also likely to involve more abstract sorts of reasoning about the meaning and implications of the fictitious events, and a consideration of the plausible scenarios within which they might have transpired. This sort of elaborative processing may serve to establish stronger and more numerous connections between the misleading suggestions and other information in memory. To the extent that suggested memories that are embedded in a coherent network of relations are likely to be confused for "real" memories, it is possible that simply elaborating on the meaning and implications of suggested events might serve to increase false memory.

In a follow-up to the Drivdahl and Zaragoza (2001) study, Zaragoza, Mitchell, Payment, and Drivdahl (2006) examined the relative contributions of perceptual and meaningful elaboration on false-memory creation by manipulating the type of follow-up questions participants received about the suggested information. Participants in the semantic-elaboration group answered follow-up questions that led them to think about the meaning and implications of the suggested details, but not their perceptual characteristics. For example, some participants in the semantic-elaboration condition who received the misleading suggestion that the "thief stole a ring" were asked the follow-up question "How incriminating would a jury find it if they were told that the thief was found with a stolen ring in his possession?" If the suggestion was repeated, participants answered a different type of follow-up question every time they encountered it (e.g., "Was the fact that the thief stole a ring central to the plot?" "Do you think the thief was disappointed that he did not find other jewelry besides the ring?"). As in the Drivdahl and Zaragoza study, participants in the perceptual-elaboration group were asked follow-up questions about the perceptual characteristics of the suggested items. Relative to a repetition-control group that had repeated exposure to the suggested information but no elaboration, participants in both elaboration groups evinced higher levels of false memory for the suggested detail. The proportion of times participants claimed they "definitely" remembered seeing suggested details was .28, .41, and .59 in the repetition-control, perceptual-elaboration, and semantic-elaboration groups, respectively. Hence, a novel and unexpected finding was that semantic elaboration led to greater increases in false memory than perceptual elaboration (even though type of elaboration had no effect on any other dependent measure). Zaragoza et al. proposed that semantic elaboration promotes false memory by establishing stronger and more numerous connections between the misleading suggestions and other well-developed knowledge structures in memory (e.g., schemas regarding juries, what constitutes incriminating evidence, etc). In sum, it appears that misinformation that is embedded in a coherent network of relations is more likely to be confused for a "real" memory. (See also Drivdahl, 2001, for the related finding that inducing participants to think about the emotional consequences of suggested events also increases false memory.)

*Photograph Review.* The foregoing studies on perceptual and semantic elaboration induced participants to mentally elaborate on suggested items that pertained to recently experienced events. When participants are misled about events from their remote past—such as their childhood—their relatively impoverished memory of their distant past may make it more difficult for them to construct a perceptually and semantically detailed image of the suggested childhood event. On the other hand, if participants are given cues, such as photographs, that help them retrieve aspects of their childhood, they may be better equipped to form a compelling and plausible image of the suggested (i.e., fictitious) childhood event. This, in turn, should increase their susceptibility to developing a false memory for the suggested event. A fascinating study by Lindsay, Hagen, Read, Wade, and Garry (2004) provides evidence consistent with this prediction.

In the Lindsay, Hagen et al. (2004) study, participants were asked to remember three school-related childhood events: two true events provided by parents, and a third, fictitious event (putting slime in the teacher's desk in Grade 1 or 2). For participants in the photo group, the experimenter provided a color photo of their class picture at the time of the suggested event, and participants in all groups were encouraged to recall as much as possible using mental-context reinstatement and guided-imagery exercises over a period of several days. In a final test session, participants in the photo condition were twice as likely as participants in a no-photo condition to experience false memories, and their ratings of the extent to which remembering the event was like reliving it was comparable to the ratings they gave for true events. The authors proposed that although the photo did not depict the slime prank, the photo may have enabled participants to speculate about plausible scenarios involving the suggested event (e.g., "Who would my collaborator in the slime prank have been?"). Participants in the no-photo condition may have had difficulty constructing such scenarios because of their inability to recall relevant elements, such as who was in their classroom and the appearance of the teacher. The authors further proposed that participants may have used perceptual details from the photo (e.g., the teacher's appearance) to produce vivid images of the fictitious event, thus producing especially compelling false memories (see Lindsay et al., 2004).

## NEW DIRECTIONS AND EXTENSIONS OF THE MISINFORMATION PARADIGM

### Misinformation Encountered Outside the Interview Context

The misinformation paradigm provides a laboratory analogue of real-world situations involving eyewitnesses to forensically relevant events who are interviewed suggestively about the events they have witnessed. For this reason, most studies of misinformation effects have presented misinformation in the context of postevent questions or postevent narratives about the witnessed event. Recent studies have begun to document that eyewitness memories can also be contaminated by misinformation encountered outside the postevent interview context.

Studies of the social-contagion effect (Meade & Roediger, 2002; Roediger, Meade & Bergman, 2001) have shown that when two people witness the same event, a person's memory for the witnessed information can be contaminated by false information provided by the cowitness. In these studies, two participants (one of whom is a confederate) view a series of scenes and then engage in a collaborative-recall task where they each recall several items from each scene. However some of the items "recalled" by the confederate are false in that they suggested objects that had not actually appeared in the scene (and thus serve as misinformation). The finding of interest is that when participants are later tested individually they recall these suggested items even when told to recall only those items they remembered from the scenes. Moreover, neither warning participants that others' responses might influence their recall, nor giving them a source-monitoring test (which oriented them to discriminate between items they saw and those the cowitness reported) eliminates the social-contagion effect (Meade & Roediger, 2002). These findings extend research on the misinformation effect by showing that even information provided by an unfamiliar peer can affect participants' memories for events they have witnessed.

Perhaps even more surprising than the social-contagion effects is the recent finding that participants will sometimes intrude details from one event into their memory of a different event (Allen & Lindsay, 1998; Lindsay, Allen, Chan, & Dahl, 2004).

In these studies, participants viewed a movie clip depicting a museum burglary and read a narrative description of either (a) the same event (i.e., the museum burglary they had seen), (b) a different, but thematically related, event (a palace burglary), or (c) a less closely related event (a school field trip to a palace). In every case, the narratives contained information that was not in the original movie clip. The finding of interest was that when participants were given a cued-recall test of their memory for the video, participants in all three conditions falsely recalled information from the narratives, though false recall was greater when the narrative described the witnessed event rather than a different event. A striking finding was that these intrusions occurred even when the narrative described an event (a school field trip to a palace) that was in many ways quite different from the event depicted in the movie clip participants had seen (a burglary in a museum).

## False Memories for Forced Confabulations and False Confessions

To date, most studies in the eyewitness suggestibility literature have focused almost exclusively on suggestive interviews involving false-memory implantation. In the implantation paradigm, the witness is given misinformation about a witnessed event, and suggestibility is measured as the extent to which the witness then (or later) assents to the misinformation provided by the interviewer. However, in real-world forensic and therapeutic settings, suggestive interview practices are not restricted to situations involving the explicit provision of misinformation. Rather, in some cases interviewers attempt to elicit from witnesses accounts that support their beliefs about what transpired (cf. Bruck, Ceci, & Hembrooke, 1998). To this end, interviewers may forcibly press witnesses to describe those events they believe transpired, even when witnesses cannot remember or never witnessed the events they are pressed to testify about (cf. Gudjonssson, 1992; Leo, 1996).

Might witnesses eventually develop false memories for events they had earlier been forced to confabulate? Intuitively, it seems unlikely they would do so.

Presumably, events that are confabulated deliberately and under duress will be remembered as mere fabrications, even over the long term. However, contrary to this intuition, a recent study (Zaragoza, Payment, Ackil, Drivdahl, & Beck, 2001) showed that participants who were pressed to confabulate information about a witnessed event later evidenced false memories for some of the events they had earlier confabulated knowingly (see also Ackil & Zaragoza, 1998, for similar evidence with children), a phenomenon they call the "forced confabulation effect." In this study, participants viewed a movie clip and were then asked specific questions about both true and blatantly false events. In order to answer these false-event questions, the participants were required to confabulate, or make something up. For example, in going over a scene from the video, the experimenter said, "It [the chair] broke, and Delaney fell on the floor. Where was Delaney bleeding?" This question required a confabulated response because although Delaney did fall off a chair in the video, he clearly did not bleed nor hurt himself in any way.

As one might expect, participants firmly resisted answering such questions, but were repeatedly pressed to guess until they eventually acquiesced. To illustrate, the following is a transcript from a forced-confabulation interview:

| | |
|---|---|
| Interviewer: | After he fell, where was Delaney Bleeding? |
| Participant: | He wasn't. He was? I didn't see any blood. |
| Interviewer: | What's your best guess? |
| Participant: | Where was he bleeding? |
| Interviewer: | Yeah. |
| Participant: | But he wasn't bleeding. Oh, I don't have a best guess. I didn't think he was bleeding. *His knee?* |
| Interviewer: | Okay, his knee. |
| Participant: | *It's not his knee!* (Zaragoza et al., 2001, p. 476) |

Throughout the interview, the interviewer selectively reinforced some of the participants' confabulated responses by providing confirmatory feedback (e.g., "Knee is the correct answer!") and provided neutral (uninformative feedback for the remaining confabulated responses (e.g., "OK, knee"—see earlier transcript) (see Wells & Bradfield, 1998, for other evidence that confirmatory feedback leads to distortions in eyewitness testimony). One week later, a large proportion of participants misremembered witnessing the events they had earlier confabulated knowingly (even though they were warned in advance that they had been questioned about fictitious events). Moreover, confirmatory feedback increased false memory for forcibly confabulated events, increased confidence in those memories, and increased the likelihood that participants would freely report the confabulated events 1 to 2 months later. Important to note, the authors were able to show that these false-memory effects were not dependent on memory for the feedback.

In an ingenious experiment, Kassin and Kiechel (1996) demonstrated that false incriminating evidence can lead people to believe—and even remember—that they committed a crime they did not commit. Research on this topic is of great practical importance as the presentation of false incriminating evidence is a common interrogation technique, and studies have shown that coerced confessions increase the conviction rate even when participants recognize they are coerced, even when it is stricken from the record, and even when jurors claim it had no influence on their verdict (Kassin & Sukel, 1997). In their study, participants engaged in a computer reaction-time task and were incorrectly accused of hitting the wrong key and damaging the computer. All of the participants initially denied hitting the key, and indeed none of them had done so. Two variables were manipulated: First, in order to influence participants' certainty in their own innocence, the pace of the computer task was varied (either very fast paced or slow paced). Second, they varied whether or not participants received the false incriminating evidence (the "misinformation"). Specifically, for participants in the false-witness condition, an experimental confederate claimed she saw the participant hit the key, whereas for participants in the no-witness condition the same confederate said she had not seen what happened. There were three outcome measures: participants' willingness to sign a confession (a measure of compliance), participants' tendency to freely report to another participant that they had hit the key/damaged the computer (a measure of internalization), and participants' tendency to "recall" specific details to fit the allegation, such as "I hit it with the side of my right hand after you called out the 'A'" (Kassin & Kiechel, 1996, p. 127). The latter served as a measure of confabulation (or false memory). The results showed that both variables influenced participants' performance on all measures: Compared to participants in the slow-pace/no-witness group, participants in the fast-pace/false-witness group were more likely to sign the confession, internalize guilt for the event, and confabulate details in memory consistent with the false belief. Interestingly, the false incriminating evidence was a critical ingredient in producing confabulations. No participants in the no-witness groups (whether slow *or* fast paced) produced confabulations. In summary, these findings extend studies of misinformation phenomena by showing that people can be misled about their own actions, not just events they have observed. Moreover, like the forced-confabulation studies, these studies show that coercing witnesses to say things against their will (describing events they did not see, providing self-incriminating statements), can seriously distort their memories over the long term.

## The Scope of False Memories of Suggested Events

Most of the research on misinformation phenomena reviewed here has documented false memories for selected aspects of a witnessed event (e.g., a false memory that the thief had a gun, when in fact he had no weapon). In recent years, the controversy surrounding allegedly false recovered memories of childhood abuse has raised important questions about the extent of people's susceptibility to memory illusions. In particular, a question of central concern in this debate is whether people can be led to develop false memories for entire events that never actually transpired (see chap. 8, this volume). Once again, Elizabeth Loftus has been at the forefront of the effort to provide scientific evidence that bears on this issue of pressing social concern by developing innovative methods for addressing such questions in the laboratory (e.g., Loftus, Coan, & Pickrell, 1979/1996)

Although the recovered/false-memory debate has captured a great deal of attention in recent years, research on this problem is in many ways a natural outgrowth of research on misinformation phenomena. Although the latter focuses on participants' memories for details of recent eyewitness events, many of the factors that appear to promote the creation of false memories for suggested childhood events (e.g., imagery, repetition, forced generation, mental elaboration) were discovered in the context of basic research on the misinformation effect. Our hope is that the ongoing recovered/false-memory debate may resolve itself as the once lively debates on the misinformation effect have largely been resolved, with scientists who once took adversarial positions beginning to see that their points of agreement are more numerous than those points on which they disagree. Finally, as this chapter has shown, research on the misinformation effect is an ongoing energetic direction of investigation that continues to provide unique insights into the nature of memory and its susceptibility to error.

## REFERENCES


Ackil, J. K., & Zaragoza, M. S. (1998). Memorial consequences of forced confabulations: Age differences in susceptibility to false memories. *Developmental Psychology, 34,* 1358–1372.

Allen, B. P., & Lindsay, D. S. (1998). Amalgamations of memories: Intrusions of information from one event into reports of another. *Applied Cognitive Psychology, 12,* 277–285.

Ayers, M. S., & Reder, L. M. (1998). A theoretical review of the misinformation effect: Predictions from an activation-based memory model. *Psychonomic Bulletin & Review, 5,* 1–21.

Banaji, M. R., & Crowder, R. G. (1989). The bankruptcy of everyday memory. *American Psychologist, 44,* 1185–1193.

Bekerian, D. A., & Bowers, J. M. (1983). Eyewitness testimony: Were we misled? *Journal of Experimental Psychology: Learning, Memory, and Cognition, 9,* 139–145.

Belli, R. F. (1988). Color blend retrievals: Compromise memories or deliberate compromise responses? *Memory & Cognition, 16,* 314–326.

Belli, R. F. (1989). Influences of misleading postevent information: Misinformation interference and acceptance. *Journal of Experimental Psychology: General, 118,* 72–85.

Belli, R. F. (1993). Failure of interpolated tests in inducing memory impairment with final modified tests: Evidence unfavorable to the blocking hypothesis. *American Journal of Psychology, 106,* 407–427.

Belli, R. F., Lindsay, D. S., Gales, M. S., & McCarthy, T. T. (1994). Memory impairment and source misattribution in postevent misinformation experiments with short retention intervals. *Memory & Cognition, 22,* 40–54.

Belli, R. F., & Loftus, E. F. (1996). The pliability of autobiographical memory: Misinformation and the false memory problem. In D. C. Rubin (Ed.), *Remembering our past: Studies in autobiographical memory* (pp. 157–179). New York: Cambridge University Press.

Belli, R. F., Windschitl, P. D., McCarthy, T. T., & Winfrey, S. E. (1992). Detecting memory impairment with a modified test procedure: Manipulating retention interval with centrally presented event items. *Journal of Experimental Psychology: Learning, Memory, and Cognition, 18,* 356–367.

Bowman, L. L., & Zaragoza, M. S. (1989). Similarity of encoding context does not influence resistance to memory impairment following misinformation. *American Journal of Psychology, 102,* 249–264.

Bruck, M., Ceci, S. J., & Hembrooke, H. (1998). Reliability and credibility of young children's reports: From research to policy and practice. *American Psychologist, 53,* 136–151.

Ceci, S. J., Huffman, M. L. C., Smith, E., & Loftus, E. F. (1994). Repeatedly thinking about a non-event: Source misattributions among preschoolers. *Consciousness & Cognition: An International Journal, 3*(3–4), 388–407.

Ceci, S. J., Loftus, E. F., Leichtman, M. D., & Bruck, M. (1994). The possible role of source misattributions in the creation of false beliefs among preschoolers. *International Journal of Clinical and Experimental Hypnosis, 42,* 304–320.

Ceci, S. J., Ross, D. F., & Toglia, M. P. (1987). Suggestibility of children's memory: Psycholegal implications. *Journal of Experimental Psychology: General, 116,* 38–49.

Chambers, K. L., & Zaragoza, M. S. (2001). Intended and unintended effects of explicit warnings on eyewitness suggestibility: Evidence from source identification tests. *Memory & Cognition, 29,* 1120–1129.

Chandler, C. C. (1989). Specific retroactive interference in modified recognition tests: Evidence for an unknown cause of interference. *Journal of Experimental Psychology: Learning, Memory, and Cognition, 15,* 256–265.

Chandler, C. C., Gargano, G. J., & Holt, B. C. (2001). Witnessing postevents does not change memory traces, but can affect their retrieval. *Applied Cognitive Psychology, 15,* 3–22.

Christiaansen, R. E., & Ochalek, K. (1983). Editing misleading information from memory: Evidence for the co-existence of original and postevent information. *Memory & Cognition, 11,* 467–475.

Crowder, R. G. (1976). *Principles of learning and memory.* Oxford, England: Lawrence Erlbaum Associates.

Dobson, M., & Markham, R. (1993). Imagery ability and source monitoring: Implications for eyewitness memory. *British Journal of Psychology, 84,* 111–118.

Dodd, D. H., & Bradshaw, J. M. (1980). Leading questions and memory: Pragmatic constraints. *Journal of Verbal Learning & Verbal Behavior, 19*(6), 695–704.

Drivdahl, S. B. (2001). The role of emotion and self-reference in the creation of false memories for suggested events. *Dissertation Abstracts, 61,* 6156.

Drivdahl, S. B., & Zaragoza, M. S. (2001). The role of perceptual elaboration and individual differences in the creation of false memories for suggested events. *Applied Cognitive Psychology, 15,* 265–281.

Eakin, D. K., Schreiber, T. A., & Sergent-Marshall, S. (2003). Misinformation effects in eyewitness memory: The presence and absence of memory impairment as a function of warning and misinformation accessibility. *Journal of Experimental Psychology: Learning, Memory, and Cognition, 29,* 813–825.

Frost, P. (2000). The quality of false memory over time: Is misinformation "remembered" or "known"? *Psychonomic Bulletin & Review, 7*(3), 531–536.

Frost, P., Ingraham, M., & Wilson, B. (2002). Why misinformation is more likely to be recognised over time. A source monitoring account. *Memory, 10*(3), 179–185.

Gardiner, J. M., & Java, R. I. (1990). Recollective experience in word and nonword recognition. *Memory & Cognition, 18,* 23–30.

Gardiner, J. M., & Java, R. I. (1993). Recognition memory and awareness: An experiential approach. *European Journal of Cognitive Psychology, 5,* 337–346.

Garry, M., Manning, C. G., Loftus, E. F., & Sherman, S. J. (1996). Imagination inflation: Imagining a childhood event inflates confidence that it occurred. *Psychonomic Bulletin & Review, 3,* 208–214.

Goff, L. M., & Roediger, H. L. (1998). Imagination inflation for action events: Repeated imaginings lead to illusory recollections. *Memory & Cognition, 26,* 20–33.

Gudjonsson, G. H. (1992). *The psychology of interrogations, confessions and testimony.* Oxford, England: Wiley.

Hekkanen, S. T., & McEvoy, C. (2002). False memories and source-monitoring problems: Criterion differences. *Applied Cognitive Psychology, 16,* 73–85.

Hyman, I. E., & Billings, F. J. (1998). Individual differences and the creation of false childhood memories. *Memory, 6,* 1–20.

Hyman, I. E., Husband, T. H., & Billings, F. J. (1995). False memories of childhood experiences. *Applied Cognitive Psychology, 9,* 181–197.

Hyman, I. E., & Pentland, J. (1996). The role of mental imagery in the creation of false childhood memories. *Journal of Memory and Language, 35,* 101–117.

Jacoby, L. L., Kelley, C. M., & Dywan, J. (1989). Memory attributions. In H. L. Roediger & F. I. M. Craik (Eds.), *Varieties of memory and consciousness: Essays in honor of Endel Tulving* (pp. 391–422). Hillsdale, NJ: Lawrence Erlbaum Associates.

Jacoby, L. L., Woloshyn, B., & Kelley, C. M. (1989). Becoming famous without being recognized: Unconscious influences of memory produced by divided attention. *Journal of Experimental Psychology: General, 118,* 72–85.

Johnson, M. K., Foley, M. A., & Leach, K. (1988). The consequences for memory of imagining another person's voice. *Memory & Cognition, 16,* 337–342.

Johnson, M. K., Foley, M. A., Suengas, A. G., & Raye, C. L. (1988). Phenomenal characteristics of memories for perceived and imagined autobiographical events. *Journal of Experimental Psychology: General, 117,* 371–376.

Johnson, M. K., Hashtroudi, S., & Lindsay, D. S. (1993). Source monitoring. *Psychological Bulletin, 114,* 3–28.

Johnson, M. K., Kounios, J., & Reeder, J. A. (1994). Time-course studies of reality monitoring and recognition. *Journal of Experimental Psychology: Learning, Memory, and Cognition, 20,* 1409–1419.

Johnson, M. K., & Raye, C. L. (1981). Reality monitoring. *Psychological Review, 88,* 67–85.

Kassin, S. M., & Kiechel, K. L. (1996). The social psychology of false confessions: Compliance, internalization, and confabulation. *Psychological Science, 7,* 125–128.

Kassin, S. M., & Sukel, H. (1997). Coerced confessions and the jury: An experimental test of the "harmless error" rule. *Law & Human Behavior, 21,* 27–46.

Kelley, C. M., & Lindsay, S. D. (1993). Remembering mistaken for knowing: Ease of retrieval as a basis for confidence in answers to general knowledge questions. *Journal of Memory and Language, 32,* 1–24.

Labelle, L., Laurence, J., Nadon, R., & Perry, C. (1990). Hypnotizability, preference for an imagic cognitive style, and memory creation in hypnosis. *Journal of Abnormal Psychology, 99,* 222–228.

Lampinen, J. M., & Smith, V. L. (1995). The incredible (and sometimes incredulous) child witness: Child eyewitnesses' sensitivity to source credibility cues. *Journal of Applied Psychology, 80,* 621–627.

Lane, S. M., Mather, M., Villa, D., & Morita, S. K. (2001). How events are reviewed matters: Effects of varied focus on eyewitness suggestibility. *Memory & Cognition, 29,* 940–947.

Leo, R. A. (1996). Miranda's revenge: Police interrogation as a confidence game. *Law & Society Review, 30,* 259–288.

Lindsay, D. S. (1990). Misleading suggestions can impair eyewitnesses' ability to remember event details. *Journal of Experimental Psychology: Learning, Memory, and Cognition, 16,* 1077–1083.

Lindsay, D. S. (1994). Memory source monitoring and eyewitness testimony. In D. F. Ross, J. D. Read, & M. P. Toglia (Eds.), *Adult eyewitness testimony: Current trends and developments* (pp. 27–55). New York: Springer-Verlag.

Lindsay, D. S., Allen, B. P., Chan, J. C. K., & Dahl, L. C. (2004). Eyewitness suggestibility and source similarity: Intrusions of details from one event into memory reports of another event. *Journal of Memory and Language, 50,* 96–111.

Lindsay, D. S., Hagen, L., Read, J. D., Wade, K. A., & Garry, M. (2004). True photographs and false memories. *Psychological Science, 15,* 149–154.

Lindsay, D. S., & Johnson, M. K. (1989). The eyewitness suggestibility effect and memory for source. *Memory & Cognition, 17,* 349–358.

Loftus, E. F. (1975). Leading questions and the eyewitness report. *Cognitive Psychology, 7,* 560–572.

Loftus, E. F. (1977). Shirting human color memory. *Memory & Cognition, 5,* 696–699.

Loftus, E. F. (1979a). *Eyewitness testimony.* Cambridge, MA: Harvard University Press.

Loftus, E. F. (1979b). The malleability of human memory. *American Scientist, 67,* 312–320.

Loftus, E. F. (1979c). Reactions to blatantly contradictory information. *Memory & Cognition, 7,* 368–374.

Loftus, E. F., Coan, J. A., & Pickrell, J. E. (1996). Manufacturing false memories using bits of reality. In L. M. Reder (Ed.), *Implicit memory and metacognition* (pp. 195–220). Mahwah, NJ: Lawrence Erlbaum Associates. (Original work published 1979)

Loftus, E. F., Donders, K., Hoffman, H. G., & Schooler, J.W. (1989). Creating new memories that are quickly accessed and confidently held. *Memory & Cognition, 17,* 607–616.

Loftus, E. F., & Hoffman, H. G. (1989). Misinformation and memory: The creation of new memories. *Journal of Experimental Psychology: General, 118,* 100–104.

Loftus, E. F., & Ketcham, K. (1994). *The myth of repressed memory.* New York: St. Martin's Press.

Loftus, E. F., & Loftus, G. R. (1980). On the permanence of stored information in the brain. *American Psychologist, 35,* 409–420.

Loftus, E. F., Miller, D. G., & Burns, H. J. (1978). Semantic integration of verbal information into a visual memory. *Journal of Experimental Psychology: Human Learning and Memory, 4,* 19–31.

Loftus, E. F., & Palmer, J. C. (1974). Reconstruction of automobile destruction: An example of the interaction between language and memory. *Journal of Verbal Learning and Verbal Behavior, 13,* 585–589.

Loftus, E. F., Schooler, J. W., & Wagenaar, W. (1985). The fate of memory: Comment on McCloskey and Zaragoza. *Journal of Experimental Psychology: General, 114,* 375–380.

McCloskey, M., & Zaragoza, M. (1985a). Misleading postevent information and memory for events: Arguments and evidence against memory impairment hypotheses. *Journal of Experimental Psychology: General, 114,* 1–16.

McCloskey, M., & Zaragoza, M. (1985b). Postevent information and memory: Reply to Loftus, Schooler, and Wagenaar. *Journal of Experimental Psychology: General, 114,* 381–387.

Meade, M. L., & Roediger, H. L. (2002). Explorations in the social contagion of memory. *Memory & Cognition, 30,* 995–1009.

Metcalfe, J. (1990). Composite Holographic Associative Recall Model (CHARM) and blended memories in eyewitness testimony. *Journal of Experimental Psychology: General, 119,* 145–160.

Mitchell, K. J. ,& Zaragoza, M. S. (1996). Repeated exposure to suggestion and false memory: The role of contextual variability. *Journal of Memory and Language*l 246V260.

Mitchell, K. J., & Zaragoza, M. S. (2001). Contextual overlap and eyewitness suggestibility. *Memory & Cognition, 29,* 616–626.

Paddock, J. R., Joseph, A. L., Chan, F. M., Terranova, S., Manning, C., & Loftus, E. F. (1998). When guided visualization procedures may backfire: Imagination inflation and predicting individual differences in suggestibility [Special issue]. *Applied Cognitive Psychology, 12,* 563–575.

Payne, D. G., Toglia, M. P., & Anastasi, J. S. (1994). Recognition performance level and the magnitude of the misinformation effect in eyewitness memory. *Psychonomic Bulletin & Review, 1,* 376–382.

Porter, S., Yuille, J. C., & Lehman, D. R. (1999). The nature of real, implanted, and fabricated memories for emotional childhood events: Implications for the recovered memory debate. *Law & Human Behavior, 23,* 517–537.

Rajaram, S. (1993). Remembering and knowing: Two means of access to the personal past. *Memory & Cognition, 21,* 89–102.

Roediger, H. L., Jacoby, D., & McDermott, K. B. (1996). Misinformation effects in recall: Creating false memories through repeated retrieval. *Journal of Memory and Language, 35,* 300–318.

Roediger, H. L., Meade, M. L., & Bergman, E. T. (2001). Social contagion of memory. *Psychonomic Bulletin & Review, 8,* 365–371.

Schooler, J. W., Foster, R. A., & Loftus, E. F. (1988). Some deleterious consequences of the act of recollection. *Memory & Cognition, 16,* 243–251.

Schooler, J. W., Gerhard, D., & Loftus, E. F. (1986). Qualities of the unreal. *Journal of Experimental Psychology: Learning, Memory, and Cognition, 12,* 171–181.

Schreiber, T. A., & Sergent, S. D. (1998). The role of commitment in producing misinformation effects in eyewitness memory. *Psychonomic Bulletin & Review, 5,* 443–448.

Smith, V. L., & Ellsworth, P. C. (1987). The social psychology of eyewitness accuracy: Misleading questions and communicator expertise. *Journal of Applied Psychology, 72,* 294–300.

Suengas, A. G., & Johnson, M. K. (1988). Qualitative effects of rehearsal on memories for perceived and imagined complex events. *Journal of Experimental Psychology: General, 117,* 377–389.

Thomas, A. K., Bulevich, J. B., & Loftus, E. F. (2003). Exploring the role of repetition and sensory elaboration in the imagination inflation effect. *Memory & Cognition, 31,* 630–640.

Tousignant, J. P., Hall, D., & Loftus, E. F. (1986). Discrepancy detection and vulnerability to misleading postevent information. *Memory & Cognition, 14,* 329–338.

Tulving, E. (1985). Memory and consciousness. *Canadian Psychology, 26,* 1–12.

Tversky, B., & Tuchin, M. (1989). A reconciliation of the evidence on eyewitness testimony: Comments on McCloskey and Zaragoza. *Journal of Experimental Psychology: General, 118,* 86–91.

Underwood, J., & Pezdek, K. (1998). Memory suggestibility as an example of the sleeper effect. *Psychonomic Bulletin & Review, 5,* 449–453.

Vornik, L. A., Sharman, S. J., & Garry, M. (2003). The power of the spoken word: Sociolinguistic cues influence the misinformation effect. *Memory, 11,* 101–109.

Wells, G. L., & Bradfield, A. L. (1998). "Good, you identified the suspect": Feedback to eyewitnesses distorts their reports of the witnessing experience. *Journal of Applied Psychology, 83,* 360–376.

Windschitl, P. D. (1996). Memory for faces: Evidence of retrieval-based impairment. *Journal of Experimental Psychology: Learning, Memory, and Cognition, 22,* 1101–1122.

Zaragoza, M. S. (1991). Preschool children's susceptibility to memory impairment. In J. Doris (Ed.), *The suggestibility of children's recollections* (pp. 27–39). Washington, DC: American Psychological Association.

Zaragoza, M. S., Dahlgren, D., & Muench, J. (1992). The role of memory impairment in children's suggestibility. In M. L. Howe, C. J. Brainerd, & V. F. Reyna (Eds.), *The development of long-term retention* (pp. 184–216). New York: Springer-Verlag.

Zaragoza, M. S., & Koshmider, J. W., III (1989). Misled subjects may know more than their performance implies. *Journal of Experimental Psychology: Learning, Memory, and Cogntion, 15,* 246–255.

Zaragoza, M. S., & Lane, S. M. (1994). Source misattributions and the suggestibility of eyewitness memory. *Journal of Experimental Psychology: Learning, Memory, &and Cogntion, 20,* 934–945.

Zaragoza, M. S., & Lane, S. M. (1998). Processing resources and eyewitness suggestibility. *Legal & Criminological Psychology*, *3*(Pt. 2), 305–320.

Zaragoza, M. S., Lane, S. M., Ackil, J. K., & Chambers, K. L. (1997). Confusing real and suggested memories: Source monitoring and eyewitness suggestibility. In N. Stein, P. A. Ornstein, B. Tversky, & C. Brainerd (Eds.), *Memory for everyday and emotional events* (pp. 401–428). Mahwah, NJ: Lawrence Erlbaum Associates.

Zaragoza, M. S., & McCloskey, M. (1989). Misleading postevent information and the memory impairment hypothesis: Comment on Belli and reply to Tversky and Tuchin. *Journal of Experimental Psychology: General, 118,* 92–99.

Zaragoza, M. S., McCloskey, M., & Jamis, M. (1987). Misleading postevent information and recall of the original event: Further evidence against the memory impairment hypothesis. *Journal of Experimental Psychology: Learning, Memory, and Cogntion, 13,* 36–44.

Zaragoza, M. S., & Mitchell, K. J. (1996). Repeated exposure to suggestion and the creation of false memories. *Psychological Science, 7,* 294–300.

Zaragoza, M. S., Mitchell, K. J., Payment, K. E., & Drivdahl, S. B. (2006). *Reflective elaboration and false memory: The role of relational processing.* Manuscript in preparation, Kent State University, Department of Psychology.

Zaragoza, M. S., Payment, K. E., Ackil, J. K., Drivdahl, S. B., & Beck, M. (2001). Interviewing witnesses: Forced confabulation and confirmatory feedback increase false memories. *Psychological Science, 12,* 473–477.

CHAPTER

# 5

# Loftus's Lineage in Developmental Forensic Research: Six Scientific Misconceptions About Children's Suggestibility

Stephen J. Ceci and Maggie Bruck

In recent years, there has been an explosion of interest in children's testimonial issues among therapists, policymakers, and law enforcement officials. Increasingly, children are finding their way into the legal system to offer testimony in a broad range of cases; and even larger numbers of children are deposed, interviewed, and examined each year as part of civil and family court cases. Although prior to the early 1980s it was rare to find children testifying in criminal cases, now it has become so common that many jurisdictions have implemented special procedures to minimize children's discomfort and increase the reliability of their statements under oath (e.g., one-way screens or shields to allow the defendant to watch the child without the child being aware; videotaped testimony in judges' chambers; a support person to sit with them while they testify). Unsurprisingly, as a result of these legal trends, researchers have turned their attention to the problems faced by and caused by child witnesses. In fact, a perusal of any developmental journal today will confirm that topics pertinent to young children in the forensic arena represent one of the most active areas of child research. But this was not always the case. In our earlier reviews (Ceci & Bruck, 1993, 1995), we pointed out that forensic research with young children was almost nonexistent until the early 1990s. One of the catalysts for the surge in research since then has been the work of the individual this volume is dedicated to—Elizabeth F. Loftus.

No discussion of this topic is complete without acknowledging the seminal and prolific contributions of Beth Loftus. Her early work on suggestibility, breaking new ground in the development of paradigms, became not only citation classics among adult-memory researchers (Loftus, Miller, & Burns, 1978; Loftus & Palmer, 1974; Loftus & Zanni, 1975), but were also immensely important as a catalyst for developmental memory researchers who adopted her paradigms and reasoning to study accuracy and distortion of children's memories. For example, the misinformation paradigm that was first developed by Loftus to examine suggestibility in adults was adapted by Ceci, Ross, and Toglia (1987) to examine developmental differences in young children's suggestibility. Loftus's insights on how to study false-memory implantation for entire events (e.g., Loftus, 1993) were adapted by the authors of this chapter to study developmental differences in false beliefs (Ceci, Huffman, Smith, & Loftus, 1994a; Ceci, Loftus, Leichtman, & Bruck, 1994), and has since become a staple paradigm for research on children's memory accuracy and distortion.

In what follows, we provide an update on suggestibility research, focusing on new developments that challenge many of the basic assertions made by researchers and by expert witnesses. This presentation is intended to demonstrate recent progress in understanding the accuracy and inaccuracy of children's memory as well as to show how the science is sometimes misunderstood and misused in the courtroom. A second intention is to show how this area of research makes contributions to applied issues and to basic research on cognitive and social development. Younger scholars and graduate students will find in it an opportunity to emulate one of Beth Loftus's most enduring contributions; namely, to venture into the legal arena in the role of an educator, someone who reviews the scientific findings for fact finders in a fair and comprehensive manner.

When children report being a victim of or a witness to a crime, two primary sets of issues arise for those involved in evaluating their testimony. The first set of issues concerns memories of children who have experienced traumatic events. Topics related to this set of issues include the cognitive, motivational, and emotional factors that influence the nature of the child's report of the trauma. The research in this area is based on the assumption that the child has actually experienced the traumatic event. The second set of issues concerns whether it is possible for children to falsely report traumatic events that were not experienced, particularly as a result of suggestive interviews. The major topics in this area of research include the conditions that precipitate false reports (e.g., visually guided imagery, biased interviewing), the psychological status of false reports (false beliefs vs. lies), and developmental trends in both. In this chapter, we focus on six major misconceptions about children's reports and about their suggestibility. Each of these misconceptions has made its way into courtroom testimony as we demonstrate throughout the chapter and, sadly, many of them are harbored by researchers as well as clinicians and social workers.

## MISCONCEPTION 1: CHILDREN'S DISCLOSURES OF TRAUMATIC EVENTS ARE OFTEN DENIED, AND LATER RECANTED

A highly influential assumption that has been in wide circulation among expert witnesses and some researchers since the 1980s is that sexually abused children do not readily disclose abuse because of shame, guilt, and fear; consequently, there are long delays between abuse and disclosure, and often there is never any disclosure (see Mason, 1991, for description of expert testimony on this assumption). But beyond the phenomenon of delay in reporting, it has repeatedly been asserted that, when questioned, children will initially deny their abuse, and will only divulge its details with repeated questioning. It is further claimed that these disclosures are frequently recanted, but with additional support their disclosures will be reinstated. The most popular embodiment of this model was proposed by Roland Summit (1983) and was termed the Child Sexual Abuse Accommodation Syndrome (CSAAS). It has been invoked in the forensic arena to explain to the court why children may not readily disclose their abuse.

Finally, the majority of children who are sexually abused underreport the extent and severity of the abuse. If I would have heard about lengthy disclosures with a specific beginning, middle, and end to the story, I would have been less impressed because that type of recounting is not likely with sexually abused children, particularly preschoolers. The two most common types of reports that I hear from a sexually abused child of this age are either flat denials or fragmented segments of an incident (Expert Report prepared for *Lillie v. Newcastle City Council*, 2002, p. 11).

In *People v. Carroll* (2001, p. 70) a prosecutor questioned his expert witness:

| | |
|---|---|
| *Prosecutor:* | Doctor, you mentioned earlier that with respect to child victims it is not unusual that they would fully describe all of the events in your first interview. |
| *Expert:* | No. |
| *Prosecutor:* | And if they do, is it suspicious to you? |
| *Expert:* | To me, yes. |

The irony is that if a child victim spontaneously described an event, this expert would be suspicious of its authenticity.

The CSAAS model was based not on empirical data but rather on clinical intuitions. Given this, we recently set out to review the literature on children's disclosure to determine whether there was any empirical support for the claims (London, Bruck, Ceci, & Shuman, 2005). As will be seen, some of the literature we reviewed did support claims inherent in the CSAAS model, although some of the literature refuted other assumptions of this model. Ten studies were identified in which adults with histories of childhood abuse were asked to recall their disclosures in childhood. Results were very consistent; on average only 33% of the adults remembered disclosing the abuse during childhood. These data support the view that sexually abused children are silent about their victimization and delay disclosure for long periods of time. These data are also important in that they support the contention that prevalence data on sexual abuse (which are based on reports to official agencies) greatly underestimate the extent of the problem because so much abuse does not get reported.

Although these studies are informative on the issue of delay of reporting, because the adults in these studies were never asked, "As a child, did anyone ever ask you or question you about abuse?" the data are silent on issues of denial and recantation by sexually abused children. From these studies of delayed reporting, we have no idea whether these individuals were asked about their abuse and denied or told then recanted. For that, we need to look elsewhere. Another set of studies provides some relevant data on this point. We identified 17 studies that examined rates of denial and recantation by sexually abused children who were, in fact, asked directly about being abused when they were assessed or treated at clinics. The rates of denial at assessment interviews were highly variable (4% to 76%) as were the rates of recantation (4% to 27%). We found that the methodological adequacy of each study (sampling procedures, validation of sexual abuse) was related to denial and recantation rates, with the highest rates being associated with the weakest studies. For the six methodologically superior studies, the average rate of denial was only 14% and the average rate of recantation was just 7%.

In part, the myth of children's patterns of disclosure has persisted because documentation of the first stage of the CSAAS model (children are silent, they delay disclosures) has been interpreted as evidence for the full model. Also, as shown by our recent review and analysis, the most commonly cited studies were those that supported the model; sadly, these were the weakest of the 17 studies on methodological grounds.

## MISCONCEPTION 2: SEXUALLY ABUSED CHILDREN'S STATEMENTS OF ABUSE CAN BE ELICITED ONLY BY SPECIFIC AND LEADING QUESTIONS

Even if it is conceded that children will not "deny" being sexually abused when directly asked, this does not address the issue of how to elicit disclosures. A corollary of CSAAS is that in order to overcome emotional and motivational barriers that inhibit spontaneous disclosure of their abuse, children must be asked specific questions about it over a period of time. In part, this assumption is supported by the developmental literature that shows that children will provide more detailed answers to specific or cued questions than to open-ended questions. With the acquisition of cognitive structures that assist the organization of events into coherent narratives, the need for specific questions declines with age. The following expert testimony illustrates how these two concepts become intertwined:

> *Prosecutor*: In your experience in interviewing children, have you ever found it necessary to use a leading question, give them cues for recall?
>
> *Expert:* Oh, yes. Children who don't have [the] ability to free recall, they are nervous; they are scared, or they are just resistant for various reasons to talk about the abuse. ... When anybody encodes information in their memory, they usually do that through their sensory input. ... If they did not put the details into their brain then they have trouble retrieving that of course. Also, children are more likely not to have the categories in their brain for certain information; so they have a harder time with retrieval. So the details come out slowly as they are going back and being comfortable with being able to relate the information. That's why therapy is needed so badly so long, is that it takes a while for them to feel comfortable enough to let the information come up and come out. (*Respondent v. Ryan D. Smith,* Tr. 865)

Recent research by Michael Lamb, Kathleen Sternberg, and colleagues challenges the common claim that children need to be asked specific questions because they are cognitively or emotionally unprepared to provide reports in response to more general questions. This team has constructed a structured interview protocol and then trained interviewers of suspected child abuse victims in its use. The major characteristic of the protocol is to encourage the child to provide detailed life-event narratives through the guidance of open-ended questions (e.g., "Tell me what happened"; "And then what happened next?"; "And you said it happened at the store. Tell me about the store."). The use of specific questions is allowed only after exhaustive free-recall prompting. Suggestive questions are highly discouraged. In their latest study, Lamb et al. (2003) examined the interviews of 16 trained police officers with 130 children (4–8 years old), all of whom had made allegations of sexual abuse. They found that 78% of preschoolers' allegations and disclosures were elicited through free-recall questions, and 66% of all children identified the suspect through open-ended question (60% for preschoolers). These data dispel the belief that children need to be bombarded with specific questions in order to elicit details of their traumatic events; in fact, children can provide detailed information through open-ended prompts and, if a child denies abuse when asked directly, there is no scientifically compelling evidence that the child is "in denial." Abused children usually disclose when directly asked.

## MISCONCEPTION 3: SUGGESTIVE INTERVIEWS CAN BE INDEXED BY THE SHEER NUMBER OF LEADING QUESTIONS

The following testimony by an expert witness illustrates the view that leading questions are an index of the suggestiveness of an interview:

> I usually say, "Mama talked about that somebody did some bad touching." And that's still pretty open ended. I'm not saying who and I'm not saying exactly what. I'm just introducing the subject ... or I will say, "I see many children, and children come and tell me when bad things happen to them, and I've heard other kids tell me when bad things happen. So it's okay if you want to tell me." (*Respondent v. Ryan D. Smith,* Tr, 875)

Contrary to this expert's opinion, the suggestiveness (and thus the risk of eliciting false information) of an interview is not merely reflected by the number of leading questions or the lack thereof but rather in how the concept of "interview bias" plays out in the various interviewing techniques and interactions during the interview as well as in previous interviews. Sometimes suggestive interviews can be void of leading questions; on the other hand, leading questions *may* not pose a risk to the reliability of children's reports in the absence of interview bias. (We emphasize the word *may* because it is an inference derived from some of our studies in which leading questions failed to taint report accuracy when interviewer bias was absent. Clearly, more and better evidence is needed to elevate this conjecture to the level of an empirical reality.)

For example, Garven, Wood, and Malpass (2000) asked kindergarten children to recall details when a visitor named Paco came to their classroom and read a story, gave out treats, and wore a funny hat. Half the children were asked questions that included misleading questions about plausible events (e.g., Did Paco break a toy?) and about bizarre events (e.g., Did Paco take you to a farm?). Between 5% and 13% of the children falsely agreed with the misleading questions. A second group of children were also questioned, but these children were given feedback after their answers to the misleading questions. "No" responses were negatively evaluated:

*Interviewer:* Did Paco take you somewhere in a helicopter?
*Child:* No.
*Interviewer:* You're not doing good.

"Yes" responses were positively evaluated:

*Interviewer:* Did Paco break a toy?
Child: Yes.
*Interviewer:* Great, you're doing excellent now.

This group of children provided the desired but false answer to 35% of the plausible questions and to 52% of the bizarre questions. This study demonstrates that a simple count of misleading/leading questions would not reflect the suggestiveness of the interview; it was the added combination of the selective reinforcement that provided the child with sufficient information concerning the bias of the interviewer. In a follow-up interview 2 weeks later, when children were simply asked nonleading questions with no selective reinforcement feedback, the same level of between-group differences were obtained. Thus interviewer bias in a prior interview can produce false reports in a later unbiased/neutral interview that contains no leading questions.

## MISCONCEPTION 4: SUGGESTIBILITY IS PRIMARILY A PROBLEM FOR YOUNGER AGE GROUPS

This fourth point concerns the status of developmental differences in suggestibility. Although much of the literature pays lip-service to the concept that suggestibility exists at all ages, including adults, the primary view is that preschool children are disproportionately suggestible, and that there should be less concern about the tainting effects of suggestive interviews with older children. This view reflects the disproportionate attention to the study of preschool children at the end of the 20th century, a practice that was directly motivated by current forensic concerns. During that time, there were a number of high-profile criminal cases in which preschool children's horrific claims about sexual abuse by day-care workers, parents, and other unfamiliar adults were presented to the jury. Although the case facts showed that these children had been subjected to highly suggestive interviews, at that time there was no relevant body of scientific literature to indicate the risk of these interviewing techniques in producing false allegations about a range of salient events. When researchers began to fill in this empirical void, most of the studies focused on preschoolers with few examining age-related differences in susceptibility to misleading suggestions between preschoolers and older individuals. Studies that did include age comparisons in suggestibility usually found ceiling effects for the older children, leading to the conclusion that only preschoolers were suggestible (e.g., Ceci et al, 1987).

The conclusion that suggestibility was minimal in grade school children was discrepant with the findings of another body of literature showing that many of the suggestive techniques used in the child studies also produced tainted reports or memories in adults (e.g., see Loftus, 2003). By inference, one might assume that children in elementary school must also be quite suggestible, given that both the younger and older groups were. Recent evidence supports this view: Susceptibility to suggestion is highly common in middle childhood, and under some conditions there are small or even no developmental differences in susceptibility to misleading suggestions. For example, Finnila et al. (2003) staged an event (a version of the Paco visit described earlier for Garven et al., 2000) for two age groups of children (4- to 5-year-olds and 7- to 8-year-olds). One week later half the children were given a low-pressure interview that contained some misleading questions with abuse themes that were taken from a previous study by Goodman and

Aman (1990, e.g.. "He took your clothes off, didn't he?"). The other children received a high-pressure interview during which they were told that their friends had answered the leading questions affirmatively. These latter children were praised for assenting to the misleading questions, and when they did not assent the question was repeated. In both conditions, there were no significant age differences although a significant number (68%) of misleading questions were assented to in the high-pressure condition (see also Bruck, London, Landa, & Goodman, in press; Zaragoza et al., 2001). It has also been found that under some conditions, older children are more suggestible than younger children (e.g., Finnila et al., 2003; Scullin & Ceci, 2001; Zaragoza et al. 2001). These newer findings reshape current views of the developmental trends in suggestibility, and also challenge current conceptualizations of the developmental mechanisms in children's suggestibility. Specifically, current candidate mechanisms (e.g., theory of mind; social compliance) are commonly those known to have developed by the end of the preschool years. Clearly, a wider perspective needs to be taken and skills that develop throughout the childhood years should become the focus of future study (e.g., appreciation of the ramifications of false statements; insight into questioner's motives).

## MISCONCEPTION 5: MULTIPLE SUGGESTIVE INTERVIEWS ARE NEEDED TO TAINT A REPORT

A fifth misconception concerns the view that it is very difficult to implant memories or to taint reports, especially reports about salient events such as bodily touching, in a single interview. Those holding this view claim that repeated suggestions over the course of multiple interviews are needed to taint a child's report of a salient event. We have been as responsible as anyone for this view (e.g., Ceci & Bruck, 1995). In part, this conclusion was based on results of studies in which children made false reports after a series of suggestive interviews (Bruck, Ceci, Francoeur, & Barr, 1995; Leichtman & Ceci, 1995). However, because there was no comparison condition in which children received only one suggestive interview, or because children in these studies were not questioned after each suggestive interview but only at the end of a series of interviews, it was premature to reach definitive conclusions about the added power of multiple suggestive interviews. There are two lines of evidence that have led to a revised view of the effects of one versus multiple suggestive interviews on the accuracy of children's reports.

First, a number of researchers have found that children's reports for significant events can be greatly distorted after a single interview that contains a number of suggestive elements (Garven et al., 2000; Thompson, Clarke-Stewart, & Lepore, 1997).

Second, recent evidence suggests that, contrary to common psychological principles, there are a number of circumstances when one suggestive interview produces the same amount of taint as two or more suggestive interviews. The benefits of a second interview depend on the spacing of the interviews from the initial events and from the final interview. In other words, it depends on the strength of the original memory trace at the time of suggestion and on the strength of the memory for the suggestion at the time of the memory test (Marche, 1999; Melnyk & Bruck, 2004). For example, Melnyk and Bruck found that providing children misinformation on one occasion had the same deleterious effects as presenting the misinformation on two occasions when there was a long delay between the actual event and the suggestive interview, and a long delay between the suggestive interview and the final memory interview. However, two interviews were more damaging than one if children were provided with the misinformation soon after the event and soon before the final interview.

For several reasons, these studies should not lead to the conclusion that one need not worry about the cumulative effects of repeated suggestive interviews. First, it appears that false-assent rates for entire nonexperienced events *do* rise as a function of the number of suggestive interviews (e.g., Bruck, Ceci, & Hembrooke, 2002; Ceci, Loftus, Leichtman, & Bruck, 1994). Studies in which children come to provide narratives of episodes that never occurred may be more relevant to the legal arena than other studies in which children falsely insert suggested details. Second, the exact conditions under which two interviews are more harmful than one are still unknown (e.g., in terms of the exact timing or the number of suggestive features). Finally, as should be clear, enormous damage can be done after only one interview and thus there may be ceiling effects such that a second interview may not significantly increase the already high rate of false reports.

## MISCONCEPTION 6: THE SCIENTIFIC LITERATURE ALLOWS ACCURATE PREDICTION OF INDIVIDUAL CHLDREN'S SUGGESTIBILITY

The following expert's testimony reflects the view that one can determine whether a child has in fact fallen sway to suggestion based on personality, social, or cognitive profiles or based on the characteristics of the report:

Prosecutor: So is it fair to say that you do not see that the interviews and/or the repeated questioning interfered with their memory for these events?

Expert Witness: That's correct. I do not see the evidence for that. ... So the likelihood is high that what you saw in the tape is a child who represents that small minority of 2 or 5 percent of children who are highly suggestible.[1] They have the personality characteristics of high memory suggestibility. Now, if you have such a child and you supply, systematically, misinformation suggestions, then there are several characteristics of that that we would look for.

> Number one is that we'd see a high number of false assents over time, for central actions not just peripheral details. But, for example, with child witness A I counted 14 different interview occasions, and every time she reported the father touched her tee-tee, as just one example. Then there was no change in the central action.
>
> Number two, what you saw on the Mousetrap tape [see Ceci, Huffman, Smith, & Loftus, 1994] there was a fair amount of embellishment of a child who has a personality characteristic of embellishing. We call that high memory suggestibility. If that were the case here, we would suggest a good deal of embellishment about the central actions on the part of Child A and Child B. There is absolutely no evidence of embellishments over time. (*Commonwealth of Pennsylvania v. Gerald J. Delbridge,* 2004, pp. 273–274).

The logic used by this expert, who is both a clinician and a researcher, is poor. In the laboratory, researchers have control over and thus know exactly what a participant in a study has experienced; therefore, they can exactly determine which statements are correct and incorrect. Furthermore, because of the designs of studies (again something that researchers control), one can also determine the degree to which statements are the result of suggestive interviewing processes.

Unfortunately, in real life, unless there is an eyewitness, it is usually impossible for experts to determine the degree to which statements are true or false because they were not there to view the events or to verify whether an event took place. All they have is the word of the child. The scientific evidence provides the best guidance; if the child's first statements were associated with suggestive interviews, there is a high risk that they might be tainted.

Not having information about the original event, this expert relied on the characteristics of the child's report and relied on some studies that show that children's false reports that result from suggestion are sometimes embellished and inconsistent. Because the reports of the child witnesses in the case at hand did not contain these characteristics, the expert argued that they cannot be the product of suggestive interviewing and therefore must be true. Although there is some literature to support the view that false narratives that are the product of suggestive interviews contain more elaborations and fewer consistencies across time than true narratives, this cannot be used to differentiate which narratives are true and which are false because true and false narratives overlap on these dimensions (see Bruck et al., 2002). Thus this research cannot be used for classification or diagnostic purposes.

Next, this expert testifies that there are "personality characteristics of high memory suggestibility." In a recent review of the literature on the psychosocial characteristics associated with suggestibility in children, Melynk and Bruck (2004) failed to identify any specific dimensions that consistently predicted with high precision suggestibility in individual children. Although there were a few promising domains, these could not be used to accurately identify individual children who would be the most suggestible. Based on our reading of the current literature, individual-difference studies have not been that informative; significant effects are effervescent and small. The same children are not always necessarily suggestible across multiple contexts. Rather, the best predictors we have to date concern the factors inherent to the interview itself (the mode of questioning, the delay, etc.).

Despite the substantial advances that developmental forensic researchers have made to application and theory as a result of the seminal contributions of paradigms and methodologies by Beth Loftus, there continues to be a need to disabuse misconceptions that make their way into scholarly writings and expert testimony, including expert testimony by researchers as well as practitioners. In this chapter, we unveiled six particularly common misconceptions that in each case have made their way into expert testimony in court cases. We have shown that no compelling evidence supports the belief that victims of abuse deny their abuse when they are directly questioned about it, nor do they usually recant, as some have claimed. Furthermore, we document that even older children can be quite susceptible to the deleterious effects of suggestive interviews, and that sometimes a single suggestive interview is sufficient to taint a report, notwithstanding claims that multiple suggestive interviews are needed to taint reports about salient events. And finally, we described research on the contextual and individual-difference variables that differentiate children's error rates in response to misleading information and therefore should qualify statements that experts have made. We expect that over the next few years, as research continues in this area there may be new evidence to challenge other common beliefs; this is the role of science. Experts who come to court need to be continually up-to-date on the state of the current research, lest they provide the courts with erroneous depictions of children's strengths and weaknesses. One of Beth Loftus's most enduring legacies will be that she was among the earliest in our field to realize that researchers can venture outside their laboratories and into the courtroom to assume the role of an educator. We can only hope that those who assume this role as educator of fact finders will be as up-to-date on the state of the current research as she.

## REFERENCES

Bruck, M., Ceci, S. J., Francoeur, E., & Barr, R.J . (1995). I hardly cried when I got my shot! Influencing children's reports about a visit to their pediatrician. *Child Development, 66,* 193–208.

Bruck, M., Ceci, S. J., & Hembrooke, H. (2002). Nature of true and false narratives. *Developmental Review, 22*i 520–554.

Bruck, M., London, K., Landa, R., & Goodman, J. (in press). Autobiographical memory and suggestibility in children with Autism Spectrum Disorder. *Development and Psychopathology.*

Ceci, S. J., & Bruck, M. (1993). The suggestibility of children's recollections: An historical review and synthesis. *Psychological Bulletin, 113,* 403–439.

Ceci, S. J., & Bruck, M. (1995). *Jeopardy in the courtroom: A scientific analysis of children's testimony*. Washington, DC: APA Books.

Ceci, S. J., Huffman, M. L., Smith, E., & Loftus, E. F. (1994b). Repeatedly thinking about a non-event. *Consciousness & Cognition, 3,* 388–407.

Ceci, S. J., Loftus, E. F., Leichtman, M., & Bruck, M. (1994). The possible role of source misattributions in the creation of false beliefs among preschoolers. *International Journal of Clinical & Experimental Hypnosis, 42,* 304–320.

Ceci, S. J., Ross, D., & Toglia, M. (1987). Suggestibility of children's memory: Psycholegal implications. *Journal of Experimental Psychology: General, 116,* 38–49.

Finnila, K., Mahlberga, N., Santtilaa, P., Sandnabbaa, K., & Niemib, P. (2003). Validity of a test of children's suggestibility for predicting responses to two interview situations differing in their degree of suggestiveness. *Journal of Experimental Child Psychology, 85,* 32–49.

Garven, S., Wood, J. M., & Malpass, R. S. (2000). Allegations of wrongdoing: The effects of reinforcement on children's mundane and fantastic claims. *Journal of Applied Psychology, 85,* 38–49.

Goodman, G. & Aman, C. (1990). Children's use of fanataomically detailed dolls to recount an event. *Child Development, 61*, 1859–1871.

Lamb, M. E., Sternberg, K. J., Orbach, Y., Esplin, P. W., Stewart, H., Mitchell, S. (2003). Age Differences in young children's to open-ended invitations in the course of forensic interviews. Journal of Consulting and Clinical Psychologhy, *7* (5), 926–934.

*Lillie and Reed v. Newcastle City Council & Others*, EWHC 1600 (QB) (2002).

Leichtman, M. D., & Ceci, S. J. (1995) The effects of stereotypes and suggestions on preschoolers' reports. *Developmental Psychology, 31*(4), 568–578.

Loftus, E. F. (1993). The reality of repressed memories. *American Psychologist, 48,* 518–537.

Loftus, E. F. (2003). False memory. In L. Nadel (Ed.), *Encyclopedia of cognitive science* (Vol. 2, pp. 120–125). London: Nature.

Loftus, E. F., Miller, D., & Burns, H. (1978). Semantic integration of verbal into a visual memory. *Journal of Experimental Psychology: Human Learning and Memory, 4,* 19–31.

Loftus, E. F., & Palmer, J. C. (1974). Reconstruction of automobile destruction: An example of the interaction between language and memory. *Journal of Verbal Learning and Verbal Behavior, 13,* 585–589.

Loftus, E. F., & Zanni, G. (1975). Eyewitness testimony: The influence of wording of a question. *Bulletin of the Psychonomic Society,* 5, 86–88.

London, K., Bruck, M., Ceci, S. J., & Shuman, D. (2005). Disclosure of child sexual abuse: What does the research tell us about the ways that children tell? *Psychology, Public Policy & Law, 11,* 194–226.

Marche, T. (1999). Memory strength affects reporting of misinformation. *Journal of Experimental Child Psychology, 73,* 45–71.

Melnyk, L., & Bruck, M. (2004). Timing moderates the effect of repeated suggestive interviewing on chilren's suggestibility. *Applied Cognitive Psychology, 18,* 613–631.

Mason, M. A. (1991). A judicial dilemma: Expert witness testimony in child sex abuse cases. *The Journal of Psychiatry and Law, Fall/Winter,* 185–219.

*People v. Carroll,* Ind. No. B-10431 (Rensselaer County, New York, 2001).

Soullin, M. H. & Ceci, S. J. (2001). A suggestibility scale for children. Personality & Individual Differences, 30, 843–856.

Summit, R. C. (1983). The child sexual abuse accommodation syndrome. *Child Abuse & Neglect, 7,* 177–193.

Thompson, W. C., Clarke-Stewart, K. A., & Lepore, S. (1997). What did the janitor do? Suggestive interviewing and the accuracy of children's accounts. *Law & Human Behavior, 21*(4), 405–426.

Zaragoza, M., Payment, K., Kichler, J., Stines, L., Drivdahl, S. (2001). *Forced confabulation and false memory in child witnesses*. Paper presented at the 2001 biennial meeting of the Society for Research in Child Development.

CHAPTER

6

# Verbal Recall of Preverbal Memories: Implications for the Clinic and the Courtroom

Harlene Hayne

Zealous conviction is a dangerous substitute for an open mind (Loftus, 1993b, p. 534).

In 1993, Elizabeth Loftus published a landmark paper titled "The Reality of Repressed Memories." In that paper, Loftus explored the claim that people could experience a traumatic event, banish their memory of that event from consciousness, and then uncover it again—sometimes decades later. This kind of traumatic forgetting is often referred to as repression. Like so many other issues in psychology, the notion of repression originated with Sigmund Freud. According to his view, repression involved the selective forgetting of memories that caused the individual psychological pain. Although these painful memories remained stored in pristine condition, they were blocked from consciousness by psychological defence mechanisms. One goal of Freud's psychoanalysis was to lift the veil of repression, allowing patients to recall their painful past in a psychologically safe environment.

For decades, interest in the notion of repression was restricted to psychoanalysts and other therapists. During the early 1990s, however, there was a cavalcade of court cases involving repressed and recovered memories. In these cases, the plaintiffs reported memories for a host of crimes including sexual abuse, murder, and satanic ritual. Although the specific details varied from case to case, at the heart of each was a plaintiff who claimed that he or she had lost all memory of the crime in question, but that the memory had returned years, and often, decades later. The large number of ensuing legal battles forced lawyers, judges, experimental psychologists, clinicians, and members of the general public to take a more careful look at the validity of repressed and recovered memories.

In her paper, "The Reality of Repressed Memories," Loftus (1993b) reviewed a number of celebrated cases involving claims of repressed and recovered memory. Although she did not discount the authenticity of the plaintiffs' recovered memories entirely, she did express healthy skepticism about the phenomenon of repression and she provided a number of alternative explanations about the potential source of these recently unearthed memories including popular books for abuse survivors, dubious clinical practices, and the general malleability of human memory (for a recent review of repression, see chap. 8, this volume). Furthermore, given the lack of empirical evidence for the concept of repression, Loftus cautioned therapists (and presumably, judges, lawyers, and members of the general public) against blind acceptance of uncorroborated instances of repressed and recovered memory.

I first encountered "The Reality of Repressed Memories" in the context of teaching clinical trainees, but as a researcher, my primary interest is memory development, and several of the examples of repressed and recovered memory that Loftus provided piqued my interest from this point of view. In her paper, Loftus described a number of cases in which adults recovered their memory of abusive events that presumably took place during their infancy. For example, during the course of visualization with her therapist, Patti Barton recalled eye surgery that took place when she was 7 months old. She also recalled being sexually abused by her father at the age of 15 months. During the course of the trial against her father, John Peters, Patti's testimony included a verbal account of her infant attempts to communicate the sexual abuse to her mother at the time that it occurred.

The issue of repression notwithstanding, Patti Barton's claims are particularly intriguing from the perspective of infant memory development. In particular, if Patti's recovered memories are authentic, then at least two things have to be true. First, the basic neural mechanisms required for memory processing must be sufficiently mature during infancy to support the encoding, storage, and retrieval of specific memories over retention intervals of 20, 30, or 40 years. Second, given that whatever information infants learn and remember is likely to be stored in a nonverbal format, then it must be possible, at some point in development, to translate those early preverbal memories into language.

Is there any empirical evidence to support these two assumptions? Is it possible to recall the experiences of our infancy over a lifetime? If so, is it possible to translate those memories into words as we acquire language? With these questions in mind, the goal of the present chapter is threefold. First, I outline some of the theoretical issues that researchers must consider in the study of verbal recall of preverbal memories. Second, I review the empirical evidence that has been gathered to date. Finally, I discuss the clinical and legal implications of the current database for both children and adults.

## THEORETICAL ISSUES TO CONSIDER

At least three well-established psychological phenomena are relevant to our discussion of adults' ability to provide coherent verbal accounts of their preverbal memories.

### Childhood Amnesia

Freud coined the term childhood amnesia to describe the inability of adults to recall experiences from their infancy and early childhood. During the course of psychoanalysis, Freud often asked his patients to describe events that had taken place during their lifetime. On the basis of these patient reports, Freud discovered that most people had limited recollection of events that occurred prior to the age of 6 to 8 years (1905/1953). Subsequent normative studies of adults' earliest memories have since shown that most adults can recall at least some events that occurred when they were approximately 3 to 4 years of age or perhaps even slightly younger (e.g., MacDonald, Uesiliana, & Hayne, 2000; Mullen, 1994; Usher & Neisser, 1993). Although these data have redefined the boundary of childhood amnesia as it was originally defined by Freud, the fact remains that most of our infancy is inaccessible to recall later in development. The pervasive nature of childhood amnesia suggests that even if some memories leak through the childhood amnesia barrier, they may be few and far between.

### Encoding Specificity Hypothesis

Most theories of memory processing are based on a common set of three assumptions. First, it is generally assumed that a *memory* consists of a hypothetical collection of attributes that represents information present at time of original encoding. Second, it is generally assumed that those attributes represent both focal and contextual stimuli that were part of the original event. Finally, it is generally assumed that memory retrieval will occur if, and only if, there is a match between attributes stored in memory and cues present at the time of retrieval. This latter notion is commonly referred to as Tulving's encoding specificity hypothesis (Tulving, 1983; Tulving & Thomson, 1973).

A large body of empirical research has now shown that human infants exhibit a high degree of encoding specificity, particularly early in development (for a review, see Hayne, 2004, 2006). That is, despite impressive memory skills, infants fail to retrieve their memories if they are tested with cues or in contexts that differ from those present during original encoding. Given this high degree of specificity, it seems likely that children and adults might find it extremely difficult to use language cues to access preverbal memories that are composed primarily of perceptually based attributes (Hayne & Rovee-Collier, 1995; Howe & Courage, 1993; Peterson & Rideout, 1998). Furthermore, given the large number of changes that occur in ourselves and in our environment between infancy and adulthood, the probability that we would ever reencounter effective retrieval cues for our infant memories is likely to be low.

## Verbal Memory Skills Emerge Late in Development

Human infants are born with a remarkable capacity to attend to and process language. At the time of birth, infants recognize the sound of their own mother's voice and can discriminate her voice from that of another woman (DeCasper & Fifer, 1980). Newborns can also make fine discriminations between different speech sounds (e.g., "ba" vs. "pa"). In fact, their ability to discriminate speech sounds that are not part of their native language (but are part of other languages) is actually better than that of adults (Jusczyk, 1995). Most infants begin to say their first words sometime around their first birthday and by the age of 2½ years, they have a productive vocabulary of approximately 600 words. Comprehension of language precedes production throughout the infancy period, which means that infants understand more words than they can say.

Despite these impressive language skills, the ability to use language in the service of memory lags behind the ability to use language to talk about events in the here and now (Simcock & Hayne, 2002, 2003). At approximately 2½ years of age, children begin to talk about past events, typically within the context of their families, but even then, their verbal accounts are sketchy and require substantial scaffolding from an adult conversational partner (for a review, see Nelson & Fivush, 2004). Even by the age of 4 years, children still rely more heavily on their nonverbal memory skills than on their emerging verbal memory skills (Simcock & Hayne, 2003). Thus, although it is obvious that infant memories must be stored in some nonverbal format, even during early childhood, the linguistic content of a child's memory representation is likely to be very lean. Given the nature of these representations, verbal recall of early memories later in development would require some kind of translation from a nonverbal to a verbal format. I consider whether this kind of translation is actually possible later in this chapter.

Taken together, the phenomenon of childhood amnesia and the principle of encoding specificity, coupled with the nonverbal nature of our early memories suggest that finding empirical evidence for the verbal recall of preverbal memories may be a bit like looking for a needle in a haystack. Although the cards are clearly stacked against the possibility that adults will have ready, verbal access to a large number of memories for events that occurred during their infancy, the rarity of the phenomenon, if it exists at all, should not discourage us from trying to study it further. Psychologists have long been fascinated by rare events. For example, color blindness and schizophrenia affect less than 2% of the general population, but we have learned a great deal about the visual system and about the biochemistry of the human brain by studying these rare disorders. In the same vein, even if only a handful of people were able to bridge the language barrier recalling infant memories later in development or if most people could do so under a particular set of circumstances, the phenomenon would still have important theoretical implications for our understanding of memory processing and important practical implications in both clinical and legal contexts.

The extremely long delay between infancy and adulthood in humans makes it logistically impractical to trace a given individual's memories from one developmental endpoint to the other. For this reason, the bulk of research on the verbal recall of preverbal memories has focussed on *children's* memory of their *infant* experiences. In the review that follows, I examine empirical research on children's ability to remember events from their infancy. In the course of this review, I attempt to answer two fundamental questions: Can children recall their preverbal experiences? If so, can children provide a verbal report of their preverbal experiences using language that they have acquired since the original event took place? Given that most children begin to talk about the past at approximately 2½ to 3 years, this review focuses on children's ability to recall events that took place prior to the age of 3.

## CAN CHILDREN RECALL THEIR PREVERBAL EXPERIENCES?

For centuries, psychologists expressed a relatively dim view of infants' mnemonic capacities. Most experts believed that infants lived in the world of here and now and encoded and retained very little of their prior experience. This view was so pervasive that neonates were rarely given anaesthesia during painful medical procedures because it was widely assumed that they would forget the traumatic experience so quickly (for a review, see Porter, Grunau, & Anand, 1999).

Over the last four decades, researchers have demonstrated that these early views about infant memory are fundamentally incorrect. In a series of elegant studies conducted by Rovee-Collier and her colleagues, for example, even very young infants have been shown to remember over days, weeks, months, and most recently, over more than a year. In Rovee-Collier's original studies, infants were trained to kick their feet to produce movement in an overhead crib mobile using the mobile conjugate reinforcement paradigm (Rovee & Rovee, 1969; for reviews, see Rovee-Collier & Barr, 2001; Rovee-Collier, Hayne, & Colombo, 2001). During original learning, one end of a white satin ribbon was connected to the infant's ankle and the other end was connected to a flexible metal stand that supported the mobile (see Figure 6.1, right panel). In this arrangement, kicking produced movement in the mobile. During the test periods, the ankle ribbon was connected to a second, empty mobile stand that was positioned opposite the first (see Fig. 6.1, left panel). In this arrangement, kicking did not produce movement in the mobile allowing the researchers to assess infants' memory in the absence of additional learning.

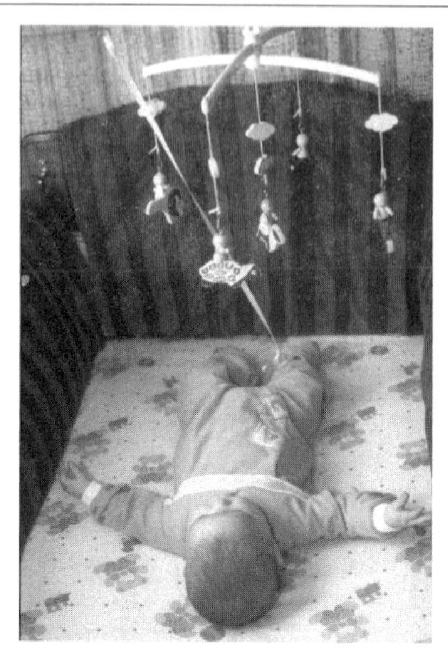

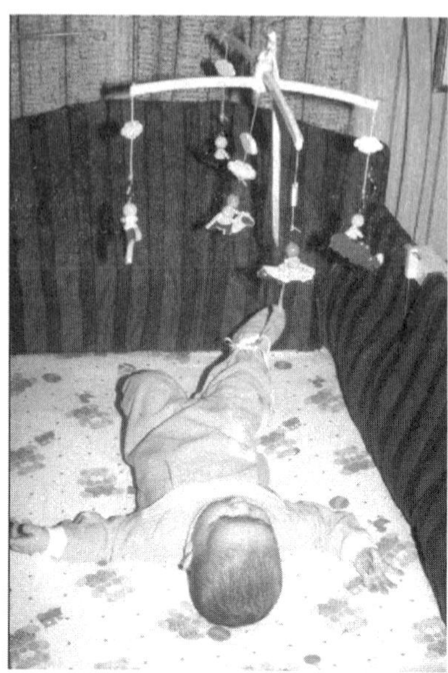

Figure 6.1. Right panel: A 3-month-old infant during a retention test in the mobile conjugate reinforcement paradigm. Note that the ankle ribbon is attached to the "empty" mobile stand. Left panel: A 3-month-old infant during acquisition in the mobile conjugate reinforcement paradigm. This procedure can be used with infants who range in age from 2 to 6 months.

The mobile conjugate reinforcement paradigm has provided the unique opportunity to study memory development between 2 and 6 months of age. To study memory by older infants, Rovee-Collier developed another procedure that has been used with 6- to 18-month-olds. In this task, infants learn to press a large lever to make a miniature train move around a track (see Fig. 6.2). During periods of reinforcement, each lever press produces 1 to 2 seconds of train movement. During periods of nonreinforcement, including all test periods, the lever is inactivated. In this way, the train task is procedurally identical to the mobile task, and when infants of the same age are tested in both, they perform equivalently (Hartshorn & Rovee-Collier, 1997). This finding has allowed researchers to use the train task as an upward extension of the mobile task, providing the unique opportunity to trace age-related changes in memory from 2 to 18 months of age (Hartshorn, Rovee-Collier, Gerhardstein, Bhatt, Klein et al., 1998a; Hartshorn, Rovee-Collier, Gerhardstein, Bhatt, Wondoloski et al., 1998b).

Using the mobile conjugate reinforcement and train paradigms, researchers have identified at least two important characteristics of infant memory. First, the absolute duration of retention increases dramatically over the infancy period. Figure 6.3 shows the maximum duration of retention for infants tested in thc mobile or the train paradigm as a function of age. As shown in Figure 6.3, there is a linear increase in retention as a function of age; 2-month-olds exhibit retention for only 24 hours, but 18-month-olds exhibit retention for as long as 12 weeks (Hartshorn et al., 1998b).

Figure 6.2. A 6-month-old infant being tested in the train paradigm. During original acquisition, each press of the lever produces a 1- to 2-s movement in the train. During the test, the lever is deactivated and presses are ineffective in moving the train. The train procedure can be used with infants who range in age from 6 to 18 months. Reprinted with permission of John Wiley & Sons, Inc.

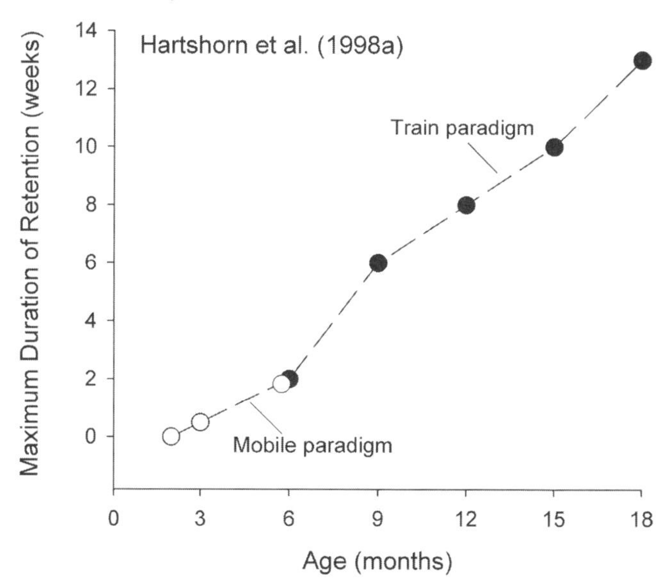


Figure 6.3. Age-related changes in the duration of retention by 2- to 18-month-old infants tested in the mobile conjugate reinforcement and train paradigms. Data have been redrawn from Hartshorn, Rovee-Collier, Gerhardstein, Bhatt, Wondolosk et al. (1998b). Reprinted with permission of John Wiley & Sons, Inc.

Second, even after infants appear to have forgotten what to do to make the mobile or the train move, retention can be restored through the presentation of a brief reminder. In the original demonstration of the reminding phenomenon, 3-month-olds were trained for 2 consecutive days in the mobile conjugate reinforcement paradigm (Rovee-Collier, Sullivan, Enright, Lucas, & Fagen, 1980; Sullivan, 1982). Thirteen days later, some infants were briefly exposed to the training mobile. During the reminder treatment, the experimenter, rather than the infant, made the mobile move (see Figure 6.4, left panel). Infants were tested 24 hours after the reminder treatment, or 14 days after the conclusion of original training. There were also two control conditions. First, to determine whether infants had forgotten in the absence of a reminder, infants in the *forgetting control group* were also trained for 2 consecutive days and they were tested after a 14-day delay, but they did not receive the reminder treatment. Second, to determine the effects of the reminder per se, infants in the *reminder control group* were never trained, but they received the reminder treatment and the test.

In the absence of the reminder treatment, infants in the forgetting control group exhibited complete forgetting during the 14-day test (see Figure 6.4, right panel). Their kick rate during the test was no different from their kick rate prior to training (i.e., baseline). Furthermore, in the absence of prior training, the reminder had no effect on performance; infants in the reminder control group exhibited no evidence of retention during the test. When infants were both trained and reminded, however, they exhibited excellent retention during the test. In fact, their kick rate during the test was no different from their kick rate at the end of training 14 days earlier.

Subsequent research using the reminder procedure in conjunction with the mobile and train paradigms has shown that repeated reminder treatments prolong retention over very long delays (Hartshorn, 2003; Hayne, 1990). In a spectacular demonstration of the effect of repeated reminder treatments, Hartshorn trained 6-month-old infants in the train paradigm. Infants initially received two 8-minute training sessions and a brief reminder 1, 2, 3, 6, and 12 months later. The infants were tested 6 months after the final reminder treatment when they were now 2 years old. During this test, infants exhibited excellent retention. Control groups who received only the original training without the interpolated reminder treatments or who received the reminder treatments without original training exhibited no retention whatsoever (see Fig. 6.5).

What do these studies tell us about the longevity of infant memory? First, contrary to historical opinion, human infants exhibit remarkable memory abilities, retaining the effects of their prior experiences over very long delays. Second, repeated retrieval opportunities may help to keep a particular memory available and accessible to subsequent retrieval. In fact, under circumstances like those employed by Hartshorn (2003), it is possible to maintain a memory established during early infancy into early childhood. Given these findings, the central nervous system must be sufficiently mature during infancy to store and retain infor-

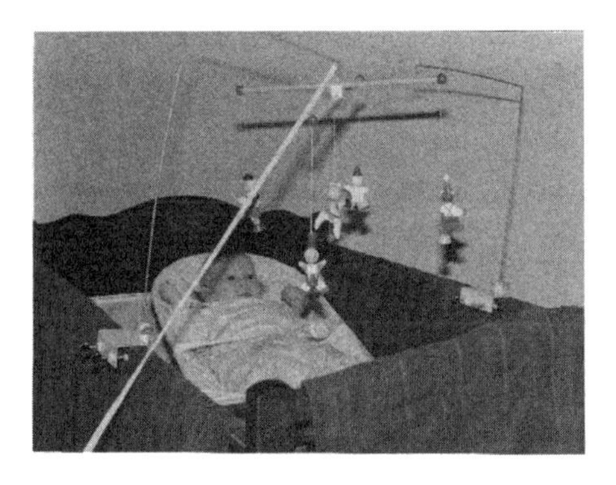

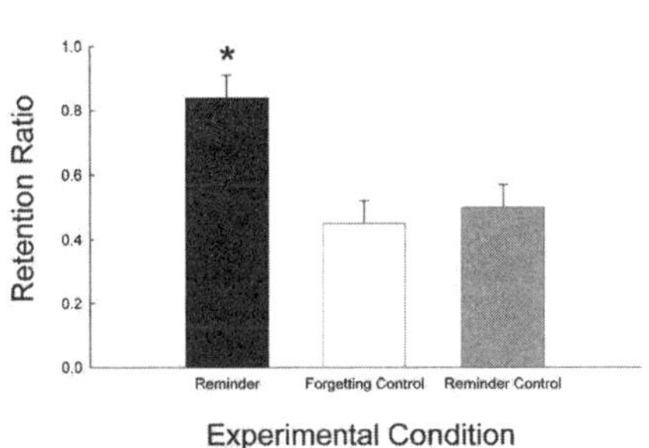


Figure 6.4. Left panel: A 3-month-old infant during a reminder treatment in the mobile conjugate reinforcement paradigm. During the reminder, the experimenter pulls the ribbon, moving the mobile for a 3-min period. Right panel: The effect of a single reminder on retention after a 14-day delay. Infants in the reminder condition received 2 days of training, a 3-min reminder 13 days after the conclusion of training, and were tested 24 hrs later on Day 14. Infants in the forgetting control condition received 2 days of training and were tested on Day 14. Infants in the reminder control condition received only the 3-min reminder and the test, but were never trained. The asterisk indicates that only infants in the reminder condition responded above baseline (i.e., exhibited retention) during the test.

mation over significant periods of development. What happens to these memories over even longer delays is not known and awaits further experimental research.

## Can Children Provide Verbal Reports of their Preverbal Experiences?

Research conducted by Rovee-Collier, Hartshorn, and others has clearly shown that infants can remember over very long delays, particularly if they are periodically reminded about their prior experience. The finding that a memory that was originally established at 6 months of age can be maintained over a period of 1½ years makes it theoretically possible that it could be maintained over a lifetime. In fact, Campbell and Jaynes (1966) were among the first to propose that repeated exposure to potential retrieval cues might be the mechanism that allows our early experiences to influence our later behavior—a phenomenon that they referred to as *reinstatement*.

In all of the research described thus far, researchers have examined infants' nonverbal, rather than verbal, memory for the target event. Given that infants can retain some of their early experiences, at least under some circumstances, is there any evidence that they can translate these preverbal experiences into language once they have acquired the requisite vocabulary to do so?

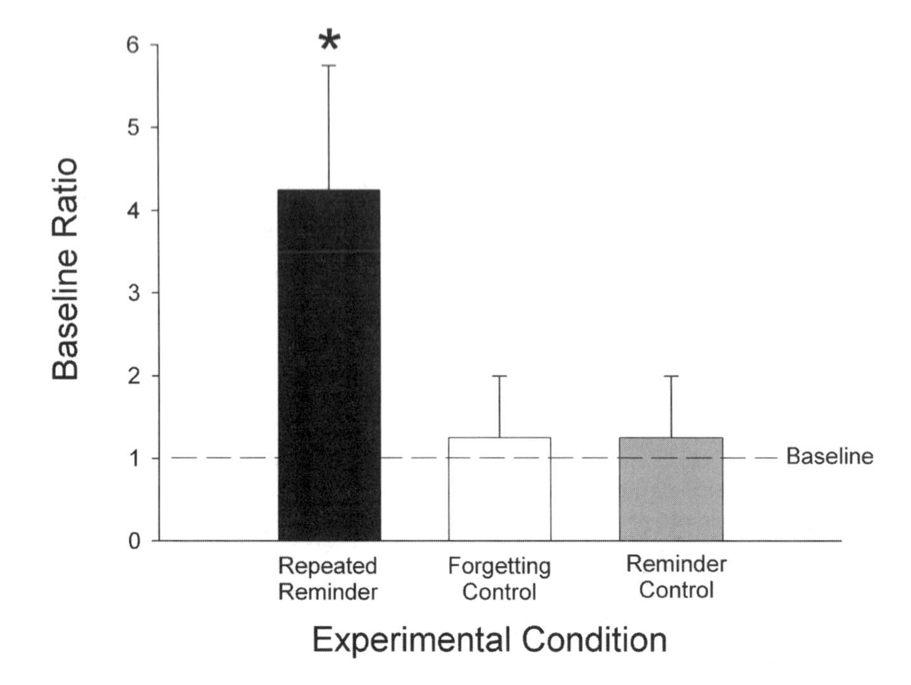


Figure 6.5. The effect of repeated reminder treatments on retention after an 18-month delay. Infants in the repeated reminder condition received 2 days of training in the train paradigm when they were 6 months old. These infants received a reminder treatment 1, 2, 3, 6, and 12 months later. These infants were tested 6 months after the final reminder treatment when they were 2 years old. Infants in the forgetting control condition received training and testing but were not reminded and infants in the reminder control condition received only the reminder treatments and the test, but were never trained. The asterisk indicates that only infants in the repeated reminder condition responded above baseline (i.e., exhibited retention) during the test.

## Anecdotal Reports

One way that researchers have attempted to study children's verbal recall of their preverbal experiences is to examine their memory for events that have occurred during the course of their everyday lives. In these naturalistic studies, the researchers do not control the nature or the content of the target event, but rather use the child's own experiences as the topic of discussion.

Some of the first attempts to study verbal recall of preverbal experiences relied on mothers' anecdotal reports of their young children's spontaneous verbal comments about past events under naturalistic conditions at home (Nelson & Ross, 1980; Todd & Perlmutter, 1980). In these original studies, mothers were asked to keep diary records of their child's verbal comments that reflected memory for a prior event. For example, one mother indicated that after looking at a picture of Santa Claus, her 2-year-old child recalled putting Sesame Street ornaments on the Christmas tree 9 months earlier, when the child was only 15 months old. Similarly, another mother reported that after watching a commercial advertising honey, her 3-year-old recalled that honey used to be added to her bottle, which had been taken away when the child was 14 months old.

Although these two examples provide some tentative support for the view that verbal recall of preverbal memories may be possible, there are a number of relevant caveats to consider. First, as we might have predicted, instances of verbal recall of these kinds of preverbal memories were extremely rare. In the Todd and Perlmutter (1980) study, for example, the two examples described previously were the only examples of verbal recall of preverbal events that mothers reported. Second, due to the retrospective nature of these anecdotal reports, children's language skill was not assessed at the time of original encoding. Instead, children's age at the time of the event was used as a proxy for their language skill; we have no idea what specific words the children could understand or say at the time that the memory was initially established. As such, the "preverbal" nature of the original memory has been assumed rather than demonstrated. Finally, given that these events took place in the context of the child's everyday life, we do not know how much they have been talked about with parents, siblings, or others during the retention interval. If discussion has taken place, then the child may be recalling these family stories rather than the event per se.

## Experimental Research

In an attempt to circumvent some of the problems outlined earlier, researchers began to interview children about more structured events that had taken place in the context of the laboratory. The initial studies of this kind involved follow-up interviews with children who had participated in specific research activities during their infancy. In a classic study by Myers, Clifton, and Clarkson (1987), for example, five children who had participated in an auditory localization task 15 to 19 times between the ages of 6 and 40 weeks of age were invited back to the laboratory when they were approximately 2½ years old. The focus of the original experiment was children's ability to localize and reach for objects in the dark.

During the follow-up visit 2 years later, the experimenter asked the child, "Do you remember this room?" Next, the experimenter pointed to a white screen that had covered the original apparatus and asked, "Can you guess what's under here?" Regardless of whether the child recalled that a whale sticker had previously been attached to the front of the apparatus, he or she was given a three-choice recognition test with two similar stickers. To conclude the verbal interview, the child was asked to "Guess what happens next."

Following the conclusion of the verbal interview, the child's nonverbal memory for the original experience was assessed. Three stimuli (one original and two new) were rattled, one at a time, in front of the child, and his or her reaction to each was recorded. Next, children's looking at, reaching to, and grasping of the rattling toys was assessed in the light and then in the dark using the exact same procedures that had been used during the original infant experiment on reaching in the dark.

Myers et al. (1987) found virtually no evidence for verbal recall of the prior experience. No child reported that he or she had been in the experimental room on a prior occasion. Four of the five children exhibited no verbal recall whatsoever; one child correctly said "whale" when asked to guess what picture had originally been on the front screen of the apparatus. Evidence for nonverbal memory was also extremely limited. The children who had participated in the original experiment responded more to the stimuli than children who were visiting the laboratory for the very first time, but there was no difference between the groups on most of the measures of nonverbal memory. Subsequent studies by a number of different researchers are highly consistent with the data reported by Myers et al. That is, researchers have found no evidence of verbal recall of laboratory-based experiences that occurred when the children were between 7 and 20 months of age (e.g., Boyer, Barron, & Farrar, 1994; Myers, Perris, & Speaker, 1994; Perris, Myers, & Clifton, 1990).

One limitation of the studies just described is that there has been limited evidence for *nonverbal* recall of the target experiences. Thus, it is impossible to know whether children's lack of verbal recall was due to their inability to translate a preverbal memory into language or to forgetting per se. That is, could children translate their preverbal memories into language if the original representation was stronger at the time of retrieval? Using the elicited imitation paradigm, Bauer and her students have examined young children's verbal recall of multistep events for which they demonstrate some nonverbal recall after a delay (Bauer, Kroupina, Schwade, Dropik, & Wewerka, 1998; Bauer et al., 2004; Bauer & Wewerka, 1995). In the general procedure, 13- to 20-month-old infants watch as an experimenter demonstrates a series of actions with novel objects. In some conditions, infants are allowed to imitate these actions immediately and in other conditions, they are not. After a delay (e.g., 1 month to 3 years later), the experimenter re-presents the objects and records what the infant does and what he or she says.

On the basis of the results of these studies, Bauer has concluded that "memories likely encoded without language can, nevertheless, later be accessible to verbal report" (Bauer et al., 1998, p. 673). But do the data actually support this claim? It is important to note that the absolute level of verbal recall in these studies is extremely small. For example, in Bauer et al., (1998) 20-month-old infants who were tested after a 6- to 12-month delay produced an average of 1.30 mnemonic units of information about events for which they had prior experience; they also produced .43 mnemonic units of information about events that they had never seen before. By way of subtraction, less than one piece of verbal information provided during the test could be attributed to some kind of memory. Furthermore, although infants' general verbal skill was measured in these experiments, there was no measure of the specific words required to describe the task. It is entirely possible that the word or words that infants used during the test had been part of their productive vocabulary at the time of the original event, eliminating the need for "translation" to a verbal code at the time of the test. The correlation between children's general verbal skill at the time of encoding and their verbal recall after a delay adds additional weight to the possibility that children's verbal memory in these studies reflects their vocabulary at the time of the event.

There are other aspects of the elicited imitation procedure that we should consider before concluding that infants can translate preverbal aspects of their memory into language after a delay. In many of the experiments, infants who are tested after long delays (e.g., 3 years) have been reexposed to the target events during the retention interval. For example, in Bauer et al. (1998), infants who were tested after a 3-year delay had been tested already, 6 to 12 months after the original event. Thus, whether infants were recalling the original event or the subsequent test cannot be determined. The implication for the present discussion is that infants' verbal status at the time of the last test, rather than at the time of the event, should be used as the benchmark against which verbal recall of preverbal memory is assessed. Finally, in all of the studies of elicited imitation, the objects that were present during original encoding are re-presented at the time of the test. This procedure makes it impossible to distinguish infants' verbal memory for the original event from their spontaneous labeling of the objects or their narration of their own actions at the time of the test.

In an attempt to circumvent some of these interpretive problems, we have conducted a series of prospective studies of children's verbal and nonverbal recall over long delays (Simcock & Hayne, 2002, 2003). In our studies, we assess children's language skill at the time of the event and again at the time of the test. In addition to general language measures, we also assess children's comprehension and production of the specific words that are required to describe the target event. That is, we assess what words children can say and understand at the time that the memory was encoded and what new words they have learned by the time of the test. In this way, it is possible to determine whether children can translate preverbal aspects of their memory into language after a delay. Furthermore, each child is tested only once, eliminating the opportunity for verbal recoding that undoubtedly occurs when children are tested repeatedly. Finally, the verbal-recall portion of the test occurs in the absence of the objects that were present at the time of the event.

The target event in these studies involved a "Magic Shrinking Machine." Two experimenters visited the child at home and showed him or her how to make the machine work. The child placed a large object in the machine (e.g., a ball, a bell, a box of raisins), turned a handle on the side of the machine, and extracted a smaller, but otherwise identical version of the object from a special opening on the front of the machine (see Fig. 6.6). Following a 6- to 12-month delay, children's verbal recall was assessed by asking them questions about what had happened during the event. This part of the test took place in the absence of the Magic Shrinking Machine and the target objects. In this way, we were able to assess children's ability to provide a verbal report of the contents of their memory that was not contaminated by ongoing narration or labeling of the Machine and the objects. Once the verbal-recall portion of the interview was complete, children's nonverbal recall was assessed using photograph recognition and behavioral reenactment.

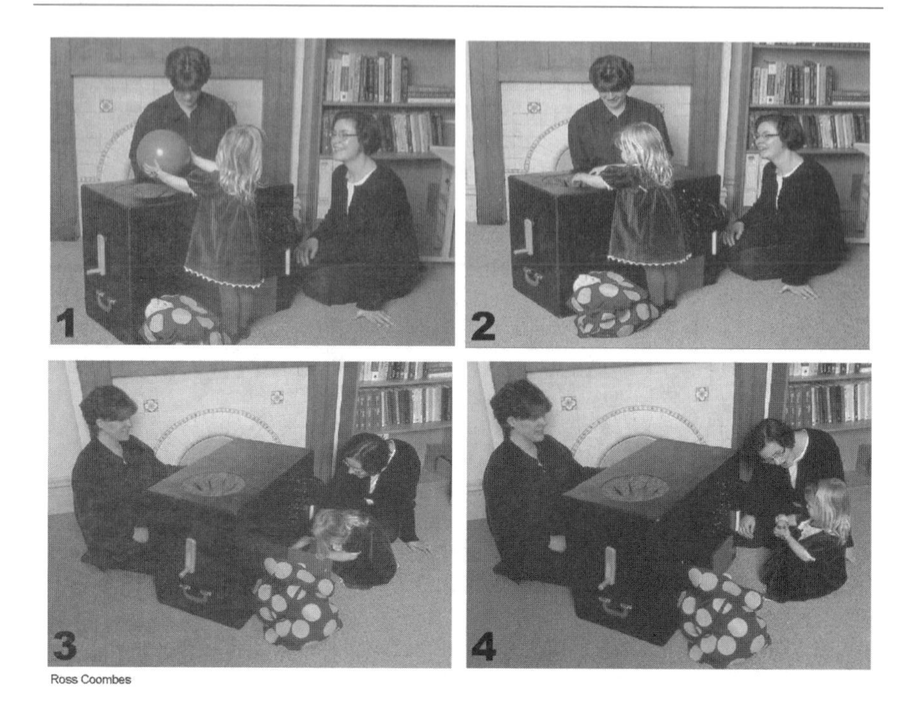


Figure 6.6. The Magic Shrinking Machine used by Simcock and Hayne (2002, 2003) to study verbal and nonverbal memory by 2- to 4-year-old children. During each session, the child was shown how to turn the machine on, place an object in the hole at the top, turn the handle on the side, and open the door on the front to retrieve a smaller, but otherwise identical version of the original object.

Three important findings emerged from these studies. First, as indicated by their photograph recognition and behavioral reenactment scores, children remembered the event over the delay. The data from children tested after a 1-year delay are shown in Figure 6.7 (see left panel). Although there was clearly an age-related increase in children's photograph recognition and behavioral reenactment scores, even the youngest participants exhibited some degree of nonverbal recall. Second, children's language ability improved over the delay. By the time of the test, most children had acquired all of the words that they needed to verbally describe the Magic Shrinking Machine and the objects that were placed inside (see Fig. 6.7, right panel). Finally, children displayed no ability whatsoever to translate what they remembered into language after the delay. That is, despite clear evidence of nonverbal memory (and some evidence of verbal memory), children never used a word or words to describe the event during the test that had not been part of their productive vocabulary at the time of original encoding. From a theoretical perspective, these data suggest that children's early nonverbal memories and their emerging verbal memories are stored relatively independently. Contrary to what we might expect, emerging language skills are not simply mapped onto existing preverbal memory representations.

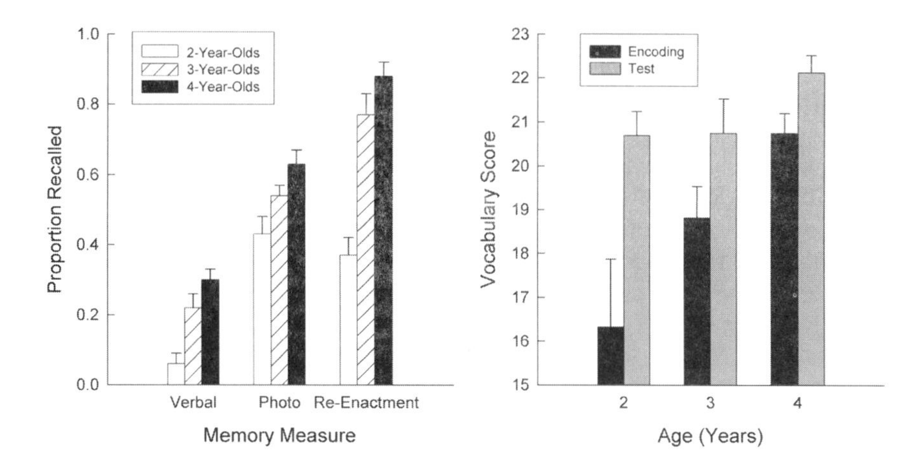


Figure 6.7. Left panel: Verbal and nonverbal memory performance by 2- to 4-year-olds who participated in the Magic Shrinking Machine event and who were tested 1 year later. Right panel: Children's production of the target words required to describe the Magic Shrinking Machine event at the time of the original experience and at the time of the test.

## Traumatic Events

Well-controlled prospective studies of children's memory for innocuous events like the ones described previously have yielded no compelling evidence that children can provide verbal reports of their preverbal experience (see also, Fivush, Pipe, Murachver, & Reese, 1997). But perhaps researchers have been looking in the wrong place. Although children's memory for innocuous events may not survive the transition to language, it is still possible that their memory for more salient preverbal experiences, particularly traumatic experiences, might be translated into language after a delay.

*Clinical Case Studies.* The clinical literature is replete with case studies of children's ability to provide verbal accounts of their preverbal, traumatic experiences (for recent reviews, see Gaensbauer, 2002; Paley & Alpert, 2003). In one classic example, Bernstein and Blacher (1967) describe the case of Laura who underwent a spinal tap at the age of 3 months to relieve the pressure created by her hydrocephalus. During this painful medical procedure, the spinal needle was left in place for a 2-hour period during which Laura screamed continuously. At the age of 28 months, Laura's new neighbors began some construction work on their home. Laura appeared to be terrified of the noise and when she awoke from her nap one afternoon she spontaneously said, "Man stuck me in the tushie and knocked my head off." Laura's mother interpreted "knocked my head off" as synonymous with "made my head hurt." According to her mother, Laura's verbal report was triggered by construction noises that were presumably similar to noises at the hospital at the time that Laura had experienced the original painful medical procedure.

Hewitt (1994) has also described the cases of two children who were suspected victims of sexual abuse when they were approximately 2 years old. In one case, the child's first mention of the event was prompted by a conversation with her mother about good and bad touch that took place when the child was 4. During the course of a more formal clinical interview, the child reenacted the sexual contact with her babysitter and provided additional verbal details of what happened.

In yet another example, Gaensbauer, Chatoor, Drell, Siegel, and Zeanah (1995) describe the dramatic case of "Audrey," who at the age of 12½ months witnessed her mother's death by a letter bomb that had been sent by an old boyfriend. Following her mother's murder, Audrey went to live with a series of temporary foster families until she was finally placed with one of her mother's relatives. From the time that she arrived in her final placement, Audrey showed signs of distress that occurred frequently throughout the day (e.g., rocking, self-stimulation, screaming episodes). According to her adoptive mother, Audrey's first verbal account of her mother's death occurred after she awoke from a nightmare at the age of 3 years (e.g., "It's messy all over!"). Audrey continued to experience developmental difficulties, which lead her adoptive mother to seek additional help. During the course of therapy at the age of 5, Audrey was told for the first time of how her mother had died. At that point, she provided a graphic verbal description of her mother's corpse that was subsequently confirmed through police records.

These clinical case reports are extremely provocative, but the nature of the "data" raises a number of interpretive problems. At least some (albeit not all) of these traumatic events may have been discussed between other family members during the period between the event and the therapists' interview with the child. The opportunity for family discussion raises the possibility that, during therapy, the child recalled a family story of the event rather than the event, per se. Although it is often impossible to distinguish between these two alternative sources of information, children sometimes offer clues that allow us to differentiate what they "know" from what they actually "remember." By way of example, my 10-year-old daughter was eating breakfast the other morning when I decided to clean the microwave oven. My complaints about the mess sparked a conversation about the time that her grandfather had placed an egg in the microwave. With no prompting, she provided a highly detailed account about how the egg had exploded and about how angry her grandmother had been about the mess. When I asked her what happened next she said, "I don't know. I don't actually remember it. I was only a baby when it happened, but you talk about it all the time." Thus, despite the clarity of my daughter's "recollection," her account of the event was based on a family story that she had overheard repeatedly rather than on her own experience. Without probing the source of her knowledge, however, it would have been very easy to mistake her narrative for a memory of the actual event.

In clinical contexts, family stories and discussions are also likely to infiltrate children's accounts of traumatic events. For example, Sugar (1992) describes a case study of a child who experienced a plane crash at the age of 16 months. When the child entered therapy at the age of 26 months, she provided an accurate verbal description of the location of fire and smoke in the plane. Her account was highly detailed despite the fact that the plane crash had rendered her unconscious. Given this, it is likely that the child's verbal report may have been a product of conversations about the crash that took place after it happened rather than her actual memory for the event. Because young children have trouble differentiating between these two different sources of information, the family story may become a proxy for actual experience.

Not all clinicians agree that children have ready, verbal access to their early traumatic experiences. In her highly cited paper, Terr (1988) describes the verbal and nonverbal recall of 20 children who experienced documented traumatic experiences during their infancy or early childhood. Children who were under the age of 36 months at the time of the trauma exhibited very little evidence of memory of any kind. The youngest child in her sample to provide a verbal account of a traumatic experience was 28 months old when he survived a plane crash with his mother. Although Terr argues that this child provided a full and accurate account of the event, she does not provide the reader with the content of the child's report; in the portion of the transcript that she does provide, the child does not describe the accident; rather, he complains that his Mickey Mouse suitcase was never recovered. On the basis of the information provided, we have no way of knowing whether this statement reflects the child's memory for the event or simply a statement of historical fact.

Case reports are limited in other ways as well (for a review, see Loftus & Guyer, 2002). For example, because the interviews are conducted in the clinic or at home rather than in the context of research, we know very little about the nature of the questions that were asked or about the actual content of the child's response. Often no details are provided at all. When they do appear, they typically consist of the therapist's (or the caregiver's) paraphrase of their own questions and the child's answers. How accurate are these accounts likely to be? To answer this question, Bruck, Ceci, and Francoeur (1999) asked mothers to interview their preschool-age children about a contrived event and then asked mothers to recall the format of their questions and the content of the child's answers after a delay. Bruck et al. found that even after a delay of only 3 days, mothers had difficulty recalling whether the information that their child provided during a conversation occurred in response to free-recall questions or was elicited through repeated and highly suggestive prompts. Furthermore, mothers misattributed their own contributions to the conversation to their child. These findings were obtained even when mothers were specifically warned that they would be asked to recall the details of the conversation after the delay.

When deciding how much weight should be given to clinical case reports, the results of the Bruck et al. (1999) study suggest that it may not be wise to rely on retrospective accounts of who said what to whom. Along the same lines, in many case reports, the child's actual response is heavily interpreted by an adult (e.g., Bernstein & Blacher, 1967; Hewitt, 1994). For example, in the case described by Hewitt, the comment that caused concern was "Hawwie spwedded and wipped me." Although the mother interpreted this statement as "Howie spreaded and ripped me," suggesting that some kind of sexual abuse took place, the same statement could have been interpreted as "Howie spreaded and wiped me," which may be more indicative of toileting. In the absence of additional information, it is impossible to differentiate between these two alternatives (or others).

*Structured Interviews.* One way to rule out adults' contributions to a child's report is to question children about their past experiences under more standardized interview conditions. In a recent wave of studies, researchers have interviewed large numbers of children about potentially traumatic events including medical accidents and natural disasters using a highly structured set of questions (e.g., Fivush, Sales, Goldberg, Bahrick, & Parker, 2004; Quas et al., 1999). In one of the first studies of this kind that included very young participants, Howe, Courage, and Peterson (1994) interviewed 25 children about traumatic injuries that required treatment in a hospital emergency room. The children ranged in age from 18 to 60 months at the time of their hospital treatment; each child was interviewed a few days after their visit to the hospital and again 6 months later. During both interviews, children were asked highly structured free-recall (e.g., "What happened?") and cued-recall (e.g., "Where were you when you got hurt?") questions. Children's responses to these questions were transcribed verbatim. In this way, the adult interviewers contributed nothing to the child's report and the child's exact words were used to evaluate what he or she remembered about the event. Howe et al. found that children who were younger than 30 months at the time of the trauma provided virtually no evidence of verbal recall of their experience when they were interviewed either immediately or after a 6-month delay.

Subsequent studies involving interviews with children about traumatic events have confirmed Howe et al.'s (1994) findings (Pillemer, Picariello, & Pruett, 1994; Quas et al., 1999). That is, very young children exhibit virtually no verbal recall for traumatic experiences even when they are interviewed after a period of rapid language development (i.e., after delays of months to years). These findings are highly consistent with prior research on children's lack of verbal recall for nontraumatic experiences and suggest that, irrespective of the nature of the target memory (traumatic or innocuous), few if any memories survive the transition to language, at least in a recognizable verbal format.

There is, however, at least one published exception to the pattern of findings just described. In a series of studies, Peterson and her colleagues interviewed children about injuries that required outpatient treatment in a hospital emergency room (Peterson, 1999; Peterson & Bell, 1996; Peterson, Moores, & White, 2001; Peterson & Whalen, 2001). In one study of this kind, Peterson and Rideout (1998) interviewed children multiple times about the same injury over a period of 18 to 24 months. At the time of their initial injury, children ranged in age from 12 to 34 months. Peterson and Rideout divided the children into three groups on the basis of their age at the time of injury: The *young toddler group* included children who were between 12 and 18 months old, the *older toddler* group included children who were between 20 and 25 months old, and the *2-year-old narrator group* included children who were between 26 and 34 months old.

During each interview, all children were asked a series of standard free-recall and cued-recall questions. The interviews were audio-recorded and were transcribed verbatim. The percentage of questions for which children provided correct, relevant information is shown in Figure 6.8. Across all interviews, older children reported more information than younger children. Furthermore, the amount of information that children reported increased across subsequent interviews. Importantly, although the two youngest groups provided no verbal account of their injury at the time that it happened (see Fig. 8, 0 Delay), these children did provide a verbal account when they interviewed after a delay.

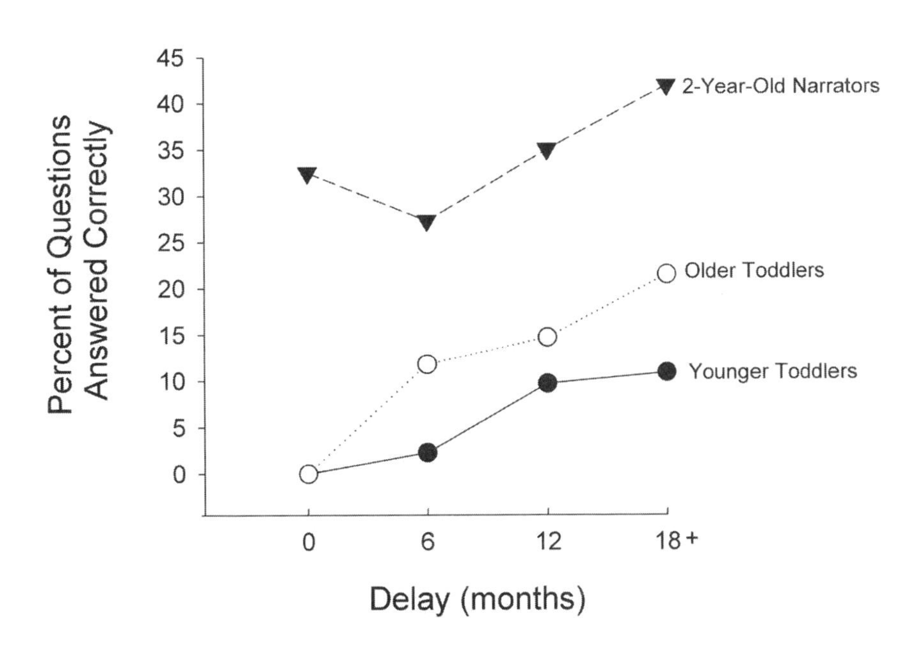


Figure 6.8. Children's verbal recall of a traumatic injury over repeated interviews as a function of delay. Children in the young toddler group were between 12 and 18 months old at the time of their injury, children in the older toddler group were between 20 and 25 months old at the time of their injury, and children in the 2-year-old narrator group were between 26 and 34 months old at the time of their injury.

What possible explanations can we offer for these findings? On the one hand, it is possible that the youngest participants initially encoded their experience in a nonverbal format, but as their language skills improved, they gradually translated their preverbal representation into language. It is also possible that the repeated interviews in the Peterson and Rideout (1998) study, like the repeated reminders used in the study by Hartshorn (2003), may have helped to maintain the original memory over time. If these two possibilities are correct, then these data provide the first empirical evidence that children might have some verbal access to their preverbal memories.

Although this explanation is consistent with the data, we cannot rule out another, equally plausible, explanation for the same findings. As Peterson and Rideout acknowledge, it is also possible that, over the course of time and over the course of repeated interviews, children simply incorporated more of what they had been told by others about the event into their own account of their injury. That is, during the later interviews, children may not have recalled their memory for the target event, but rather recalled and reported information from other sources of information that had been encountered somewhere down the track. At this stage, we have no way of knowing which explanation is actually correct; additional research will be required to disentangle these competing accounts of the same findings.

## CONCLUSIONS

The data that I have reviewed in this chapter support two general conclusions. First, carefully controlled experimental research has shown that infants and toddlers can remember their early experiences over very long delays when their memory is expressed through behavior rather than language (Hartshorn, 2003; Simcock & Hayne, 2002; for a review, see Hayne, 2004). Second, carefully controlled experimental research has provided no clear evidence that children can translate these preverbal memories into language even after they have acquired the verbal skills necessary to describe the events in question.

What are the clinical implications of the data reviewed here? The finding that children (and presumably adults) may have little or no ability to provide explicit, verbal reports of their early preverbal experiences does not mean that early traumatic experiences are psychologically benign. Although childhood amnesia may buffer some individuals from the long-term effects of early negative experiences, not everyone escapes unscathed. In extreme cases, repeated trauma and neglect have been shown to alter the course of normal brain maturation, yielding abnormalities in both structure and function (Glaser, 2000; Ito, Teicher, Glod, & Ackerman, 1998; Perry, 1997; Teicher et al., 2004). Many of these biological changes are reflected in abnormal patterns of behavior during childhood, adolescence, and adulthood (Fisher, Ames, Chisholm, & Savoie, 1997; Marcovitch et al., 1997). Psychological difficulties that originate from early experiences may be particularly difficult to treat because their effects become entrenched in an individual's behavior and personality. In short, early trauma, abuse, and neglect can cause long-term psychological difficulties even though we may have no recollection of the events that lead to the problem in the first place. In fact, the issue of child abuse and neglect poses a major mental health concern throughout the world.

Finally, what are the legal implications of the data reviewed here? I originally cast this chapter in the context of court cases involving repressed and recovered memory for events that presumably took place during infancy (see Loftus, 1993b). Recall that Patti Barton claimed that she had recovered memories for sexual abuse that had taken place when she was a toddler. On the basis of empirical research collected to date, there is no convincing evidence that adults like Patti could provide forensically relevant information about an event that occurred during infancy. Although some researchers have argued that adults can verbally recall events that occurred when they were as young as 2 years old (Usher & Neisser, 1993), it has been argued that these "memories" may consist of nothing more than educated guesses about what might have happened (Loftus, 1993a). The fact remains that most adults are completely amnestic for events that took place prior to the age of 3 or 4 years (MacDonald et al., 2000; Mullen, 1994); even when memories do slip through the childhood amnesia barrier, they tend to be sketchy and disconnected. There is also no evidence that children can provide verbal accounts of events that took place during their infancy. Even when some verbal recall for infant events leaks into early childhood, the content of those reports is extremely sparse and would have virtually no value in a court of law (cf. Peterson & Rideout, 1998).

Like Loftus (1993b), I continue to express healthy skepticism about claims of infant memories that persist into adulthood. At the same time, I want to emphasize that *absence of evidence* should never be mistaken for *evidence of absence* in this context. We can never prove that people *cannot* remember and recount the experiences of their infancy; we can only continue to explore and document the conditions under which this kind of recall may or may not occur (for a similar argument, see Loftus & Loftus, 1980). Future empirical attempts to study this problem must include a salient event for which participants exhibit at least some nonverbal recall after a delay, explicit measures of language ability both at the time of the event and at the time of the test, limited opportunities for postevent discussion, and standardized test procedures that include minimal prompting and stimulus support. Very few studies conducted to date meet these basic requirements. Furthermore, the information gathered to date has been restricted to young children's verbal recall of their preverbal experiences. We know nothing about the long-term fate of any of these early memories. In the final analysis, the answer to our questions rests exclusively on the quality of our science. Elizabeth Loftus has made a career out of posing hard questions and finding new, creative, and scientifically rigorous ways of answering them. My students and I plan to follow her lead as we continue to explore the fate of early, preverbal memories.

## REFERENCES

Bauer, P. J., Kroupina, M. G., Schwade, J. A., Dropik, P. L., & Wewerka, S. S. (1998). If memory serves, will language? Later verbal accessibility of early memories. *Development and Psychopathology, 10,* 655–679.

Bauer, P. J., Van Abbema, D. L., Wiebe, S. A., Cary, S. S., Phil, C., & Burch, M. M. (2004). Props, not pictures, are worth a thousand words: Verbal accessibility of early memories under different conditions of contextual support. *Applied Cognitive Psychology, 18,* 373–392.

Bauer, P. J., & Wewerka, S. S. (1995). One- to two-year-olds' recall of events: The more expressed, the more impressed. *Journal of Experimental Child Psychology, 59,* 475–496.

Bernstein, A. E. H., & Blacher, R. S. (1967). The recovery of a memory from three months of age. *Psychoanalytic Study of the Child, 22,* 156–167.

Boyer, M. E., Barron, K. L., & Farrar, M. J. (1994). Three-year-olds remember a novel event from 20 months: Evidence for long-term memory in children? *Memory, 2,* 417–445.

Bruck, M., Ceci, S. J., & Francoeur, E. (1999). The accuracy of mothers' memories of conversations with their preschool children. *Journal of Experimental Psychology: Applied, 5,* 89–106.

Campbell, B. A., & Jaynes, J. (1966). Reinstatement. *Psychological Review, 73,* 478–480.

DeCasper, A. J., & Fifer, W. P. (1980). Of human bonding: Newborns prefer their mothers' voices. *Science, 208,* 1174–1176.

Fisher, L., Ames, E. W., Chisholm, K., & Savoie, L. (1997). Problems reported by parents of Romanian orphans adopted to British Columbia. *International Journal of Behavioral Development, 20,* 67–82.

Fivush, R., Pipe, M.-E., Murachver, T., & Reese, E. (1997). Events spoken and unspoken: Implications of language and memory development for the recovered memory debate. In M. A. Conway (Ed.), *Recovered memories and false memories. Debates in psychology* (pp. 34–62). London: Oxford University Press.

Fivush, R., Sales, J. M., Goldberg, A., Bahrick, L., & Parker, J. (2004). Weathering the storm: Children's long-term recall of Hurricane Andrew. *Memory, 12,* 104–118.

Freud, S. (1953). Three essays on the theory of sexuality. In J. Strachey (Ed.), *The standard edition of the complete psychological works of Sigmund Freud* (Vol. 7, pp. 135–243). London: Hogarth. (Original work published 1905)

Gaensbauer, T. J. (2002). Representations of trauma in infancy: Clinical and theoretical implications for the understanding of early memory. *Infant Mental Health Journal, 23,* 259–277.

Gaensbauer, T., Chatoor, I., Drell, M., Siegel, D., & Zeanah, C. H. (1995). Traumatic loss in a one-year-old girl. *Journal of the American Academy of Child and Adolescent Psychiatry, 34,* 520–528.

Glaser, D. (2000). Child abuse and neglect and the brain—A review. *Journal of Child Psychology and Psychiatry, 41,* 97–116.

Hartshorn, K. (2003). Reinstatement maintains a memory in human infants for 1½ years. *Developmental Psychobiology, 42,* 269–282.

Hartshorn, K., & Rovee-Collier, C. (1997). Infant learning and long-term memory at 6 months: A confirming analysis. *Developmental Psychobiology, 30,* 71-85.

Hartshorn, K., Rovee-Collier, C., Gerhardstein, P. C., Bhatt, R. S., Klein, P. J., Aaron, F., Wondoloski, T. L., & Wurtzel, N. (1998a). Developmental changes in the specificity of memory over the first year of life. *Developmental Psychobiology, 33,* 61-78.

Hartshorn, K., Rovee-Collier, C., Gerhardstein, P.C, Bhatt, R.S., Wondoloski, T.L., Klein, P., Gilch, J., Wurtzel, N., & Campos-de-Carvalho, M. (1998b). Ontogeny of long-term memory over the first year-and-a-half of life. *Developmental Psychobiology, 32*, 69-89.

Hayne, H. (1990). The effect of multiple reminders on long-term retention in human infants. *Developmental Psychobiology, 23*, 453–477.

Hayne, H. (2004). Infant memory development: Implications for childhood amnesia. *Developmental Review, 24*, 33–73.

Hayne, H. (2006). Bridging the gap: The relation between learning and memory during infancy. In Y. Munakata & M. H. Johnson (Eds.), *Processes of change in brain and cognitive development: Attention and performance XXI*, (pp. 209–232), London: Oxford University Press.

Hayne, H., & Rovee-Collier, C. (1995). The organization of reactivated memory in infancy. *Child Development, 66*, 893–906.

Hewitt, S. K. (1994). Preverbal sexual abuse: What two children report in later years. *Child Abuse & Neglect, 18*, 821–826.

Howe, M. L., & Courage, M. L. (1993). On resolving the enigma of infantile amnesia. *Psychological Bulletin, 113*, 305–326.

Howe, M. L., Courage, M. L., & Peterson, C. (1994). How can I remember when "I" wasn't there? Long-term retention of traumatic memories and emergence of the cognitive self. *Consciousness and Cognition, 3*, 327–355.

Ito, Y., Teicher, M. H., Glod, C. A., & Ackerman, E. (1998). Preliminary evidence for aberrant cortical development in abused children. A quantitative EEG study. *Journal of Neuropsychiatry and Clinical Neuroscience, 10*, 298–307.

Jusczyk, P. W. (1995). Language acquisition: Speech sounds and phonological development. In J. L. Miller & P. D. Eimas (Eds.), *Handbook of perception and cognition: Vol. 11. Speech, language, and communication* (pp. 263–301). Orlando, FL: Academic Press.

Loftus, E. (1993a). Desperately seeking memories of the first few years of childhood: The reality of early memories. *Journal of Experimental Psychology: General, 122*, 274–277.

Loftus, E. (1993b). The reality of repressed memories. *American Psychologist, 48*, 518–537.

Loftus, E. F., & Guyer, M. J. (2002, May–June). Who abused Jane Doe? *Skeptical Enquirer*, pp. 1–14.

Loftus, E. F., & Loftus, G. R. (1980). On the permanence of stored information in the brain. *American Psychologist, 35*, 409–420.

MacDonald, S., Uesiliana, K., & Hayne, H. (2000). Cross-cultural differences in childhood amnesia. *Memory, 8*, 365–376.

Marcovitch, S., Goldberg, S., Gold, A., Washington, J., Wasson, C. Krekewich, K., Handley-Derry, M. (1997). Determinants of behavioural problems in Romanian children adopted in Ontario. *International Journal of Behavioral Development, 20*, 17–31.

Mullen, M. K. (1994). Earliest recollections of childhood: A demographic analysis. *Cognition, 52*, 55–79.

Myers, N. A., Clifton, R. K., & Clarkson, M. G. (1987). When they were very young: Almost-threes remember two years ago. *Infant Behavior and Development, 10*, 123–132.

Myers, N. A., Perris, E. E., & Speaker, C. J. (1994). Fifty months of memory: A longitudinal study in early childhood. *Memory, 2*, 383–415.

Nelson, K., & Fivush, R. (2004). The emergence of autobiographical memory: A social cultural developmental theory. *Psychological Review, 111*, 486–511.

Nelson, K., & Ross, G. (1980). The generalities and specifics of long-term memory in infants and young children. In M. Perlmutter (Ed.), *Children's memory: New directions for child development* (pp. 87–101). San Francisco: Jossey-Bass.

Paley, J., & Alpert, J. (2003). Memory of infant trauma. *Psychoanalytic Psychology, 20,* 329–347.

Perris, E. E., Myers, N. A., & Clifton, R. (1990). Long-term memory for a single infancy experience. *Child Development, 61,* 1796–1807.

Perry, B. D. (1997). Incubated in terror: Neurodevelopmental factors in the "cycle of violence." In J. D. Osofsky (Ed.), *Children in a violent society* (pp. 124–149). New York: Guilford.

Peterson, C. (1999). Children's memory for medical emergencies: 2 years later. *Developmental Psychology, 35,* 1493–1506.

Peterson, C., & Bell, M. (1996). Children's memory for traumatic injury. *Child Development, 67,* 3045–3070.

Peterson, C., Moores, L., & White, G. (2001). Recounting the same events again and again: Children's consistency across multiple interviews. *Applied Cognitive Psychology, 15,* 353–371.

Peterson, C., & Rideout, R. (1998). Memory for medical emergencies experienced by 1- and 2-year-olds. *Developmental Psychology, 34,* 1059–1072.

Peterson, C., & Whalen, N. (2001). Five years later: Children's memory for medical emergencies. *Applied Cognitive Psychology, 15,* S7–S24.

Pillemer, D., Picariello, M., & Pruett, J. C. (1994). Very long-term memories of a salient preschool event. *Applied Cognitive Psychology, 8,* 95–106.

Porter, F. L., Grunau, R. E., & Anand, K. J. S. (1999). Long-term effects of pain in infants. *Developmental and Behavioral Pediatrics, 20,* 253–261.

Quas, J. A., Goodman, G. S., Bidrose, S., Pipe, M.E., Craw, S., & Ablin, D. S., (1999). Emotion and memory: Children's long-term remembering, forgetting, and suggestibility. *Journal of Experimental Child Psychology, 72,* 235–270.

Rovee, C. K., & Rovee, D. T. (1969). Conjugate reinforcement of infant exploratory behavior. *Journal of Experimental Child Psychology, 8,* 33–39.

Rovee-Collier, C., & Barr, R. (2001). Infant learning and memory. In G. Bremmer & A. Fogel (Eds.), *Blackwell handbook of infant development. Handbooks of developmental psychology* (pp. 139–168). Malden, MA: Blackwell.

Rovee-Collier, C., Hayne, H., & Colombo, M. (2001). *The development of implicit and explicit memory*. Amsterdam: John Benjamins.

Rovee-Collier, C., Sullivan, M., Enright, M., Lucas, D., & Fagen, J. W. (1980). Reactivation of infant memory. *Science, 208,* 1159–1161.

Simcock, G., & Hayne, H. (2002). Breaking the barrier: Children do not translate their preverbal memories into language. *Psychological Science, 13,* 225–231.

Simcock, G., & Hayne, H. (2003). Age-related changes in verbal and nonverbal memory during early childhood. *Developmental Psychology, 39,* 805–814.

Sugar, M. (1992). Toddler's traumatic memories. *Infant Mental Health Journal, 13,* 245–251.

Sullivan, M. W. (1982). Reactivation: Priming forgotten memories in human infants. *Child Development, 53,* 516–523.

Teicher, M. H., Dumont, N. L., Ito, Y., Vaituzis, C., Giedd, J. N., & Andersen, S. L. (2004). Childhood neglect is associated with reduced corpus callosum area. *Biological Psychiatry, 56,* 80–85.

Terr, L. (1988). What happens to early memories of trauma? A study of twenty children under age five at the time of documented traumatic events. *Child Adolescent Psychiatry, 27,* 96–104.

Todd, C. M., & Perlmutter, M. (1980). Reality recalled by preschool children. In M. Perlmutter (Ed.), *Children's memory: New directions for child development* (pp. 69–86). San Francisco: Jossey-Bass.

Tulving, E. (1983). *Elements of episodic memory*. New York: Oxford University Press.

Tulving, E., & Thomson, D. M. (1973). Encoding specificity and retrieval processes in episodic memory. *Psychological Review, 80,* 352–373.

Usher, J. N., & Neisser, U. (1993). Childhood amnesia and the beginnings of memory for four early life events. *Journal of Experimental Psychology: General, 122,* 155–165.

CHAPTER

# 7

# Illusory Recollection in Older Adults: Testing Mark Twain's Conjecture

Henry L. Roediger III and Mark A. McDaniel

Late in his life Mark Twain said: "When I was younger, I could remember anything, whether it had happened or not, but my faculties are decaying now and soon I shall be so I cannot remember any but the things that never happened. It is sad to go to pieces like this but we all have to do it."

In 1997, the authors of this chapter were ignorant of the preceding quote, but we began a project for which the quote serves as an apt abstract. The thrust of the question we asked was whether older adults are more susceptible to illusory memories than are younger adults. If we examine Twain's quote as a scientific hypothesis making three assertions, two parts of it are well established. Younger adults can indeed remember events that never happened and in some situations their levels of false recall can equal levels of accurate recall (Roediger & McDermott, 1995). In addition, the fact that older adults forget more information than younger adults (especially on tests of unaided recall) has been observed in numerous experiments (see Balota, Dolan, & Duchek, 2000, for a review). However, in the late 1990s there was little evidence about the last part of Twain's conjecture: Are older adults more susceptible to memory illusions than younger adults?

In making predictions about this issue, one could make a strong argument either way—that older adults would be more prone to illusory memories or that they would be less prone—as is so often true in psychology. For example, in making the case that older adults are more likely to suffer from illusory memories, we could point to the well-documented source-monitoring difficulties in older adults (e.g., Henkel, Johnson, & De Leonardis, 1998; McIntyre & Craik, 1987). Given this tendency, older adults might be more likely to mix up the order of events and confuse events, and therefore suffer more illusions of memory than younger adults, all else being equal. On the other hand, one needs to remember *something* in order to have a false memory; in order to have source confusions, one must remember information from more than one source. Perhaps older adults remember events so poorly that they will not show the illusions of memory that younger adults show (or they will show them only in diminished form). A study of certain types of memory-impaired patients reviewed later indicates that these patients do not show the levels of illusory memories that age-matched controls show, so it may be that whatever factors encourage normal levels of retention are also responsible for memory illusions (Schacter, Verfaellie, & Pradere, 1996).

Before launching into the substance of our chapter, we might pause a moment to marvel at the fact that at the turn of the millennium there was so little evidence about memory illusions in older adults. The renaissance of studies of illusory memories began in the early 1970s, and one important stream of this research was initiated by Elizabeth Loftus, the honoree of this volume. In 1974, she published her famous study with John Palmer that began decades of work on eyewitness memory and the misinformation effect (Loftus & Palmer, 1974). This paradigm and others (e.g., Bransford, Barclay, & Franks, 1972) have been the objects of study for many years and we have learned much from them. An overlapping line of research on illusory memories in young children used some of these paradigms and other adaptations (see Ceci & Bruck, 1995, for a review). This research was driven in part by the many court cases of alleged childhood sexual abuse (in day-care centers and other situations). As a population of interest, children have been frequently studied. Older adults, on the other hand, have not been studied, at least until recently. This is surprising because older adults are disproportionately susceptible to crime and must frequently testify, so it is unclear to us why researchers studying memory and aging expended so little of their energies in studying this topic. Of course, there were occasional experiments published that are relevant, a few even dating to the 1970s (e.g., Rankin & Kausler, 1979). Still, there was no systematic program of research in the many laboratories directed at illusory memory processes in older adults, unlike the booming interest in illusory recollection in children and in young adults. It is heartening that the situation is different today than from even a few years ago. Many researchers besides us are studying illusory memories in older adults (e.g., Memon & Bartlett, 2002; Norman & Schacter, 1997; Searcy, Bartlett, & Memon, 1999, 2000).

This chapter reports progress we have made in our own program of research, which was conceived collaboratively in the late 1990s and is still in progress today. We bring in related findings from other labs as needed, but our intent is not to review the literature but rather to provide a summary of our own work with our collaborators (whom we acknowledge along the way). In overview, we report research comparing illusory memories in younger and older adults using four different illusory memory paradigms. These are the Deese–Roediger–McDermott (DRM) associative word paradigm (Deese, 1959b; Roediger & McDermott, 1995), a related categorized word list paradigm (Meade & Roediger, 2006; S. M. Smith, Ward, Tindall, Sifonis, & Wilkenfeld, 2000), the Loftus misinformation paradigm (e.g., Loftus, Miller, & Burns, 1978), and an imagination inflation paradigm in which people confuse imagined actions with ones actually performed (Goff & Roediger, 1998). We review the nature of these paradigms in the coming pages, but in preview we do find elevated levels of illusory recollection in older adults in all four paradigms.

The other focus of our chapter is to consider individual differences among older adults using neuropsychological measures. We know that individual differences are important in all of cognition, and we may suspect that their importance grows as adults age. At the simplest level, measures of variability in all studies of cognitive aging show increases with age, so if individual differences are great among younger adults—and they are—this variability and its importance waxes with age. The primary research strategy used in the field (and in our own prior work) is to compare groups of healthy older adults with younger adults, with them being equated to some degree on other factors. The older adults are usually screened for health risk factors and depression and have equal or higher levels of education relative to younger adults, which controls some variability. In addition, vocabulary scores (a measure of crystallized intelligence or general knowledge) are typically a bit higher in older than younger adults in these studies. Despite these steps, older adults' performance remains consistently more variable than that of younger adults.

In our research, we examined measures that are assumed to assess older adults' frontal-lobe functioning by employing a battery of tasks identified by Glisky, Polster, and Routhieaux (1995). Glisky and her colleagues identified five neuropsychological tests that provide converging measures of frontal functioning. These five tests resulted from a factor-analytic examination of a number of putative frontal tests and other psychometric cognitive/memory tests. The five chosen tests robustly and consistently loaded on a single factor and did not load highly on any other factor. Using a battery of five tests permits more powerful convergent measurement of putative frontal functioning than would be obtained with a single measure (as has been the practice in much neuropsychological research).

The refinement of neuropsychological measures of frontal functioning also permits advances in testing theories of cognitive aging. One prominent theory of cognitive aging attributes older adults' memory difficulties to declining frontal-lobe functioning (Balota, Dolan and Duchek, 2000; Craik, Morris, Morris, & Loewen, 1990; Mather, Johnson, & De Leonardis, 1999; Moscovitch & Winocur, 1995), so using Glisky's battery of frontal tests permits an assessment of whether frontal functioning is critical in memory performance and whether these tests predict recollection of veridical and illusory memories. We used Glisky et al.'s (1995) battery of tests to see if it predicted performance of older adults in the four paradigms we used to study false memories.

## ASSOCIATIVE ILLUSORY MEMORIES

Roediger and McDermott (1995) revised a paradigm originally introduced by Deese (1959). Deese (1959a, 1959b, 1965) was interested in associative factors that affect recall and his studies used lists of associatively related words from the Russell and Jenkins (1954) word association norms. The lists were the most commonly listed associates to single words. So, for example, the list of words that were associates to the word *window* were *door, glass, pane, shade, ledge, sill, house, open, curtain, frame, view, breeze, sash, screen,* and *shutter.* Deese (1959b) observed that a few of his lists had a high propensity to elicit recall of the word that had generated (but not appeared in) the list as an intrusion. Other lists created by the same means did not, however, have the same tendency to elicit intrusions. Many years later, Roediger and McDermott (1995) noted Deese's (1959b) observation and developed the paradigm as a means of studying illusory memories. Roediger and McDermott (1995, Experiment 2) developed 24 lists (including some of Deese's lists and others they derived from the norms) that generally produced high levels of false recall, false recognition, and false remembering (using Tulving's [1985] remember/know procedure) in younger adults. The revised paradigm has been frequently studied in the past decade and, as mentioned earlier, is called the DRM paradigm, for Deese–Roediger–McDermott, owing to a suggestion by Endel Tulving. The basic recall results from Roediger and McDermott (1995, Experiment 2) are shown in Figure 7.1 and the recognition results are shown in Figure 7.2.

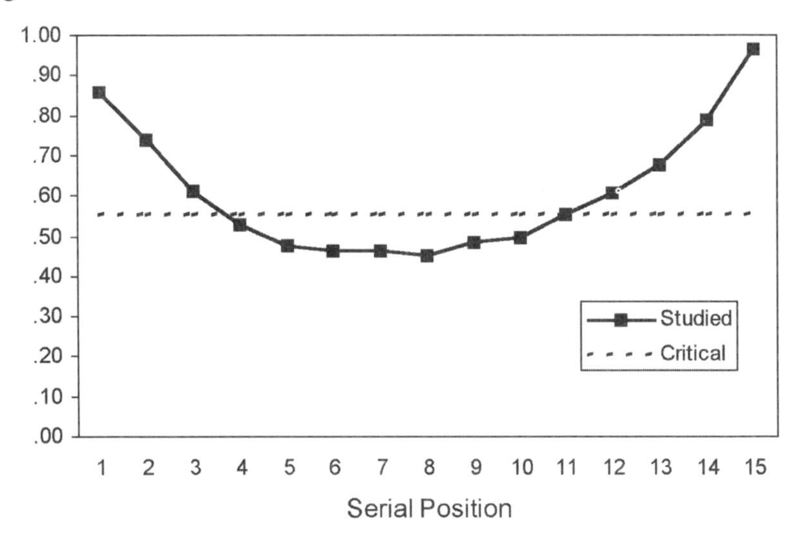


Figure 7.1. Probability of accurate and false recall in the DRM paradigm. The data show a standard serial position curve for the 15 list items, with the strong primacy and recency effects that are standard for single-trial free recall. The datum represented in the dashed line is the probability of false recall of the critical nonpresented items from which the lists were derived. False recall was about at the level of recall of presented items that occurred in the middle of the list. (Data are from Roediger & McDermott, 1995, Experiment 2.)

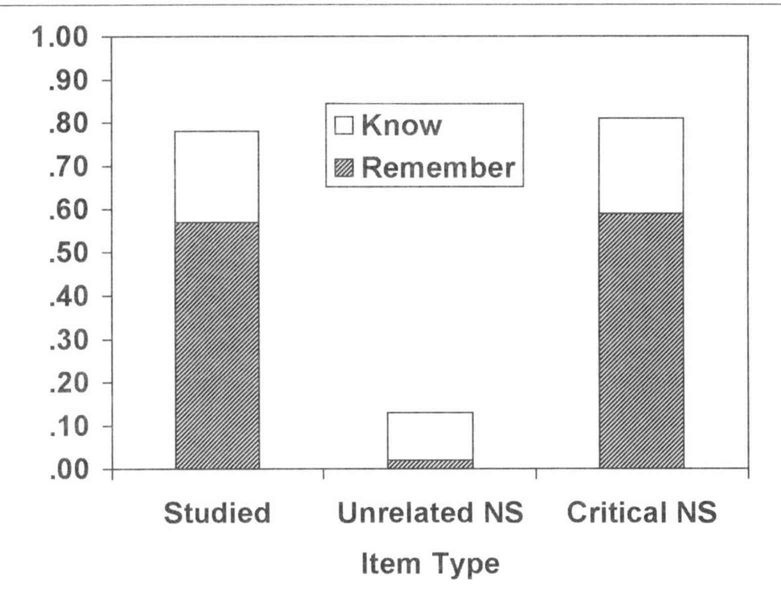


Figure 7.2. Probabilities of recognition in the DRM paradigm. The bars show the hit rate for the studied items and the false-alarm rates for two kinds of nonstudied (NS) items, those generally unrelated to the list words and the critical lure. Each bar is decomposed into the proportion of items judged old to which subjects gave remember or know judgments. The proportions of both false alarms and remember judgments were quite similar for list items and critical lures. (Data are from Roediger & McDermott, 1995, Experiment 2.)

## INDIVIDUAL DIFFERENCES IN ASSOCIATIVE ILLUSIONS

Study of individual differences in the DRM paradigm began with an experiment by Schacter, Verfaellie, and Pradere (1996). They tested a group of amnesic patients and matched controls in the DRM paradigm on both veridical recall of list items and false recall of the critical nonstudied items from which the lists had been created. As expected, they found that the memory-impaired patients performed much worse on the list items than did the controls. The interesting finding was that patients also showed much less false recall for the critical items than did the controls. This outcome might indicate that any group of people (children, older adults, depressed people, etc.) or any manipulation that produces poorer retention of the studied items might also show less propensity to elicit false recall or false recognition, which would suggest that occurrence of false memories is necessarily dependent on level of list recall. This assumption was not unreasonable as a starting place in 1996, because experimental manipulations, for example, blocked versus random presentation of several DRM lists, showed a correlation between list recall and false recall. Such as, McDermott (1996) showed that blocked presentation of lists increased both accurate and false recall relative to random presentation of lists. However, this general proposition of a cause-and-effect relation between veridical and false recall was dashed on the shoals of further research. Several experimental manipulations have opposite effects on veridical and false recall, including list length (Robinson & Roediger, 1997), presentation rate (Gallo & Roediger, 2002), and item repetition (McDermott, 1996). Most relevant for present purposes, the same negative correlation between veridical and false recall was reported in an experiment by Norman and Schacter (1997) that compared younger and older adults in the DRM paradigm. They found that older adults recalled DRM lists less well than younger adults (not surprisingly), but they also showed that older adults were *more* likely to falsely recall the critical items. This is exactly opposite the pattern Schacter et al. obtained with amnesic patients. Norman and Schacter's outcome with older adults was confirmed by Balota et al. (1999) and was extended to patients with diseases of the Alzheimer's type. Balota et al. showed greater false recall and false recognition in older adults than in younger adults, as well as greater false memory in dementia of the Alzheimer's type (DAT) patients than in age-matched older adults. However, not all studies have found higher absolute levels of false retention in older adults using the DRM paradigm (e.g., McCabe & Smith, 2002; Tun, Wingfield, Rosen, & Blanchard, 1998), but most do show a higher ratio of false recall/recognition in older adults. Differences in outcome among studies in older adults may be due to varying characteristics of the sample of older adults, an issue that we address later.

Because Balota et al. (1999) employed fairly large numbers of subjects, they were able to match subjects in the various groups on levels of veridical recall and recognition by eliminating some young subjects with the best recall and some older subjects with the poorest recall. When they performed this matched-subjects analysis, they confirmed that older adults showed greater levels of false recall and recognition relative to younger adults. The same analysis held for the comparison of DAT patients and older adults. The data are shown in Figure 7.3. Because frontal-lobe atrophy is thought to occur in older adults and to be accelerated in patients with Alzheimer's disease, these results are consistent with theories that attribute declines in memory functioning in aging to impaired frontal functioning.

Butler, McDaniel, Dornburg, Price, and Roediger (2004) compared younger and older adults in the DRM paradigm. The older adults had been previously tested using Glisky et al.'s (1995) battery of tests so that roughly half were high frontal functioning and half were low frontal functioning, using the criteria of the original Glisky et al. sample. Both groups of older adults scored higher (and equally well) on a standard vocabulary test than did younger adults, and the older adults had been screened for depression and for mental state (using the mini-mental state examination or MMSE). Subjects were given DRM lists for immediate free recall. The results are shown in Table 7.1. The left side of the panel indicates that prior work of Norman and Schacter (1997) and Balota et al. (1999) was replicated. Older adults' recall of list items was worse than that of younger adults (.52 to .61), but their false recall was reliably higher than the younger adults' recall (.42 to .31).

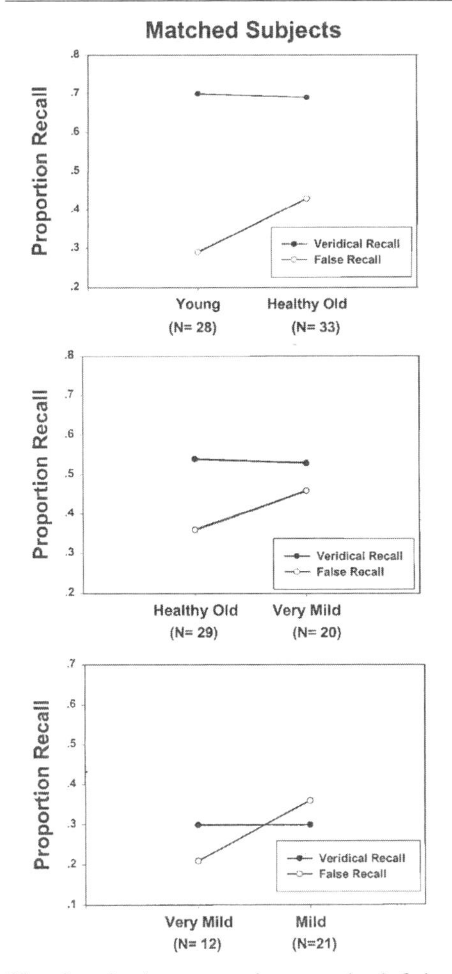


Figure 7.3. Matched-subjects analysis for younger adults, healthy older adults, and two groups of patients with Alzheimer's disease. When matched on veridical recall with a comparison group, the more impaired group always shows a greater level of false recall than the less impaired group. (Data are from Balota et al., 1999.) Reprinted by permission of psychology Press. http://www.psypress.co.uk /journals.asp

The data in the comparison on the left include the entire sample of older adults. The data on the right side of the table decompose the older adults' performance into the high-functioning and low-functioning groups. This analysis makes clear that the "aging effect" seen in the data on the left side of the table is borne entirely by the low-frontal-functioning group. Veridical recall was not significantly different between young and high-functioning older adults and neither was false recall. False recall was about 20% higher in the low-frontal-functioning group than in either the young or the high-functioning old groups.

If these results are replicable and generalize to other paradigms, the implications are profound and highly supportive of the view that cognitive aging is attributable to breakdowns in frontal functioning. Effects attributed to "cognitive aging" by comparing groups of younger and older adults would not be due to "age" per se; if one finds older adults who score highly on tests of frontal functioning (presumably like young adults score) they show neither impaired veridical recall nor increased false recall. Butler et al. (2004) examined scores of putative tests of medial temporal lobe functioning (adopted from the Glisky et al., 1995, factor-analytic study) in many of their older adults and the pattern appearing in Table 7.1 seems to be securely tied to frontal-lobe functioning rather than to some other ability, although further work is needed to bolster this conclusion.

## INTERVENTIONS TO ATTENUATE FALSE MEMORY IN LOW-FRONTAL ADULTS

Having found that low-frontal older adults display exaggerated false recall, one of our objectives in our more recent research has been to examine techniques that might attenuate this memory deficit for older adults with low frontal functioning. This work has led to several surprising twists.

One straightforward explanation for the increase in false recall in low-frontal older adults hinges on the observation that the frontal systems seem intimately involved in encoding of source information. In particular, Glisky et al. (1995; see also Glisky, Rubin, & Davidson, 2001) reported that low-frontal older adults showed significant declines relative to high-frontal older adults at remembering perceptual information (gender of speaker's voice) associated with target items. With regard to the Butler et al. finding, the idea here is that perceptual source information from presented words would not be well encoded by low-frontal older adults. Consequently, during recall the low-frontal adults would have few, if any, source features to distinguish presented list items from associatively related nonpresented items that are presumably activated at study (Roediger, Watson, McDermott, & Gallo, 2001) or generated as possible candidates during the recall process (cf. Guynn et al., 2005; Jacoby & Hollingshead, 1990).

One of us (McDaniel), in collaboration with Karin Butler and Courtney Dornburg (Butler, McDaniel, & Dornburg, 2005), reasoned that, in lieu of perceptual source information, perhaps low-frontal older adults could be encouraged to encode distinctive semantic information that would help distinguish target items

**Table 7.1**

**Proportion of List Items and Critical Nonpresented Items Recalled by Younger and Older Adults.[a]**

| | | | Frontal Status[b] | |
|---|---|---|---|---|
| Item Type | Younger | Older | High | Low |
| List | .61 | .52 | .57 | .46 |
| Critical | .31 | .42 | .32 | .52 |

*Note.* Data are from Butler et al. (2004).
[a](left side of the table)
[b]The two columns on the right show recall of older adults decomposed as a function of their frontal status (high or low).

from nonpresented associated items and therefore decrease false recall of the critical associates. McCabe, Presmanes, Robertson, and Smith (2004) developed just such a technique with younger adults. In their study, subjects who were required at encoding to generate a distinctive feature of each presented target word showed lower false recognition than an uninstructed group of subjects. We adapted this distinctive-feature technique for a parallel study conducted with high- and low-frontal-functioning older adults. Because this study has not yet been reported, we provide some of the details.

To more convincingly tie the patterns in recall to frontal functioning (rather than to general neuropsychological health), we also assessed medial temporal functioning (using five psychometric tests from the Glisky et al., 1995 and 2001, battery) for the entire sample of 36 older adults (18 high-frontal and 18 low-frontal). Medial temporal scores were not significantly different across the high- and low-frontal adults (.03 and -.13, respectively). Sixteen college-age adults were also tested. Several procedural changes from that of McCabe et al. (2004) were implemented to accommodate the present objectives. Because the neuropsychological assessment of the older adults was extensive and restricted to older adults with MMSE scores of 26 or higher, the encoding manipulation (standard encoding, distinctive-feature encoding) was varied within subjects. So that the older adults could easily apprehend the target items, we used visual presentations (rather than auditory presentations). To allow older adults time to think of a distinctive characteristic for each target word, we extended the presentation rate to 5 seconds per word (from 4 seconds). A final modification was that in the distinctive-feature condition, we had older and younger adults say aloud the distinctive characteristic they generated in response to each word. We felt that explicit production would make the generated distinctive characteristic of each target more memorable, thereby making it easier for older adults to access that information to help reduce false recall. Explicit production also allowed us to gauge whether older adults were able to implement the strategy.

In the distinctive-features condition, subjects were asked to think of one unique characteristic for each word in the list and to say this characteristic aloud. As an example, subjects were told that upon seeing the word *dog* they might say their dog's name ("Oscar") or upon seeing the word *cat* they might say "allergic" to describe their reaction to cats. Subjects practiced this technique using a list of thematically related words and were given feedback as to how successful they were in generating a unique characteristic to each practice word. Then, for each encoding condition, subjects were given nine DRM lists (blocked by condition), with recall following each list. Several sets of lists were constructed for counterbalancing purposes across each encoding condition, with the sets constructed to produce false recall of approximately .40 on average, according to the Stadler, Roediger, and McDermott (1999) norms.

Table 7.2 shows the false-recall results. Examining the results from the standard encoding condition first (left side), it is apparent that false recall for younger adults was substantially lower than the norms for these lists (.19 vs. .40, respectively). The low level of false recall was probably a consequence of relatively long visual presentations (e.g., see Gallo, McDermott, Percer, & Roediger, 2001; Gallo & Roediger, 2002; Kellogg, 2001; R. Smith & Hunt, 1998). Visual presentations (and longer presentation rates) presumably afford the encoding of perceptual (visual) information that can be used to discriminate between presented targets and nonpresented critical items (which would have little or no visual graphemic information). The idea is that visual information is more distinctive than auditory information in terms of distinguishing targets from nonpresented items (Kellogg, 2001; R. E. Smith, Lozito, & Bayen, 2005).

More important, the high-frontal-functioning older adults also displayed relatively low false recall, and at levels that were not significantly different from that of younger adults. Also consistent with Butler et al. (2004), the low-frontal-functioning older adults displayed significantly higher levels of false recall than the younger adults. For what it is worth, false-recall levels in the low-frontal-functioning group were still lower than the normed level with younger adults (with auditory presentation and a relatively fast presentation rate) of .40 (Stadler et al., 1999). R. E. Smith et al. (2005) reported that visual presentations did not reduce false recall in older adults relative to auditory presentations, but did so for young adults. This finding could be accounted for by the hypothesis that older adults are generally deficient in distinctive processing (R. E. Smith et al., 2005) or in engaging in controlled processes necessary for certain types of distinctiveness to influence retention (Geraci, McDaniel, & Roediger, 2006).

Our new results on the left side of Table 7.2 suggest that, with sufficient processing time, even low-frontal older adults can encode perceptual information that provides distinctive encodings for target items relative to nonpresented associates, and these encodings can successfully be used to reduce false recall. That is, with the current presentation conditions, low-frontal false recall (.29) was not significantly worse than that false recall for high-frontal older adults (.23). Thus, low-frontal older adults appear capable of encoding perceptual source information under favorable conditions and exploiting that perceptual information to avoid memory illusions. Clearly, however, this claim warrants more direct comparison of false recall under auditory and visual presentations for low-frontal adults.

**Table 7.2**
**Proportion of Nonpresented Critical Items Recalled in the Distinctive-Feature Experiment**

| | Standard Encoding | Distinctive Feature Encoding |
|---|---|---|
| Younger (16) | .19 | .19 |
| High Frontal Older (18) | .23 | .35 |
| Low Frontal Older (18) | .29 | .48 |

*Note.* Data are from Butler et al. (2005).

The most central and startling result is found in the right-hand side of Table 7.2. False-recall levels *increased* by at least 50%, relative to the standard encoding condition, for both low-frontal and high-frontal older adults, whereas there was no change for younger adults. Unexpectedly, the strategy of attempting to reduce memory illusions in low-frontal older adults by fostering distinctive semantic encoding not only was damaging to the low-frontal adults, but also created conditions under which high-frontal older adults displayed exaggerated false recall relative to the young. The strategy we used to reduce false recall in older adults actually increased errors in both groups, although more for the low-frontal adults.

We had adopted a relatively generous presentation rate to allow older adults to complete the encoding task, but perhaps the rate was still too fast to allow older adults to effectively generate distinctive characteristics. To examine this possibility, we evaluated the responses generated during encoding. On several measures, the older adults' response did not appear significantly different from the younger adults'. The number of trials on which a response was omitted was relatively low for all groups, the proportion of times a critical nontarget item was generated was low, and the proportion of times that the generated response was an associate to the target varied little across groups.

We conclude that the older adults were able to implement distinctive-feature encoding to the same extent as the younger adults. Why then were their memory illusions increased by this encoding technique, one that theoretically and empirically (McCabe et al., 2004) should reduce memory illusions? We cannot say for sure, but several possibilities come to mind. Kouststaal et al. (2003) found that a semantic-labeling orienting task used to encode pictures increased false memories for pictorial materials. They suggested that intentional semantic processing during encoding interfered with perceptual processing that ordinarily would allow discrimination between presented targets and unpresented lures. For the present experiment, it may be that reduced processing resources (or processing speed) of the older adults precluded adequate processing of the perceptual characteristics of the visually presented words when they had to perform the distinctive features task. Consequently, useful perceptual information would be diminished by the distinctive-features task for older subjects.

Another possibility is that the items generated for the distinctive-feature task created additional source-monitoring demands for older adults, who are already challenged by source memory tasks (e.g., Craik et al., 1990; Naveh-Benjamin & Craik, 1995). The idea here is that the words generated for the distinctive-feature task created additional source interference for the older adults because they were faced with three possible sources for candidate items that might be recalled: presented words, words generated during encoding, and nonpresented thematic associates of presented words. Dehon and Bredart (2004) present evidence consistent with this idea. In the next section, we return to this idea that forced responding of extraneous material may be problematic for exaggerating memory illusions, especially in low-frontal older adults. Before doing so, however, we describe another finding that reinforces the emerging picture that the exaggerated memory illusions displayed by low-frontal older adults can be resistant to improvement even under favorable encoding conditions.

Thomas and Sommers (2005) modified the typical DRM procedure so that target words would be more richly encoded with elaborative detail and thus presumably more distinguishable from the nonpresented thematic lures. In the elaborative condition, target words were presented in sentential contexts (e.g., "The weary worker laid down on the bed," with *bed* representing one of the items in the list whose critical lure is *sleep*). With college-age subjects, the sentential contexts significantly improved the discrimination of targets from the critical thematic lures in recognition, primarily by reducing the endorsement of the critical lures. Thomas and McDaniel (2006) examined whether sentence elaboration would similarly reduce false recognition for high- and low-frontal older adults. Table 7.3 displays the endorsement rates for targets and the critical lures and the d′ values for discriminating target items from lures. The findings are dramatic. Both young adults and high-frontal older adults showed substantially reduced false recognition and substantially increased discriminability (d,) with sentence elaboration relative to the standard word-only presentation. In contrast, the low-frontal older adults have nominally *higher* false recognition and *lower* discriminability when the targets are presented in elaborative sentence contexts than when presented in isolation. The upshot of these findings reinforces that found by Butler et al. (2005). Supportive encoding techniques that ordinarily reduce memory illusions can have the opposite effect on older adults, especially low-frontal older adults.

**Table 7.3**
**Proportion of Studied Targets and Critical Lures Endorsed by Younger and Older Adults.**

| | Younger | Older | |
|---|---|---|---|
| | | High Frontal | Low Frontal |
| *Isolated words* | | | |
| Studied | .73 | .65 | .62 |
| Critical | .64 | .65 | .70 |
| d′ | .36 | -.29 | -.83 |
| *Sentence contexts* | | | |
| Studied | .69 | .56 | .57 |
| Critical | .31 | .40 | .74 |
| d′ | 1.58 | .75 | -1.29 |

*Note.* Datat are from Thomas and McDaniel (2006).

Other memory enhancement techniques have also been shown to increase false memories in low-frontal older adults. Dornburg and McDaniel (2006; see Dornburg & McDaniel, 2005, for complete details) reported a related pattern for mnemonic retrieval techniques that is worth mentioning here. Low- and high-frontal older adults (determined by the Glisky et al., 1995, assessment) read a narrative about the courtship of two college students, Bob and Margie. Several weeks later the subjects recalled the narrative either with standard free-recall instructions or with cognitive-interview instructions (Fisher, Geiselman, & Amador, 1989) designed to facilitate recall (e.g., thinking of original encoding context, recalling from different perspectives). Even after a several-week delay, the cognitive-interview technique was successful in significantly increasing recall of information relative to the standard recall condition for both high- and low-frontal older adults. Critically, however, recall of false details increased as well with the cognitive interview for older adults with low frontal scores. That is, the cognitive interview increased production of incorrect information relative to the standard recall condition for low-frontal but not for high-frontal older adults. This pattern appeared to be linked to frontal processes, because medial temporal lobe tests were not correlated with the production of incorrect information.

Taken in concert, the practical implications of the findings described in this section for everyday memory functioning (and possibly for eyewitness memory contexts) are great. Techniques designed to improve memory accuracy and reduce memory illusions may, in some cases, amplify the already exaggerated memory illusions of low-frontal-functioning older adults. Thus, well-intentioned attempts to engineer contexts to reduce memory illusions in older adults may unwittingly exacerbate the problem for those adults with low frontal functioning.

We turn next to results in another word list paradigm that has been developed to study false memories to see if the provocative divergence of results as a function of older adults' frontal status will replicate in a somewhat different domain.

## ILLUSORY MEMORIES OF CATEGORY MEMBERS

A tactic long used by psychologists interested in the organization of memory is to use items belonging to common categories such as articles of furniture, birds, famous cities, and so on. Bousfield (1953) began the study of how people remember items belonging to common categories and, over the years, a huge number of studies have been done using this technique (see Murphy & Puff, 1982, for a partial review). One problem sometimes noted in this literature is the issue of guessing. If *robin* is presented in the bird category and a person later produces *robin* on a recall test, how can one be sure that *robin* was remembered? Perhaps instead the subject remembered that some birds were on the list and simply produced the first item that came to mind. Robin is the most probable bird to be produced when people are asked to generate members of this category, so it could have been recalled via free association rather than remembering. Tulving and Pearlstone (1966) considered this issue in their famous study of free and cued recall of categorized lists. Their solution was simply to omit the most probable items in a category from the presented members. If a researcher uses less frequent category members (e.g., oriole or even ostrich) presumably subjects are not merely free associating if they recall them on the test (unless they produce a huge number of intrusions). Other corrections for guessing are also possible (Roediger, 1973; Watkins & Gardiner, 1982). However, in retrospect, all these efforts to "correct" for guessing in categorized-list recall (or free recall or even recognition) appear, 40 years later, to be somewhat misguided. In the 1960s, researchers did not find errors to be interesting in their own right—no one was studying false memories—but rather as a source of noise, which needed to be corrected (see Roediger, 1996, for a review). Perhaps when someone produces *robin* while recalling various birds they are really remembering its occurrence, even though the word was not actually in the list. If so, its recollection would have the same status as DRM false-memory errors.

S. M. Smith, Ward, Tindell, Sifonis and Wilkenfeld (2000) used a categorized-list technique to study arousal of false memories. They created lists that omitted the most frequently produced categorized members to examine their intrusion in recall. They showed that the categorized-list paradigm produced false recall similar to that observed in the DRM paradigm, although they did find differences between the two paradigms in priming of nonpresented items on an implicit memory test.

Meade and Roediger (2006) developed a similar paradigm to examine age differences in false recollection in both free and forced recall with younger and older adults. They used 17 items from each category but omitted the first 5. In the category *birds,* subjects studied *crow, bluebird, canary, parakeet, hawk, blackbird, wren, oriole, parrot, pigeon, hummingbird, starling, woodpecker, vulture, swallow, chicken,* and *dove,* items 6 to 22 in the norms. The interest was not only in how well younger and older adults would recall these words in various conditions but also in whether they would recall the five birds that were omitted: *robin, sparrow, cardinal, blue jay,* and *eagle*. Unlike the DRM paradigm, which permits examination of only one possible critical item per list, the categorized list paradigm allows examination of five potential opportunities of false recall (and of course other category items may be intruded).

Meade and Roediger (2006) conducted two experiments, but we report only selected data of Experiment 1 here. After studying the six categorized lists, subjects were given an initial test under either normal cued-recall conditions or under forced-recall conditions. In both cases, they were given the category names one at a time and asked to recall the list items. In the cued-recall condition, they were warned not to guess and were instructed to recall only items from the category that they were reasonably sure had occurred in the list. Under forced-recall conditions, they were told that 20 items had been presented in each category (there were actually only 17) and that they should produce 20 items for each category, guessing if necessary. The subjects were then given a second test.

The results of the first test are shown in Table 7.4. In the cued-recall condition, the data replicated quite well the findings of Norman and Schacter (1997) and

Balota et al. (1999), among others. Older adults recalled more critical items (robin, etc.) than did younger adults, .22 to .09, whereas there was no difference in veridical recall. This last finding is not a real surprise, because on tests that provide strong retrieval cues, often older adults can recall about as well as younger adults, presumably due to greater retrieved support provided by the cues (Craik, 1977). The forced-recall results show much higher levels of production because subjects were required to free-associate and generate appropriate category members. Notice that for the critical items, both older and younger adults produced about 70% of the critical items. This equivalence is critical in interpreting the results on the second test.

The second test was of the most interest. All subjects were tested under cued recall conditions with instructions to recall only items that they were reasonably sure had occurred on the original study list and not to guess. The category names were presented one at a time and subjects had 3 minutes for recall of items from each category. In addition, they were instructed to make a *remember* or *know* judgment on each word recalled, using instructions adapted from Rajaram (1993; see also Gardiner, 1988; Tulving, 1985). Of course, for subjects who had previously taken a cued-recall test, the second test was essentially the same with the addition of remember/know instructions. Our interest was focused on the subjects whose first test had involved forced recall because prior work has shown that forcing subjects to guess on a first test leads them to make more errors on a later test (e.g., Roediger, Wheeler, & Rajaram, 1993; Schooler, Foster, & Loftus, 1988). We also predicted that older adults would have more difficulty in monitoring their responses on the second test and would be more bothered by having created their own retroactive interference in the form of guessed responses on the prior forced-recall test than would younger adults. The prior forced-recall phase should make interfering items come to mind in the cued-recall test and older adults should have more difficulty in ignoring this enhanced fluency. Jacoby (1999) has shown that older adults are more likely to attribute highly accessible items to memory than are younger

**Table 7.4**
**Mean Proportion of Items Recalled by Younger and Older Adults on an Initial Cued Recall or Forced Recall Test.**

| | Cued Recall | | Forced Recall | |
|---|---|---|---|---|
| | Younger | Older | Younger | Older |
| List recall: | .39 | .39 | .65 | .59 |
| Critical recall: | .09 | .22 | .70 | .69 |

*Note.* From Meade & Roediger (2006), Experiment 1.

adults, even when factors other than prior presentation make the items highly accessible. High accessibility makes people (young and old) more confident that a retrieved item was recently experienced, but the impact of this factor is greater in older adults. Kelley and Sahakyan (2003) have shown that older adults show a lower correspondence between confidence ratings (subjective judgments) and accuracy of recall (objective correctness) than do younger adults (see also Koriat & Goldsmith, 1996).

The results of Meade and Roediger's (2006) second test are shown in Table 7.5 and they bear out these predictions. Recall of list items is shown at the top as a function of whether the first test had been cued recall (on the left) or forced recall (on the right). Once again, older and younger adults did not differ too much in either overall recall or in remember/know judgments, although performance was somewhat higher for both groups following forced recall. The real interest is in critical-item recall, shown at the bottom of the table. A second cued-recall test after a first one produced higher levels of false recall for old than young adults, as shown in the lower left cells of Table 7.5. Furthermore, the effect was one of false remembering because the older adults' *remember* judgments exceeded those of younger adults on the critical items (16% to 6%). The data on the bottom right of the table show the most dramatic finding in the experiment: On the cued-recall test following a forced-recall test, older adults were twice as likely as younger adults to falsely recall the critical items and their false remembering was eight times higher than that of younger adults (.33 to .04). *Know* judgments did not differ between younger and older adults.

**Table 7.5**
**Mean Proportion of Items Recalled and Mean Proportion of Remember and Know Responses on a Second Cued Recall Test.**

| | Prior Cued Recall | | Prior Forced Recall | |
|---|---|---|---|---|
| | Younger | Older | Younger | Older |
| *List Recall* | | | | |
| Total | .48 | .43 | .51 | .51 |
| Remember | .39 | .34 | .40 | .37 |
| Know | .09 | .09 | .12 | .14 |
| *Critical Recall* | | | | |
| Total | .17 | .28 | .32 | .60 |
| Remember | .06 | .16 | .04 | .33 |
| Know | .11 | .12 | .28 | .27 |

*Note.* From Meade and Roediger (2006), Experiment 1.

These results show that older adults are especially susceptible to interference from their own self-produced responses given on the earlier forced-recall test. (Recall that older and younger adults produced equivalent numbers of responses on that first test.) Comparing the data from the first (forced) and second (cued) recall tests, younger adults reduced responding with critical items from .70 to .32, and although .32 is still a high error rate, younger adults claimed to remember the occurrence of only .04 of the critical items. On the other hand, older adults reduced production of critical items from .69 on the forced-recall test (when they were told to guess) to only .60 on the cued-recall test (when they were told not to guess). Furthermore, the older adults *remembered* .33 of the erroneously produced items, a remarkable level of false remembering. These results add to those of Jacoby (1999; Jacoby, Bishara, Hessels, & Toth, 2005) in showing spectacular levels of false memories in older adults.

The next step in this program of research was to determine if frontal status of older adults (high or low) would be related to illusory remembering in the categorized-list paradigm developed by Meade and Roediger (in press). Roediger, Meade, and Geraci (2006) conducted two experiments on this issue with similar results. We report one experiment here. Younger adults and two groups of older adults (high frontals and low frontals, as classified by Glisky et al.'s [1995] criteria) studied the six 17-item categorized lists used in Meade and Roediger and then took two successive cued-recall tests. On both tests subjects rated their confidence in their responses, so that subjects would place an emphasis on accurate responding; for the same reason, we did not include a forced-recall condition in these experiments.

The results from the experiment are shown in Table 7.6 for both tests for younger and older adults. On the left are shown data comparing younger adults to older adults, with data collapsed across both groups of older adults. The data on the right decompose the older adults' performance by their frontal-functioning status. Examining first the data on the left, it is clear that these results replicate those of Meade and Roediger (2006) in that older adults produce more intrusions of critical items than do younger adults on both tests, and this pattern conceptually replicates the work of others with the DRM paradigm. However, when the data on the right-hand side of the table are examined, it is clear that only the low-frontal older adults are carrying the "aging effect" in false recall. The data of the high-frontal older adults lie within a percentage point or two of the younger adults' data for each of the four comparisons. It is the low-frontal older adults who show somewhat lower veridical recall and much higher false recall than the younger adults. Roediger et al.'s (2006) second experiment replicated these results.

We now have consistent patterns of data from two false-memory paradigms, although the two paradigms are similar (both involve presentation of word lists with false recall or recognition indexed by recall or recognition of words that were not presented). Older adults show greater levels of false recall than younger adults in both paradigms., However, when older adults are divided into high- and low-frontal-status groups, the effects of "age" are more properly seen to involve frontal sta-

**Table 7.6**
**Proportion Recalled of List and Critical Items for Younger and Older Adults on Two Successive Cued Recall Tests[a]**

| **Test 1: Cued Recall** | | | **Frontal Status** | |
|---|---|---|---|---|
| | Younger | Older | High | Low |
| List | .44 | .43 | .45 | .41 |
| Critical | .17 | .26 | .15 | .36 |
| **Test 2: Cued Recall** | | | | |
| | Young | Old | High | Low |
| List | .42 | .44 | .45 | .43 |
| Critical | .18 | .32 | .16 | .47 |

*Note.* From Roediger et al. (2005), Experiment 1.
[a]On the right side of the table the older adults' data are decomposed into high- and low-frontal functioning groups.

tus (except for the increase in false recall with distinctive-features encoding in Butler et al., 2005). High-frontal older adults' data resemble those of younger adults and not those of low-frontal older adults. Our next step was to determine if this pattern would hold in a rather different false-memory paradigm.

## THE LOFTUS MISINFORMATION PARADIGM

In 1974, this volume's honoree published a study that doubtless changed her life as well as forever altering our field. The Loftus and Palmer (1974) experiments began the study of how eyewitness memory for an event can be molded and reshaped by statements made to or questions asked of a witness after the event had occurred. According to the Web of Science database, that study has been cited over 300 times. A later study by Loftus, Miller, and Burns (1978) that introduced what has come to be regarded as the standard misinformation paradigm has been cited about 450 times. And Beth's great book *Eyewitness Testimony* (published in 1979) has garnered over 800 citations. Yet these remarkable figures actually seem to us to underestimate the impact that her work from the 1970s has had. Every introductory psychology textbook includes discussion of these studies and their implications, as do all cognitive psychology textbooks (and of course human memory textbooks). The eyewitness/misinformation paradigm (like others, such as the obedience studies of Milgram, 1963, or the bystander intervention experiments of Darley and Latane, 1968) is among the classics of modern psychology. Everyone who is a scientific psychologist knows (or should know) this work.

The fact that recollection of a visual event such as observing a crime or a traffic accident can be reshaped by later descriptions of the event (or even questions about the event) has changed the way people regard human memory. The tendency to think of memories as static little bundles of information stored away in the nervous system until some cue would later awaken them and display them before the bright light of consciousness with great fidelity has been thoroughly discredited, although one can still see residual effects of these ingrained assumptions in some theories. The work begun by Loftus and Palmer (1974), as well as other research begun in the early 1970s on constructive aspects of remembering (e.g., Bransford & Franks, 1972; Paris & Lindauer, 1976), firmly established the constructive approach to remembering. Of course, Bartlett (1932) had argued for the same view much earlier, but his evidence was mostly anecdotal and in fact his main finding was never successfully replicated until Bergman and Roediger (1999) did so 67 years later.

Although Beth Loftus's studies of the misinformation effect had a huge impact, with a tremendous number of studies being conducted with young adults and then, somewhat later, with children, relatively few studies have been carried out with older adults. When we wrote our first grant proposal in the late 1990s, we could find only a handful of studies. The first was by G. Cohen and Faulkner (1989, Experiment 2), who found that older adults did show a greater misinformation effect than younger adults. This outcome fits well with the idea that the misinformation effect is due to an error in source monitoring—the misinformation gets mixed up with what originally happened—and that older adults have greater source-monitoring difficulties than younger adults (see Lindsay & Johnson, 1989, for the first point and McIntyre & Craik, 1987, for the second). Although others have replicated this pattern (e.g., Mitchell, Johnson, & Mather, 2003), several studies have found no difference between younger and older adults in incorporating misinformation into memory (Coxon & Valentine, 1997; Gabbert, Memon, & Allan, 2003) and one study even found that younger adults can be more suggestible than older adults (Marche, Jordan, & Owre, 2002). As we noted earlier in the chapter, under some circumstances older adults may not encode and retain the misinformation as well as younger adults and therefore it will have less of an effect.

We began our research to first see if we could find conditions in which older adults would show a greater misinformation effect than younger adults and, if so, whether the effects would be mediated by frontal status of older adults. Roediger and Geraci (2006) conducted two experiments using basic procedures from work by Roediger, Jacoby, and McDermott (1996), who used two slide sequences (ones that had been used in earlier work), rather than the usual one sequence, to gain more power. Younger and older adults saw slide sequences depicting crimes, with the expectation that their memories would be tested for the scenes. In one sequence, a workman pulls a hammer from his toolbox while fixing a chair (and stealing money from a desk), so we will use the hammer as the example item in what follows. After seeing each sequence, subjects read a description purportedly written by another observer (but rich in detail). Some details were right and some were wrong, relative to the original slide sequence. In the inconsistent-information condition, the description referred to the item taken from the toolbox as a screwdriver, whereas in the neutral (baseline) condition the narrative simply referred to a tool.

The subjects later received both yes–no and source-monitoring recognition tests. Roediger and Geraci (2006) obtained the standard misinformation effect in younger adults and found an enhanced misinformation effect in older adults, replicating G. Cohen and Faulkner (1989) among others. Subjects were more likely to recognize screwdriver in the final test following receipt of misinformation in the narrative, and this effect was greater for older than for younger adults. Interestingly, the effect of age also appeared on a source-monitoring recognition test in which subjects were given items such as hammer or screwdriver and then asked whether it had appeared in (a) the slides, (b) the narrative, (c) both the slides and the narrative, or (d) neither the slides nor the narrative. The finding of an age difference in the misinformation effect on a source-monitoring recognition test makes sense in that older adults' source-monitoring abilities have consistently been shown to be worse than those of younger adults.

Roediger and Geraci (2006) conducted a second misinformation experiment, but only with older adults who had been pretested and shown to be high or low in frontal status (again, using Glisky et al.'s, 1995, criteria). Briefly, subjects saw the slide sequences, read a narrative, and received a later source-monitoring test. The design was a 2 x 3 with frontal status (high or low) crossed with consistent, neutral, and misinformation conditions. We added a consistent condition to this experiment in which the narrative correctly referred to items in the original slide sequence, such as hammer for the tool the man pulled from the toolbox (see Loftus et al., 1978). The critical results are shown in Table 7.7, which reports errors on the source test, such as subjects judging the misinformation item (screwdriver) to have actually appeared in the slides for the three conditions (misformation, neutral, and consistent). The data combine errors in which subjects judged the misleading item to be only in the slide sequence or to be in the slide sequence and in the narrative.

Before considering the misinformation effect, we need to address one seeming puzzle in the neutral condition. The baseline error rate of judging the "misinformation" item to have been in the slide sequence is quite high even when a screwdriver had never been presented in the experiment—about 44% overall. This outcome is understandable as the same type of error that occurs in DRM experiments in that the critical item (screwdriver, in this case) is consistent with what subjects saw (a toolbox and items in it). Furthermore, as in the Butler et al. (2004) experiment, low-frontal subjects were more likely to provide a false-recognition judgment (.51) than were high-frontal subjects (.36), thereby providing a replication of the Butler et al. research with pictorial rather than verbal materials. Therefore, at least for these purposes, the data in the neutral condition are quite useful in confirming the prior work in a new paradigm.

On the other hand, the data in the neutral condition create a problem in comparing the misinformation effect in high- and low-frontal subjects because of the dif-

**Table 7.7**

**False Recall of Misinformation Items as a Function of Experimental Condition (Misinformation, Neutral and Control) and Frontal Status of Older Adults (High or Low)**

| | Frontal Status[a] | |
|---|---|---|
| | High | Low |
| Misinformation | .49 | .80 |
| Neutral | .36 | .51 |
| Consistent | .36 | .32 |
| | **Frontal Status[b]** | |
| | High | Low |
| Misleading—Neutral | .13 | .29 |
| Misleading—Consistent | .13 | .48 |

Note. From Roediger & Geraci (2006), Experiment 2.
[a]Proportion errors on the source test in which older adults reported that an item had appeared in the scene in the three conditions.
[b]Misinformation effect as calculated against 2 different baselines

fering baselines. That is, the misinformation effect is based on a difference score between false recognition in the misinformation condition and the neutral (baseline) condition; if performance in the latter condition differs, interpretation of the misinformation effect can become clouded. Somewhat surprisingly, the consistent condition helps to solve this problem, because performance is nearly equivalent for the two frontal groups in this condition. Therefore, the consistent condition provides a good baseline with which to compare the data from the misinformation condition. (For reasons we do not understand, low-frontal subjects benefited from the consistent information in the narrative whereas high-frontal subjects did not.)

The two rows at the bottom of Table 7.7 show the misinformation effect calculated against the two possible baselines (i.e., the difference between false recognition in the misinformation condition to either the neutral or consistent condition). As can be seen there, data using either baseline lead to the same conclusion: Low-frontal subjects showed a greater misinformation effect than did high-frontal subjects, although the effect is much greater if the consistent baseline is used. The results are produced by the remarkably high false-alarm rate for low-frontal subjects in the misinformation condition: .80 false recognition.

Our results using the misinformation paradigm confirm the same patterns obtained in the DRM and categorized-list false-memory paradigms: Older adults are more susceptible than younger adults to illusory memories, and the effect is much greater in low-frontal older adults than in high-frontal older adults. Confirmation of the same basic pattern in the misinformation paradigm suggests a welcome generality to our conclusions, because this paradigm is so different from the other two.

In the next section, we report our attempts to generalize these findings to a fourth paradigm used to study illusory memories.

## IMAGINATION INFLATION

Forming mental images is a time-honored way of improving retention (McDaniel & Pressley, 1987; Paivio, 1969) and imagery techniques are included in most mnemonic devices (Roediger, 1980). However, in these cases, people form images of events they want to remember, of true events. What would happen if people were led to form misleading images, if they imagine events that did not happen? Might they come to remember the events as having actually occurred? Raye, Johnson, and Taylor (1980) presented subjects with words or had them generate the words from conceptual clues, and either presentation or generation of the object could occur varying numbers of times. Later, they asked subjects to judge how often they had actually seen the words. Raye et al. found that the internal generation of the words inflated the frequency with which subjects thought they had actually seen the words; the more frequently the word was generated, the greater the effect.

In a more naturalistic paradigm, Garry, Manning, Loftus, and Sherman (1996) asked college students if they had ever experienced rather infrequent events during their childhoods. After subjects made initial judgments, Garry et al. selected items students said they did not remember experiencing and later had the subjects vividly imagine the events. Two weeks later the subjects were again asked to rate the likelihood that the event had occurred during their childhoods. The results showed what the authors called imagination inflation: Imagining the event increased subjects' judgments that the event had occurred, relative to control events that were not imagined. Similar results were reported by Heaps and Nash (1999) and Hyman and Pentland (1996), among others.

These studies used childhood events that, of course, are not under experimental control. The possibility exists (although we believe it unlikely) that the imagination session acted as a retrieval cue on some occasions to prompt subjects to recall actual events from their childhoods. If so, then the second rating by subjects as to whether they had done the event in childhood may have increased because of enhanced accurate recollection of the events in question, not due to imagination inflation.

Goff and Roediger (1998) developed a three-part laboratory procedure designed to examine possible effects of imagination on memory for actions where the potential artifact described previously could not operate. In a first phase, subjects were engaged in the enactment (or subject-performed task) paradigm developed by R. L. Cohen (1981) and Engelkamp and Krumnacker (1980). In an encoding phase, subjects heard commands for action events such as "Push the toy car" or "Break the toothpick" (with the objects provided). Sometimes subjects just listened to the command, sometimes they actually performed the action, and sometimes they imagined performing the action but did not actually do it. In a second, imagination, phase of the experiment, subjects were given a long series of imagination trials with action events; they imagined performing an event either zero (control items), one, three, or five times. Some of these imagined items had occurred during the encoding phase and some had not. Two weeks later subjects received a final test in which they were given action statements (some that had been heard 2 weeks previously and some that had not) and asked to make two judgments: Was the item previously heard and, if so, had they performed it, imagined performing it, or only heard it?

The critical issue of interest in the Goff and Roediger (1998) research was whether repeatedly imagining performance of an action would lead people to believe that they had actually done it. In general, the answer was yes, because the more frequently subjects imagined performing an action, the more frequently they falsely reported having actually performed the action on the later test. The effect across five imaginings was in the 8% to 10% range, but later researchers discovered ways to boost the effect. Thomas, Bulevich, and Loftus (2003) changed the imagination phase from using the general instructions provided by Goff and Roediger (1998) to using specific instructions that encouraged subjects to imagine the action in several modalities—to imagine how the action would feel, how it would look, how it would sound, how it would smell or taste (when appropriate), and so on. Under these conditions, the imagination inflation effect was much larger so that in some conditions people claimed to remember performing an action after repeated imaginings around 25% of the time.

We turn now to an examination of imagination inflation in high- and low-frontal-functioning older adults. Using a somewhat more complicated study procedure than the one used by Goff and Roediger (1998), McDaniel, Butler, and Dornburg (2006) focused more generally on age-related changes in source memory for performed and imagined actions. Both younger and older subjects were presented with action events like those in Goff and Roediger, with the action events either performed or imagined or both. During study, a particular action could be performed one, two, or four times; a particular action could be imagined one, two, or four times; or a particular action could be performed and imagined (once imagined and once performed or twice imagined and twice performed). Two weeks after study, subjects returned to the laboratory to be tested on their retention for the action statements. Verbal descriptions of actions were again presented (but the actions were not performed or imagined); some of them had been previously studied and some had not. Subjects indicated how many times they "did" each described action 2 weeks earlier, and how many times they "imagined" each action (using a response scale ranging from 0 to 8 in both cases). Older adults were characterized as low- and high-frontal-functioning using the same test battery described throughout the chapter.

Of interest were the responses to the actions that had only been imagined and responses to actions that had only been performed (i.e., the actions both imagined and enacted were not included in the following analyses). There are two main memory errors that can be examined in this paradigm. Imagination inflation occurs when subjects indicate that they did an action that they had only imagined, which will presumably increase with the number of imaginings (Goff & Roediger, 1998). Another possible memory illusion in this paradigm is that subjects could indicate they only imagined an action they had actually performed.

Consider first the memory illusion in which subjects indicated that an imagined action was performed—the imagination inflation effect. McDaniel et al. (2006) examined these responses in two ways: (a) The proportion of times that subjects indicated they performed an imagined action at least once (i.e., gave a response of 1–8) was tabulated, and (b) the average number of times the subjects indicated performing an imagined action was tabulated. These scoring procedures converged on a similar pattern; accordingly, we describe the results for only the first measure (see McDaniel et al. for a more detailed report). Older adults were significantly more likely to show imagination inflation; they indicated that they had actually performed an imagined action 41% of the time, whereas younger adults made this error 28% of the time. The effect increased with repeated imaginings for both groups of subjects, replicating Goff and Roediger's (1998) finding with young adults. For actions imagined one, two, and four times, "did" responses were reported for 26%, 37%, and 40% of the items, respectively. However, this increase was not more pronounced for older adults than younger adults. Important to note for present purposes, and unlike the false-memory findings described for the other paradigms we have discussed, low- and high-frontal older adults displayed virtually identical imagination inflation and increases in imagination inflation over repeated imaginings. A more sensitive correlational test of the relation between frontal status and the incidence of "did" responses also found no evidence of an association ($r = -.05$, .09, and $-.04$ for actions imagined one, two, and four times).

For actions that were performed, the false-memory patterns were more complex. Paralleling imagination inflation, with increased number of actual enactments subjects falsely remembered imagining performance of the actions. In contrast to the aforementioned results, older adults were not significantly more likely than younger adults to falsely indicate that a performed action was imagined (38% vs. 33%, respectively). However, within the performance of older adults, low- and high-frontal older adults began to diverge; for actions performed four times low frontals were more likely (over 50% of the time) to indicate the action was imagined than were high frontals (less than 40% of the time). The difference between low- and high-frontal older adults for actions performed four times was also obtained in the scores of the average number of times the subjects indicated imagining the performed action, with low frontals judging the item to be imagined more often (average frequency of .82) than high frontals (.52). In sum, there were generally no age-related differences in falsely remembering that performed actions were imagined. This finding is reliable, because Lee (2001, Experiment 2) reported the same pattern using a similar paradigm. Yet, consistent with the emergent theme of this chapter, in the McDaniel et al. (2006) experiment low-frontal older adults showed an exaggerated imagination illusion relative to high-frontal older adults for the performed actions.

## CONUNDRUMS AND CONCERNS

We discuss three issues in this section: Why is it that three paradigms produced a consistent pattern of findings whereas the imagination inflation paradigm produced a somewhat different pattern, inasmuch as high- and low-frontal older adults did not differ in their performance for the imagination inflation illusion? (All four paradigms showed a greater incidence of illusory memories in older than younger adults.) Second, what does it mean to divide older adults into those scoring high or low on frontal tests? Can the dimension really be attributed to frontal functioning or might the differences be due to other individual differences or general cognitive ability? Third, how prevalent are high- and low-frontal subjects in the general populations of older adults that are likely to be tested in typical university settings, where older adults must travel to the campus to be tested?

Regarding the first issue, replication of the imagination inflation results for low- and high-frontal older adults would be useful, and we (McDaniel, Butler, & Dornburg) are in the process of conducting such research. If the pattern holds, it may be that the source memory judgment (judging whether an imagined item was imagined or performed) in the McDaniel et al. (2006) imagination inflation experiment is more difficult than the judgment older adults are required to make in the other paradigms. In the DRM, categorized-list, and misinformation paradigms, retention was tested immediately (in the same experimental session as study) whereas in the imagination inflation experiment performance was tested after a substantial (2-week) delay. Moreover, the study list in the imagination inflation experiments included items presented under both imagine and perform instructions, thereby complicating the subject's source decision with the possibility that an action item could have been both imagined and performed (rather than one or the other). Under these demanding conditions, even high-frontal older adults may not have the capabilities to avoid memory illusions as well as younger adults can. In line with this possibility is the result from the DRM paradigm with the distinctive-feature encoding manipulation (Butler, McDaniel, & Dornburg, 2005). Here, we found that high-frontal older adults were more susceptible to false recall than young adults when the encoding condition created potential interference (with self-generated "distinctive features") but not in the standard encoding condition.

Another possibility is that the memory illusions in the imagination inflation paradigm are mediated by somewhat different processes or neuropsychological systems than the illusions in the other three paradigms. Briefly, McDaniel et al. (2006) hypothesized that when the source of information is central to its content (e.g., the source information refers to a defining feature such as voice or color), then frontal processes will not be correlated with source memory judgments. Only when source information refers to peripheral details will frontal processes mediate recollection of source. In the imagination inflation paradigm, arguably the source of enacting or imagining an event modifies the content—it is part and parcel of the content. That is, the performed action event necessarily takes on additional features including motoric programs involved in enactment, body postures, and kinesthetic feedback (Engelkamp, 2001). In this case, more spontaneous (medial-temporal) processes, rather than controlled frontal processes, may be prominent in subserving source memory (cf. Naveh-Benjamin, 2000). We refer the interested reader to McDaniel et al. for more detailed discussion of this idea.

The second issue, about classification of older adults as a function of frontal status, will likely be better informed as neuroimaging data are brought to bear in examining older adults scoring high or low on the frontal tests. At present, however, it seems safe to say that the test batteries used in our research are not simply dividing older adults into high- and low-functioning individuals. In a number of published studies, as well as some of the newer studies described in this chapter, the group of older adults scoring better on the frontal battery does not score significantly better on average than the low-frontal group on other tests, tests that are thought to tap into medial temporal systems (Butler et al., 2004; Glisky et al., 1995, 2001; McDaniel et al., 1999). Furthermore, the assumption that the high versus low scores reflect differences in frontal neuropsychological systems in particular is supported by the finding that these differences are associated with source memory (a frontal function; e.g., Craik et al., 1990), but not with item memory (Glisky et al., 1995). Indeed, Glisky et al. (1995) reported a double dissociation such that scores on the putative frontal battery were associated with memory for the source of an item (speaker's gender); scores on the putative medial temporal battery were not associated with source memory. In contrast, scores on the medial temporal battery were associated with item memory (recognition of the content of spoken sentences); scores on the frontal battery were not.

Finally, what about the distribution of high-frontal and low-frontal older adults in the population? In a way, this is the wrong question to ask because of course the measure we are using represents a continuous dimension. In addition, samples of older adults may vary widely from lab to lab due to methods of subject recruitment. To gain solid evidence on the possible distribution of frontal measures in older adults one would need to conduct a representative sampling of the population, which we have not done. Nonetheless, we provide some observations here. When we began this research we worried that we might have difficulty finding low-frontal older adults. The reason is that we tested only older adults who were very high functioning. At both Washington University and the University of New Mexico, the older adults tested in memory experiments live in the community, drive to campus for the test, and typically have at least a college degree (and often an advanced degree). Their vocabulary scores are also quite high. Given these facts, we assumed that we were testing very high functioning older adults and that they would mostly be classified as having high levels of frontal functioning on our tests. However, we were wrong. Thus far we have tested several hundred older adults using the Glisky et al. (1995) battery of tests and have consistently found across samples that more of the older adults tested are classified as low frontals when using Glisky et al.'s cutoff scores from their original study. (Glisky's original sample was only 48 subjects and was also composed of generally high-functioning older adults who came to the lab for testing.) We suspect that if it were possible to gain a representative sample of older adults in all settings, we would find a very low proportion of "high-frontal" older adults using Glisky's original criteria. We make this assertion because samples of older adults volunteering for experiments at universities are probably already in the highest ranges of functioning. If more than half of those older adults are classified as low functioning (using Glisky et al.'s criteria), then it seems safe to say that the criteria are very strict and unlikely to generalize well to the population of older adults at large. These concerns highlight the need to consider measures of frontal functioning as a continuum (rather than as categories) and to use correlational and regression techniques to understand the data better. We hasten to add that our studies have generally used both regression analyses and separate group analyses, with similar conclusions derived from both. We have presented analyses using separate groups for ease of understanding.

## CONCLUSION

We began the chapter with Mark Twain's quote about aging and memory. We can say now, in retrospect, that he was prescient in his remarks: Our experiments show that all three of his hypotheses are correct. Younger adults can remember events that never happened, just as they can remember ones that did happen; furthermore, aging has dual effects on retention in that older adults are less able than young adults to remember events that occurred in the past, but are more likely than younger adults to remember events that did not happen (or to have illusory memories). Of course, Twain had only hypotheses. Like Twain, we are (now) from the great state of Missouri, which is called the Show Me state. The reason is said to be after a speech given by one of its native sons, Congressman Willard Duncan Vandiver. During a speech at a Navy event in Philadelphia in 1899, he said, "I come from a state that raises corn and cotton and cockleburs and Democrats, and frothy eloquence neither convinces nor satisfies me. I am from Missouri. You have got to show me." We have followed Vandiver's advice and shown through experiments that Twain was right in all essential respects. However, there was one way in which he was wrong. Apparently his conclusions about older adults do not hold for all older adults. Some, those high in frontal functioning, seem to remember much like younger adults in three of our four tasks. We suspect Twain would be happy with this finding, and we also suspect he would have been one of the older adults whose memories were well preserved.

## ACKNOWLEDGMENTS

The research reported here and the writing of this chapter was supported by National Institute of Aging grant AG17481 to the authors. We thank Rebecca Roediger for her able assistance with the chapter, and we thank Lisa Geraci, Harlene Hayne, David McCabe, and Jane McConnell for their comments on an earlier draft of the manuscript.

## REFERENCES

Balota, D. A., Cortese, M. J., Duchek, J. M., Adams, D., Roediger, H. L., III, McDermott, K. B., et al. (1999). Veridical and false memories in healthy older adults and in dementia of the Alzheimer's type. *Cognitive Neuropsychology, 16,* 361–384.

Balota, D. A., Dolan, P. O., & Duchek, J. M. (2000). Memory changes in healthy older adults. In E. Tulving & F. I. M. Craik (Eds.), *The Oxford handbook of memory* (pp. 395–409). Oxford, England: Oxford University Press.

Bartlett, F. C. (1932). *Remembering: A study in experimental and social psychology.* Oxford, England: Macmillan.

Bergman, E., & Roediger, H.L., III (1999). Can Bartlett's repeated reproduction experiments be replicate? *Memory & Cognition, 27,* 937–947.

Bousfield, W. A. (1953). The occurrence of clustering in the recall of randomly arranged associates. *Journal of General Psychology, 49,* 229–240.

Bransford, J., Barclay, J. R., & Franks, J. (1972). Sentence memory: A constructive versus interpretive approach. *Cognitive Psychology, 3,* 193–209.

Bransford, J., & Franks, J. (1972). The abstraction of linguistic ideas: A review. *Cognition, 1,* 211–249.

Butler, K. M., McDaniel, M. A., & Dornburg, C. C. (2005). *Age increases in false memory under an item-specific processing strategy.* Manuscript under review.

Butler, K. M., McDaniel, M. A., Dornburg, C. C., Price, A. L., & Roediger, H. L., III (2004). Age differences in veridical and false recall are not inevitable: The role of frontal lobe function. *Psychonomic Bulletin & Review, 11,* 921–925.

Ceci, S., & Bruck, M. (1995). *Jeopardy in the courtroom: A scientific analysis of children's testimony.* Washington, DC: American Psychological Association.

Cohen, G., & Faulkner, D. (1989). Age differences in source forgetting: Effects on reality monitoring and on eyewitness testimony. *Psychology & Aging, 4,* 10–17.

Cohen, R. L. (1981). On the generality of some memory laws. *Scandinavian Journal of Psychology, 22,* 267–281.

Coxon, P., & Valentine, T. (1997). The effects of the age of eyewitnesses on the accuracy and suggestibility of their testimony. *Applied Cognitive Psychology, 11,* 415–430.

Craik, F. I. M. (1977). Age differences in human memory. In J. E. Birren & K. W. Schaie (Eds.), *Handbook of the psychology of aging* (pp. 384–420). New York: Van Nostrand Reinhold.

Craik, F. I. M., Morris, L. W., Morris, R. G., & Loewen, E. R. (1990). Relations between source amnesia and frontal lobe functioning in older adults. *Psychology and Aging, 5,* 148–151.

Darley, J. M., & Latane, B. (1968). Bystander intervention in emergencies: Diffusion of responsibility. *Journal of Personality & Social Psychology, 8,* 377–383.

Deese, J. (1959a). Influence of the inter-item associative strength upon immediate free recall. *Psychological Reports, 5,* 305–312.

Deese, J. (1959b). On the prediction of occurrence of particular verbal intrusions in immediate recall. *Journal of Experimental Psychology, 58,* 17–22.

Deese, J. (1965). *The structure of associations in language and thought.* Baltimore: Johns Hopkins University Press.

Dehon, H., & Bredart, S. (2004). False memories: Young and older adults think of semantic associates at the same rate, but young adults are more successful at source monitoring. *Psychology and Aging, 19,* 191–197.

Dornburg, C., & McDaniel, M. A. (2005). *The cognitive interview enhances long-term free recall of older adults: Associations with frontal functioning?* Unpublished manuscript.

Dornburg, C., & McDaniel, M. A. (2006). The cognitive interview enhances long-term free recall of older adults. *Psychology and Aging, 21,* 196–200.

Engelkamp, J. (2001). Action memory: A system-oriented approach. In H. D. Zimmer, R. L. Cohen, M. J. Guynn, J. Engelkamp, R. Kormi-Nouri, & M. A. Foley (Eds.), *Memory for actions: A distinct form of memory?* (pp. 49–96). New York: Oxford University Press.

Engelkamp, J., & Krumnacker, H. (1980). Image- and motor-processes in the retention of verbal materials. *Zeitschrift fur Experimentelle und Angewandte Psychologie, 27,* 511–533.

Fisher, R. P., Geiselman, R. E., & Amador, M. (1989). Field test of the cognitive interview: Enhancing the recollection of actual victims and witnesses of crime. *Journal of Applied Psychology, 74,* 722–727.

Gabbert, F., Memon, A., & Allan, K. (2003). Memory conformity: Can eyewitnesses influence each other's memories for an event? *Applied Cognitive Psychology, 17,* 533–543.

Gallo, D. A., McDermott, K. B., Percer, J. M., & Roediger, H. L., III (2001). Modality effects in false recall and false recognition. *Journal of Experimental Psychology: Learning, Memory, and Cognition, 27,* 339–353.

Gallo, D. A., & Roediger, H. L., III. (2002). Variability among word lists in evoking associative memory illusions. *Journal of Memory and Language, 47,* 469–497.

Gardiner, J. M. (1988). Functional aspects of recollective experience. *Memory & Cognition, 16,* 309–313.

Garry, M., Manning, C., Loftus, E., & Sherman, S. (1996). Imagination inflation: Imagining a childhood event inflates confidence that it occurred. *Psychonomic Bulletin & Review, 3,* 208–214.

Geraci, L., McDaniel, M. A., & Roediger, H. L. (2006). *Aging, attention, and memory for distinctive events.* Manuscript submitted for publication.

Glisky, E. L., Polster, M. R., & Routhieaux, B. C. (1995). Double dissociation between item and source memory. *Neuropsychology, 9,* 229–235.

Glisky, E. L., Rubin, S. R., & Davidson, P. S. R. (2001). Source memory in older adults: An encoding or retrieval problem? *Journal of Experimental Psychology: Learning, Memory, and Cognition, 27,* 1131-1146.

Goff, L., & Roediger, H. L., III (1998). Imagination inflation for action events: Repeated imaginings lead to illusory recollections. *Memory & Cognition, 26,* 20–33.

Guynn, M. J., McDaniel, M. A., Strosser, G. L., Ramirez, J. M., Hinrichs, E. L., & Hayes, K. H. (2005). *Relational and item-specific influences on generate-recognize processes in recall.* Manuscript submitted for publication.

Heaps, C., & Nash, M. (1999). Individual differences in imagination inflation. *Psychonomic Bulletin & Review, 6,* 313–318.

Henkel, L., Johnson, M. K., & De Leonardis, D. (1998). Aging and source monitoring: Cognitive processes and neuropsychological correlates. *Journal of Experimental Psychology: General, 127,* 251–268.

Hyman, I., & Pentland, J. (1996). The role of mental imagery in the creation of false childhood memories. *Journal of Memory and Language* [Special issue: Illusions of memory], *35,* 101–117.

Jacoby, L. L. (1999). Ironic effects of repetition: Measuring age-related differences in memory. *Journal of Experimental Psychology: Learning, Memory, and Cognition, 25,* 3–22.

Jacoby, L. L., Bishara, A., Hessels, S., & Toth, J. (2005). Aging, subjective experience, and cognitive control: Dramatic false remembering in older adults. *Journal of Experimental Psychology: General, 134,* 131–148.

Jacoby, L. L., & Hollingshead, A. (1990). Toward a generate/recognize model of performance on direct and indirect tests of memory. *Journal of Memory and Language, 29,* 433–454.

Kelley, C. M., & Sahakyan, L. (2003). Memory, monitoring, and control in the attainment of memory accuracy. *Journal of Memory and Language, 48,* 704–721.

Kellogg, R. T. (2001). Presentation modality and mode of recall in verbal false memory. *Journal of Experimental Psychology: Learning, Memory, and Cognition, 27,* 913–919.

Koriat, A., & Goldsmith, M. (1996). Monitoring and control processes in the strategic regulation of memory accuracy. *Psychological Review, 103,* 490–517.

Kouststaal, W., Reddy, C., Jackson, E., Prince, S., Cendan, D., & Schacter, D. (2003). False recognition of abstract versus common objects in older and younger adults: Testing the semantic categorization account. *Journal of Experimental Psychology: Learning, Memory, and Cognition, 29,* 499–510.

Lee, S. (2001). *Imagination inflation for action events: Are older adults more susceptible?* Unpublished master's thesis, Washington University, St. Louis, MO.

Lindsay, D. S., & Johnson, M. K. (1989). The eyewitness suggestibility effect and memory for source. *Memory & Cognition, 17,* 349–358.

Loftus, E., & Palmer, J. (1974). Reconstruction of automobile destruction: An example of the interaction between language and memory. *Journal of Verbal Learning & Behavior, 13,* 585589.

Loftus, E. F. (1979). *Eyewitness testimony*. Cambridge, MA: Harvard University Press.

Loftus, E. F., Miller, D. G., & Burns, H. J. (1978). Semantic integration of verbal information into a visual memory. *Journal of Experimental Psychology: Learning, Memory, and Cognition, 4,* 19–31.

Marche, T., Jordan, J., & Owre, K. (2002). Younger adults can be more suggestible than older adults: The influence of learning differences on misinformation reporting. *Canadian Journal on Aging, 21,* 85–93.

Mather, M., Johnson, M., & De Leonardis, D. (1999). Stereotype reliance in source monitoring: Age differences and neuropsychological test correlates. *Cognitive Neuropsychology* [Special issue: The cognitive neuropsychology of false memories], *16,* 437–458.

McCabe, D. P., Presmanes, A. G., Robertson, C. L., & Smith, A. D. (2004). Item-specific processing reduces false memories. *Psychonomic Bulletin & Review, 11,* 1074–1079.

McCabe, D. P., & Smith, A. (2002). The effect of warnings on false memories in young and older adults. *Memory & Cognition, 30,* 1065–1077.

McDaniel, M. A., Butler, K. M., & Dornburg, C. (2006). Binding of source and content: New directions revealed by neuropsychological and age-related effects. In H. D. Zimmer, A. Mecklinger, & U. Lindenberger (Eds.), *Binding in human memory: A neurocognitive approach*. (pp. 657–675)London: Oxford University Press.

McDaniel, M. A., Glisky, E. L., Rubin, S. R., Guynn, M. J., & Routhieaux, B. C. (1999). Prospective memory: A neuropsychological study. *Neuropsychology, 13,* 103–110.

McDaniel, M. A., & Pressley, M. (Eds.). (1987). *Imagery and related mnemonic processes: Theories, individual differences, and applications*. New York: Springer-Verlag.

McDermott, K. B. (1996). The persistence of false memories in list recall. *Journal of Memory and Language, 35,* 212–230.

McIntyre, J. S., & Craik, F. I. M. (1987). Age differences in memory for item and source information. *Canadian Journal of Psychology* [Special issue: Aging and cognition], *41,* 175–192.

Meade, M., & Roediger, H. L., III (2006). The effect of forced recall on illusory recollection in younger and older adults. *American Journal of Psychology, 119,* 433–462.

Memon, A., & Bartlett, J. (2002). The effects of verbalization on face recognition in young and older adults. *Applied Cognitive Psychology, 16,* 635–650.

Milgram, S. (1963). Behavioral study of obedience. *Journal of Abnormal & Social Psychology, 67,* 371–378.

Mitchell, K. J., Johnson, M. K., & Mather, M. (2003). Source monitoring and suggestibility to misinformation: Adult age-related differences. *Applied Cognitive Psychology, 17,* 107–119.

Moscovitch, M., & Winocur, G. (1995). Frontal lobes, memory, and aging. In J. Grafman, K. J. Holyoak, & F. Boller (Eds.), *Structure and functions of the human prefrontal cortex* (pp. 119–150). New York: New York Academy of Sciences.

Murphy, M., & Puff, R. (1982). Free recall: Basic methodology and analyses. In C. R. Puff (Ed.), *Handbook of research methods in human memory and cognition* (pp. 99–128). New York: Academic Press.

Naveh-Benjamin, M. (2000). Adult age differences in memory performance: Tests of an associative deficit hypothesis. *Journal of Experimental Psychology: Learning, Memory, and Cognition, 26,* 1170–1187.

Naveh-Benjamin, M., & Craik, F.I. (1995). Memory for context and its use in item memory: Comparisons of younger and older persons. *Psychology & Aging, 10,* 284–293.

Norman, K. A., & Schacter, D. L. (1997). False recognition in younger and older adults: Exploring the characteristics of illusory memories. *Memory & Cognition, 25,* 838–848.

Paivio, A. (1969). Mental imagery in associative learning and memory. *Psychological Review, 76,* 241–263.

Paris, S., & Lindauer, B. (1976). The role of inference in children's comprehension and memory for sentences. *Cognitive Psychology, 8,* 217–227.

Rajaram, S. (1993). Remembering and knowing: Two means of access to the personal past. *Memory & Cognition, 21,* 89–102.

Rankin, J., & Kausler, D. (1979). Adult age differences in false recognitions. *Journal of Gerontology, 34,* 58–65.

Raye, C., Johnson, M., & Taylor, T. (1980). Is there something special about memory for internally generated information? *Memory & Cognition, 8,* 141–148.

Robinson, K., & Roediger, H. L., III (1997). Associative processes in false recall and false recognition. *Psychological Science, 8,* 231–237.

Roediger, H. L., III (1973). Inhibition in recall from cueing with recall targets. *Journal of Verbal Learning & Verbal Behavior, 12,* 644–657.

Roediger, H. L., III (1980). The effectiveness of four mnemonics in ordering recall. *Journal of Experimental Psychology: Human Learning & Memory, 6,* 558–567.

Roediger, H. L., III (1996). Memory illusions. *Journal of Memory and Language* [Special issue: Memory Illusions], *35,* 76–100.

Roediger, H. L., III, Geraci, L. (2006). *Aging and the misinformation effect: A neuropsychological analysis.* Manuscript submitted for publication.

Roediger, H. L., III, Geraci, L., & Meade, M. L. (2005). *Misinformation effects in older adults: A neuropsychological analysis.* Manuscript in preparation.

Roediger, H. L., III, Jacoby, J. D., & McDermott, K. B. (1996). Misinformation effects in recall: Creating false memories through repeated retrieval. *Journal of Memory and Language, 35,* 300–318.

Roediger, H. L., III, & McDermott, K. B. (1995). Creating false memories: Remembering words not presented in lists. *Journal of Experimental Psychology: Learning, Memory, and Cognition, 21,* 803–814.

Roediger, H. L., III, Meade, M. L., & Geraci, L. (2006). *Effects of neuropsychological status of older adults in false recall of catagorized words. Manuscript in preparation.*

Roediger, H. L., III, Watson, J., McDermott, K. B., & Gallo, D. (2001). Factors that determine false recall: A multiple regression analysis. *Psychonomic Bulletin & Review, 8,* 385–407.

Roediger, H. L., III, Wheeler, M. A., & Rajaram, S. (1993). Remembering, knowing, and reconstructing the past. In D. L. Medin (Ed.), *The psychology of learning and motivation: Advances in research and theory.* San Diego: Academic Press.

Russell, W. A., & Jenkins, J. J. (1954). *The complete Minnesota norms for responses to 200 words from the Kent–Rosanoff Word Association Test* (Tech. Rep. No. 11, Contract N8 ONR 66216, Office of Naval Research). University of Minnesota.

Schacter, D. L., Verfaellie, M., & Pradere, D. (1996). The neuropsychology of memory illusions: False recall and recognition in amnesic patients. *Journal of Memory and Language, 35,* 319–334.

Schooler, J. W., Foster, R. A., & Loftus, E. F. (1988). Some deleterious consequences of the act of recollection. *Memory & Cognition, 16,* 243–251.

Searcy, J., Bartlett, J., & Memon, A. (1999). Age differences in accuracy and choosing in eyewitness identification and face recognition. *Memory & Cognition, 27,* 538–552.

Searcy, J., Bartlett, J., & Memon, A. (2000). Influence of post-event narratives, line-up conditions and individual differences on false identification by young and older eyewitnesses. *Legal and Criminological Psychology, 5,* 219–235.

Smith, R., & Hunt, R. (1998). Presentation modality affects false memory. *Psychonomic Bulletin & Review, 5,* 710–715.

Smith, R. E., Lozito, J. P., & Bayen, U. J. (2005). Adult age differences in distinctive processing: The modality effect on false recall. *Psychology and Aging, 20,* 486–492.

Smith, S. M., Ward, T. B., Tindell, D. R., Sifonis, C. M., & Wilkenfeld, M. J. (2000). Category structure and created memories. *Memory & Cognition, 28,* 386–395.

Stadler, M. A., Roediger, H. L., III, & McDermott, K. B. (1999). Norms for word lists that create false memories. *Memory & Cognition, 27,* 494–500.

Thomas, A., Bulevich, J., & Loftus, E. (2003). Exploring the role of repetition and sensory elaboration in the imagination inflation effect. *Memory & Cognition, 31,* 630–640.

Thomas, A., & Sommers, M. (2005). Attention to item-specific processing eliminates age effects in false memories. *Journal of Memory and Language, 52,* 71–86.

Thomas, A., & McDaniel, M. A. (2005). *Not all older adults are equal: How cognitive functioning mediates the use of item specific information in reducing memory illusions.* Manuscript submitted for publication.

Tulving, E. (1985). Memory and consciousness. *Canadian Psychologist, 26,* 1–12.

Tulving, E., & Pearlstone, Z. (1966). Availability versus accessibility of information in memory for words. *Journal of Verbal Learning & Verbal Behavior, 5,* 381–391.

Tun, P. A., Wingfield, A., Rosen, M. J., & Blanchard, L. (1998). Response latencies for false memories: Gist-based processes in normal aging. *Psychology & Aging, 13,* 230–241.

Watkins, M. J., & Gardiner, J. M. (1982). Cued recall. In C. R. Puff (Ed.), *Handbook of research methods in human memory and cognition* (pp. 173–196). New York: Academic Press.

CHAPTER
# 8
# False Memories

Deryn Strange, Seema Clifasefi,
and Maryanne Garry

November 1989 is a landmark month in the intersection of psychology and the law. It was during this month that Eileen Franklin-Lipsker told two detectives how her father, George Franklin, raped and murdered her childhood friend Susan Nason 20 years earlier. Eileen claimed that she did not intentionally keep the details of Susan's death a secret. Instead, Eileen, her therapist, the prosecution—and eventually the jury—believed that Eileen had repressed the details of Susan's death, burying them deep in her subconscious until they came flooding back (see MacLean, 1993, for the full story). As details of the case hit the media in the weeks that followed, *repression* became a household word and Eileen Franklin-Lipsker the media darling. By contrast, Elizabeth Loftus's thoughtful skepticism and subsequent research were characterized as the work of the Devil. The goal of this chapter is to discuss how the research Loftus pioneered influenced how we see the issue of repression and recovered memories today.

## A BRIEF HISTORY ON THE CONCEPT OF REPRESSION

November 1989, did not come out of nowhere. It was simply a "tipping point" (Gladwell, 2000) in a succession of events that led the United States toward a legal and social fiasco. To understand how events culminated in criminal prosecution, it is necessary to understand how the concept of repression evolved.

Repression is a fundamental tenet of Freud's psychoanalysis. Yet even he wavered on the details of how it works (Crews, 1995; Erdelyi, 1990). Despite Freud's lack of clarity, today's advocates are clear that repression is an unconscious mechanism that involves banishing a traumatic event from consciousness until such a time that it can be appropriately dealt with (e.g., Herman, 1992). However, although the event itself may be locked safely away, temporarily inaccessible, the emotion associated with the event is not. Instead, the emotion associated with the repressed event is left to seep into the person's everyday life, manifesting itself in poor relationships and psychological illnesses, such as depression and anxiety. As Crews (1995), and later McNally (2003), described, the primary objective of psychoanalysis is not to treat the presenting problem but to dig up the repressed event responsible for the problem. In other words, the goal is to recover the original memory and deal with it so that the patient may regain psychological health.

Despite a lack of evidence to suggest that memory works in the way Freud proposed (for reviews, see Holmes, 1990, 1995; Loftus & Loftus, 1980), the concept of repression was quickly adopted, and psychoanalysis went on to become the dominant clinical approach of the early 20th century (Gay, 1988). However, as McNally (2003) notes, the rise of a certain brand of feminism in the 1970s saw repression redefined as an almost political concept. Repression went from a mental process to a tool the patriarchy used to continue the oppression of women and children (Miller, 1997). Ultimately, seminal papers such as Herman and Schatzow's (1987) asserted that "massive repression"(p. 12) accounted for the (albeit alleged) rapid increase in rape and child sexual abuse cases.

In his examination of historical moral panics, Jenkins (1998) reports that it was books such as Diane Russell's *The Politics of Rape: The Victim's Perspective* (1974), that helped to highlight the prevalence of rape and child abuse, and dispelled the myth that rape was an issue for marginalized societal groups. In Jenkins's view, by the early 1980s, the widespread literature and media interest in the prevalence and effects of child abuse had led to a groundswell of public opinion: There was simply not enough being done to protect women and children. The public pressure led to the introduction of mandatory reporting laws in some states, a 1984 U.S. Department of Justice conference on child molestation, as well as the investigation and prosecution of rape and abuse cases becoming funding priorities for the National Institute of Justice. As a result, there was an exponential increase in reported cases of abuse. Indeed, between 1976 and 1986, reported cases of child abuse and neglect rose from 669,000 to more than 2,000,000 across the United States. What did not make media headlines, however, was that more than 60% of these reported cases were unsubstantiated (for more on the fascinating history of moral panics, see Jenkins's book, *Moral Panics*).

Of course, the increasing number of reported cases served to fuel the flames of the repression phenomenon. The sudden increase in cases was believed to reflect increased *reporting* rather than an increase in sexual crimes (Courtois,

1992). As McNally (2003) noted, it was clear that there were many women who were either not talking about or simply did not remember their own experiences. Therapists such as Judith Herman and Emily Schatzow (1987) and Alice Miller (1997) argued for the latter explanation: that women did not remember their abuse because they had repressed it. Thus, women entering therapy were encouraged to do memory work—hypnosis, trancework, dreamwork, bodywork, and groupwork—to discover the necessary trigger that would unearth their memories (Brown, Scheflin, & Hammond, 1998; Herman & Schatzow, 1987; Olio, 1989).

As Tavris (1993) suggested however, no development was quite as crucial to the phenomenon as the advent of the "self-help book." Books such as *Secret Survivors* (Blume, 1985), *The Courage to Heal* (Bass & Davis, 1988), *Incest and Sexuality: A Guide to Understanding and Healing* (Maltz & Holman, 1991), *The Right to Innocence* (Engel, 1990), and *Repressed Memories: A Journey to Recovery From Sexual Abuse*" (Fredrickson, 1992), spread the word that emotional pain in adulthood could be overcome by dealing with the original cause: childhood trauma, specifically childhood sexual abuse. Although these books no doubt conveyed a great deal of support to true survivors, they also encouraged those who had no recollection of abuse to dig deeper. Readers were told that they were not alone in being unable to recall their abuse, and that "many women don't have memories, and some never get memories. This does not mean they weren't abused" (Bass & Davis, 1988, p. 81). In fact, any niggling possibility of childhood abuse was thought to be an indication of abuse: "If you think you were abused and your life shows the symptoms, then you were" (Bass & Davis, 1988, p. 22). A complete lack of memory was also thought to indicate abuse: "If you remember almost nothing or very little of your childhood, or if you cannot remember a period of time, such as between the ages of ten and fourteen, you have repressed memories" (Fredrickson, 1992, p. 46). Moreover, Blume and Engel included checklists to help readers identify whether they had been abused. These "symptoms" ranged from multiple personality disorder, anxiety, and depression, to general phobias, sexual difficulties, or even just a sense of helplessness or failure. As Tavris (1993) noted, they amounted to an "all-purpose female checklist"—what woman doesn't feel like a failure some of the time?

After the introduction of the self-help books, the stories in the media—respected newspapers as well as tabloid magazines and daytime talk shows—emphasized the power of repression, and published stories about people who had successfully recovered their repressed memories (Kantrowitz, 1991; Oldenberg, 1991; Ritter, 1991; Toufexis, 1991). Even celebrities (e.g., Roseanne Barr and Marilyn Van Derbur; see Darnton, 1991) divulged their recovered memories of childhood abuse. Yet, although the world devoured the stories, there was still no evidence that memory could work the way Freud proposed (Holmes, 1990, 1995; Loftus & Loftus, 1980). Instead, the concept of the "abuse-survivor machine" (Tavris, 1993) was built on entirely suspect foundations—what Carl Sagan might have called a "tower of turtles" (1979).

For Eileen Franklin-Lipsker, and many others, the self-help industry led straight to the courtroom. On October 31, 1990, the case against George Franklin was presented to a jury in San Mateo County, California. By November 30, 1990, despite Loftus's presence on the witness stand (Loftus, 1993), the jury found Franklin guilty and he was sentenced to life in prison. The conviction set the precedent for future cases, cases that did not peak until 1993 (see the Appendix for a timeline tracing both the recovered-memory movement and Loftus's role in it).

After her experience on the witness stand, Elizabeth Loftus began, in earnest, to consider an alternate route by which memories could be "recovered." In her book *The Myth of Repressed Memory* (Loftus & Ketcham, 1994), Loftus describes how the breakthrough finally came during a car ride with Denise Park. Loftus's goal was to devise an event that would be disturbing enough—yet safe enough—to demonstrate the possibility that recovered memories might simply be constructed memories. It was Park who suggested getting lost, what she called "every parent's worst fear" (p. 97). As it happened, they were driving past a shopping mall when the lightbulb went off. Thus, a mix of good science and good luck gave us the "lost in the mall" paradigm.

## THE "LOST IN THE MALL" PARADIGM

The design was simple. Loftus and Pickrell (1995; see also Loftus, 1993) recruited subjects in family pairs. One family member became the confederate; their role was to supply the true events from the subject's childhood. The other family member became the subject and was mailed a five-page booklet containing narratives describing four events, three true events, and one false event. This false event was created by Loftus and Pickrell and described the subject getting lost in a shopping mall. For example, this is what one subject read about the false event:

> You, your mom, Tien, and Tuan all went to the Bremerton K-mart. You must have been 5 years old at the time. Your mom gave each of you some money to get a blueberry Icee. You ran ahead to get into the line first, and somehow lost your way in the store. Tien found you crying to an elderly Chinese woman. You three then went together to get an Icee.

Although the specific detail differed from subject to subject, the basic structure of the narrative was the same: Subjects were with their family in a large store or mall, they got lost, and were rescued by an elderly person.

The subjects were first asked to write down everything they could remember about the events. Then they were interviewed face-to-face on two separate occasions, spaced up to 2 weeks apart. Loftus and Pickrell (1995) found that, not surprisingly, subjects could easily recall their true events. However, 25% of them also came to remember details about being lost in a shopping mall. Some of these false memories were full of sensory detail, and some of the subjects had difficulty believing that the event had never really happened when they were debriefed. In fact, they struggled to believe that their memory of getting lost was merely the product of a suggestion combined with the power of their own imagination. In summary, Loftus and Pickrell had provided the first demonstration that normal everyday people could come to recall an entirely false event.

The "lost in the mall" study was just the first in a series of what have come to be called "implantation" studies. Other researchers quickly adopted the lost-in-the-mall paradigm, modified it, and showed that false memories could be implanted for a wide range of events: wreaking havoc on a family wedding (Hyman, Husband, & Billings, 1995), being attacked by an animal (Porter, Yuille, & Lehman, 1999), and being rescued from drowning by a lifeguard (Heaps & Nash, 2001). Nevertheless, though it seemed as though Loftus and her colleagues had, quite convincingly, shown another route to a "recovered" memory, their research was criticized on several fronts.

## THE QUESTION OF PLAUSIBILITY

Perhaps the strongest criticism came from those who argued that the false events used in these studies were too mundane, that they bore no resemblance to the traumatic memories (mostly) women were uncovering and describing daily. For example, Pezdek, Finger, and Hodge (1997) asserted that plausibility was critically important in determining whether people would develop a false memory. They reasoned that people would be less likely to develop memories for more implausible events—such as having a rectal enema—because they lack the script-relevant knowledge to form the memory. Pezdek et al. repeated Loftus and Pickrell's (1995) study with one variation. Half the subjects were asked to remember getting lost in a shopping mall, what Pezdek et al. called their plausible false event. The remaining subjects were asked to recall receiving a rectal enema, or what they called their implausible false event. Just as they predicted, no subjects developed a memory of the implausible event, whereas 15% developed a memory of getting lost in a shopping mall.

Thus, Pezdek et al. (1997) concluded that memories for implausible events would be much more difficult to implant than those for plausible events. The problem with that logic is that people *do* falsely remember implausible experiences (see Ofshe & Watters, 1994). Mazzoni, Loftus, and Kirsch (2001) recognized this crucial point, and approached the issue of plausibility from a different perspective: Because we know implausible false memories happen in real life, they argued, the real question is not *whether,* but *how* implausible false memories can develop. To answer this question, Mazzoni et al. devised an experiment that showed that plausibility is far from a fixed construct. Instead, judgments concerning plausibility can change over time and even implausible events can come to be believed given enough evidence.

Mazzoni et al. (2001) first asked subjects to rate the plausibility of a list of childhood events, as well as their confidence that they had experienced those events. One of the target events from the list was plausible (almost choking) and the other was implausible (witnessing a demonic possession). Not surprisingly, subjects rated possession as less plausible than choking, and were confident they had neither witnessed a demonic possession nor choked. Three months later, subjects were invited to participate in a seemingly unrelated experiment. They read a series of short articles on four different topics, one of which was either about choking (half the subjects) or demonic possession (the other half of the subjects). These articles described the frequency of each event and included testimonies from people who had choked. One week later, subjects completed a questionnaire about their fears, the results of which were always interpreted as indicating that subjects had either choked as a young child or witnessed a demonic possession. Finally, a further week later, Mazzoni et al. asked subjects to once again rate the plausibility and their confidence that the list of childhood events had happened to them.

Mazzoni et al. (2001) found that subjects who read about demonic possession rated witnessing it as more plausible than they had initially. Not surprisingly, they still rated demonic possession as less plausible than choking, but, by the end of the study, subjects were equally likely to say that they had witnessed a demonic possession as they were to say they had choked. Clearly then, Mazzoni et al.'s (2001) results suggest that Pezdek et al.'s (1997) conclusion—that subjects will develop memories only for events that they find plausible—misses a crucial point: Even implausible events can become more plausible, and small changes in what we think is plausible can lead to large changes in our autobiographical beliefs.

In fact, Scoboria, Mazzoni, Kirsch, and Relyea (2004) have recently cast doubt on how Pezdek et al. (1997) defined plausibility. Pezdek et al. used schematic knowledge as a proxy for plausibility, a decision Scoboria et al.'s research suggests was dubious. When Scoboria et al. investigated whether subjects' schematic knowledge was related to how plausible they judged a series of events, they found no correlation. In other words, Scoboria et al. showed that schematic knowledge is a poor substitute for plausibility.

## NEW TECHOLOGY: THE ROLE OF PHOTOGRAPHIC EVIDENCE IN DEVELOPING FALSE MEMORIES

More recently, the focus of implantation research has turned to the means with which the false event is suggested to subjects. It is not hard to see how a story supposedly written by a family member—which describes a childhood event—induces subjects to think about, imagine, and talk about that event in an effort to remember it. A story, however, is not the only medium capable of inducing subjects to engage in these behaviors. In fact, there is a medium that, arguably, could be thought of as more objective, and thus more persuasive: photographs.

In a twist on the standard lost-in-the-mall procedure, Wade, Garry, Read, and Lindsay (2002) replaced the narratives describing the target events with photographs. They created the photo of the false event, which showed the subject and family members having a ride in a hot-air balloon, with Photoshop®, the powerful image-editing software that amateur photographers use to create their own high-quality photographs. Wade et al. extracted images from different sources to compose a single image. Over three interviews, Wade et al.'s subjects saw only four childhood photos: the three true events, and the false hot-air balloon ride. They received no additional information about any of the events. Once they had exhausted their recollection of the events, Wade et al. led them through a guided-imagery phase, instructing them to imagine the balloon, the weather, and what it would have felt like to be in the balloon. By the end of the third interview, 50% of the subjects had come to recall details of the event. Just like Loftus and Pickrell (1995) observed, the reports were often full of surprising detail:

> Um, just trying to work out how old my sister was; trying to get the exact...when it happened. But I'm still pretty certain it occurred when I was in form one [sixth grade] at um the local school there ... Um basically for $10 or something you could go up in a hot-air balloon and go up about 20 odd meters ... it would have been a Saturday and I think we went with, yeah, parents and, not it wasn't, not my grandmother ... not certain who any of the other people are there. Um, and I'm pretty certain that Mum is down on the ground taking a photograph.

And,

> I'm pretty sure this is um, this happened at home. Like in the weekend there's a kite fair and stuff. Me and [sister] went up when I was pretty young I'd say. I remember the smell and it was really hot ... the balloon would go up and all the warmth would come down.

Perhaps most significantly, however, the subjects expressed genuine astonishment when they were told that the photo of the balloon ride was entirely faked. For example, one subject said, "Is that right? Yeah, *truly*? How'd you do *that*?!"

## PHOTOGRAPHS VERSUS NARRATIVES

Interestingly, it turns out that a photograph is sometimes no better than a narrative at inducing a false memory. Garry and Wade (2005) pitted narratives and photographs against each other to examine their relative power in producing false memories. To ensure that subjects received the same information about each event, Garry and Wade asked judges to list all the information they could pick out of the balloon photograph, and then used that information to create the narrative.

Garry and Wade (2005) asked subjects about four events: three true events, and one false—the hot-air balloon ride. However, this time all subjects saw a mix of photos and narratives. One group of subjects saw a doctored photo of themselves and another family member taking a hot-air balloon ride, whereas another group read a narrative describing the same event. In other words, for each subject, each event was presented in only one medium, but the medium for the false event differed between the two groups. After three interviews with guided imagery, Garry and Wade found that whereas 50% of their photo subjects developed images or complete memories of the hot-air balloon ride, 80% of their narrative subjects did. Moreover, whatever initial difficulty subjects had in recalling the false event, they blamed that difficulty on the medium with which the false event had been presented. In other words, narrative subjects thought that photographs would have provided a better memory cue, whereas photograph subjects thought narratives would have been better. Garry and Wade suggested that their results fitted with a fluency-based explanation. In such an account, the rich detail in the doctored photographs might have actually constrained subjects' imagination, confining them, for example, to imagine the balloon depicted in the photograph. By contrast, the lack of constraints in the narratives should have made it easier for subjects to generate information about the balloon ride, information that would have been processed more fluently, felt more familiar, and thus been more likely to be mistaken for a real experience.

## TRUE PHOTOGRAPHS

Of course, whereas the doctored photo studies provide an interesting twist on the typical narrative paradigm, it would be far more problematic if a common holiday pastime—flipping through photo albums reminiscing about childhood experiences—could produce similar false memories. Such a discovery would be particularly problematic in therapy because some therapists encourage their clients to look through photo albums as a way of triggering their childhood memories (Poole, Lindsay, Memon, & Bull, 1995; Weiser, 2002). Lindsay, Hagen, Read, Wade, and Garry (2004) wondered what impact a false suggestion would have when it was accompanied by a true photo.

Lindsay et al. (2004) asked subjects about three school-related events: two true events from Grades 5 to 6 and 3 to 4, and a false event from Grade 1 to 2. The false event described the subject getting into trouble for putting Slime (the gooey green children's toy) into their teacher's desk drawer. They showed all of the subjects a narrative describing each event, but half of the subjects were also shown their class photo from Grade 1 to 2 to help cue their memories. After two interviews, 45% of those who just read the narrative described images or complete memories of the Slime event. By contrast, 78% of those who also saw their class photo described images or complete memories. Thus, it seems even true photographs can have dangerous consequences.

Although at first glance these results seem not to square with the results Garry and Wade (2005) found, the studies were actually very different in their rationale and method. For example, Garry and Wade set out to compare narratives and photos head-to-head, whereas Lindsay et al. (2004) wanted to understand the additional power that a photograph could bring to a narrative. In addition, Garry and Wade's photograph documented the target event, whereas Lindsay et al.'s photograph depicted the protagonists who were involved in it. Thus, nobody in

Lindsay et al.'s study would have generated the false event after having seen only the photograph. In short, Garry and Wade's study tells us what we might expect when comparing false photographs and false narratives about the same event; Lindsay et al.'s tells us what we might expect when we add supporting true photographs to a false suggestion.

Taken together, the "implantation" research shows that normal everyday people can come to remember entirely false events. Moreover, a variety of different suggestions can produce these memories: false narratives, false photos, or false narratives with true photos (Garry & Wade, 2005; Hyman & Billings, 1998; Hyman et al., 1995; Hyman & Pentland, 1996; Lindsay et al., 2004; Loftus & Pickrell, 1995; Pezdek et al., 1997; Ost, Foster, Costall, & Bull (2005), in press; Porter et al., 1999; Wade et al., 2002). Although it is true that a significant number of research subjects come to develop false memories, it is (obviously) also true that some never do. Thus we are left with an interesting question: Are the people who develop false memories really normal everyday people?

## PERSONALITY FACTORS AND FALSE MEMORIES

Though it must be true that not everyone is susceptible to developing false memories, efforts to discover what personality types are more likely than others to develop memories have yielded inconsistent results. For example, several studies have found that people who score highly on a measure of dissociation (Dissociative Experiences Scale, version C [DES–C]), are more likely to experience memory errors than those who do not score highly (Candel, Merckelbach, & Kuijpers, 2003; Hyman & Billings, 1998; Merckelbach, Muris, & Rassin, 1999; Ost, Fellows, & Bull, 1997; Ost, et al., 2005; Porter, Birt, Yuille, & Lehman, 2000). By contrast, however, other researchers have found no relationship between dissociation and memory errors (Eisen, Morgan, & Mickes, 2002; Hekkanen & McEvoy, 2002; Horselenberg et al., 2000; Platt, Lacey, Lobst, & Finkelman, 1998; Wade, 2004; Wilkinson & Hyman, 1998). Such inconsistent results have led some researchers to argue that a considerable amount of statistical power is necessary to demonstrate a correlation between dissociation and memory errors (Horselenberg et al.). Therefore, if dissociation is in fact related to memory creation, then at best it can be only a weak relationship.

Similarly inconsistent results have been found with a variety of other personality measures. For example, studies by Ost, Vrij, Costall, and Bull (2002) and Gudjonsson (1995) both found that people who scored highly on a measure of self-monitoring (Snyder, 1974)—interpreted as a strong tendency toward wanting to please other people—were more likely to go on to develop false memories. However, Ost et al. (in press) found a negative relationship—people who scored highly on a measure of self-monitoring were actually less likely to develop false memories. In addition, Porter et al. (2000) examined the relationship between the personality factors measured on the NEO Five-Factor Inventory (Costa & McCrae, 1992) and the likelihood of developing false memories. The NEO measures neuroticism (a negative approach to oneself and the world), extraversion (a positive outlook on oneself and the world), openness to experience (defined as being original, having broad interests, and willing to take risks), agreeableness (ability to get along with others, trustworthy, modest, altruistic, and compliant), and conscientiousness (the extent to which a person is careful, scrupulous, reliable, and persevering). Porter et al. found that none of the five factors bore any relationship to false-memory development. However, Porter et al. did find that people defined as introverts (those who did not score highly on the measure of extroversion) were more likely to develop a false memory. By contrast, whereas Wade (2004) replicated Porter et al.'s primary results, finding no relationship between any of the five personality factors and false-memory creation, she did not replicate Porter et al.'s findings for introverts. Instead, Wade found introversion also bore no relationship to false-memory development. Taken together, the only conclusion we can make about the relationship between personality factors and memory distortions is that we do not know what the relationship is. Yet.

## CAN WE DISTINGUISH TRUE MEMORIES FROM FALSE MEMORIES?

One of the practical questions that drives implantation research is whether it is possible to reliably distinguish false memories from true memories? Unfortunately, the research regarding this issue has also produced inconsistent results. For example, Loftus and Pickrell (1995) found that subjects used fewer words to describe being "lost in the mall" than they did to describe their true memories. They also rated the clarity of their false memory lower than that of their true memories, as if somehow they were aware that there was something odd about their memory of being lost in the mall. Not surprisingly, they were also less confident about the "lost" event. By contrast, Lindsay et al. (2004) asked subjects to rate each of their events on three different measures: their sense of reliving when describing the event, the extent to which they felt like they were remembering the event, and their confidence that the event actually happened. When subjects developed a false memory they showed no differences between their "Slime in the teacher's desk" memory and their true memories on any of these measures. In addition, Hyman and Pentland (1996) reported that subjects who did not recall their true memories from the outset rated those memories as similar to false memories in terms of their emotional strength and image clarity, and subjects were just as confident about these memories as their false ones. Thus, a definitive answer to the question of whether or not true memories can be easily distinguished from false memories is not possible based on what we know from the implantation studies so far.

Research conducted with people who have memories of highly implausible events, however, suggests that we are unlikely to ever discover a reliable method. In fact, recent research suggests that even physiological responses to false memories can appear entirely normal. For example, most of us would be willing to accept that anyone who remembers being abducted by aliens and taken back to their interplanetary spaceship for medical testing, is not remembering a genuine experience. However, for some people, memories like these are as real as, say, their memories of their 5th birthday party.

McNally et al. (2004) were interested in whether "abductees"—people who claim to have been abducted by aliens—experience a similar physiological reaction when remembering their abduction experiences as people diagnosed with posttraumatic stress disorder (PTSD). The abductees McNally et al. tested reported a comprehensive range of alien encounters: visiting spaceships, intercourse with aliens, medical probes or extraction of sperm/ova to produce hybrid babies, and later visits with their hybrid offspring.[1] McNally et al. matched each of their abductees to a control subject and then had each pair listen to tape-recorded accounts of the abductees' two most terrifying abduction experiences—what McNally et al. called an "abduction script." The researchers were specifically interested in whether simply believing that they had these farfetched experiences would be enough for the abductees to show specific physiological responses—increased heart rate, greater electrical conductance of the skin, and tensing of the muscles in the face—that PTSD patients show when they remember their traumas.

McNally et al. (2004) found that even though abductees showed no signs of psychiatric disorders, they displayed a greater physiological reaction to their abduction scripts than control subjects did. In fact, 60% of the abductees responded to their abduction scripts as though they had PTSD. Thus, just because a memory report is accompanied by strong, visible emotion does not mean that the memory is real. Put another way, the old adage—if it looks like a duck, sounds like a duck, and acts like a duck, it is a duck—cannot be applied to memories.

To summarize, we have not established a foolproof means of determining whether a memory is true or false—yet. In the meantime, researchers have made progress in determining how false memories develop.

## A THEORETICAL FRAMEWORK: HOW DO FALSE MEMORIES DEVELOP?

Once it was well established that false memories could be created experimentally, the next step was to figure out the processes involved in *how* false memories develop. Mazzoni et al.'s (2001) research was instrumental in clarifying those processes (see also Hyman & Kleinknecht, 1999; Hyman & Loftus, 1998). In fact, after a series of studies we now know that there are four distinct processes that, although best described as a linear process, are in all likelihood interrelated. First, subjects must consider the suggested event to be personally plausible, then they must develop a belief that it did in fact happen to them. Next, subjects must construct a memory. Many different factors can influence this construction process. In short, any task that involves thinking about, imagining, or talking about a false event can encourage the

[1]As an aside, in every case, the abductees' memories were "recovered" with the help of hypnosis.

generation of false information. As that generated information becomes more similar to the sorts of information we process when we experience an event, the chances of making a source-monitoring error—the final process in developing a false memory—increases. According to Johnson, Hashtroudi, and Lindsay (1993), source-monitoring errors occur because our memories are not filed away with information specifying where they came from. Instead we are forced to use certain criteria (which depend on the situation) to determine where a memory may have originated, and sometimes those criteria fail us. Though it remains unclear whether these processes (plausibility, belief, and memory construction) describe independent or related constructs, each process has been investigated a great deal, especially the "autobiographical belief" component.

## Autobiographical Beliefs

Garry, Manning, Loftus, and Sherman (1996) were the first to consider whether our autobiographical beliefs about childhood experiences could be altered after imagining an event. Although there is no doubt that even at the height of recovered-memory therapy's popularity therapists did not intentionally seek false memories from their clients, many therapists were simply convinced that guided imagery was an invaluable therapeutic tool. Indeed, many a self-help book touted the benefits of imagining an abuse scenario without worrying about accuracy (e.g., Bass & Davis, 1988). Garry et al. wondered what the effect of a seemingly innocuous imagination exercise could be if the interviewer was removed from the scenario.

To answer this question, Garry et al. designed an experiment made up of three phases. First, they asked their subjects to rate how confident they were that a list of events, on what they called a Life Events Inventory (LEI), had happened to them during childhood. Sometime later, they asked subjects to imagine some of the events and not others from the LEI. Finally, Garry et al. asked the subjects to rate their confidence a second time, claiming that their original answers had been lost. They found that subjects became more confident that events they had imagined had happened in their childhood compared to those events that they did not imagine. Garry et al. termed this increase in confidence after imagination "imagination inflation" and concluded that imagining a childhood event, even for only a few minutes, is an extremely powerful technique.

Garry et al.'s (1996) effect has since been replicated in a series of experiments (Heaps & Nash, 1999; Paddock et al., 1999). For example we now know that imagination inflation doesn't occur just for imagined childhood events, but also for imagined recent actions, and that the more times something is imagined the more inflation we can expect (Goff & Roediger, 1998; see chap. 7, this volume, for a review). In fact, more recent studies show that similar increases in confidence can be induced by asking subjects to paraphrase sentences (Sharman, Garry, & Beuke, 2004), or by asking subjects to solve anagrams (Bernstein, Godfrey, Davison, & Loftus, 2004; Bernstein, Whittlesea, & Loftus, 2002), rather than imagining the target event.

For example, Bernstein et al. (2002) had two phases to their experiment: a training phase and a test phase. In the training phase, Bernstein et al. taught subjects to solve a set of anagrams. These anagrams were difficult and this phase was designed to set up an expectation that any task involving anagrams would also be difficult. In the test phase, subjects' task was to rate their confidence that they had experienced a series of events in childhood. Some of those events were presented intact (e.g., "broke a window playing ball") and some were presented with an anagrammed word (e.g., "broke a nwidwo playing ball"). Subjects had to solve the anagram before they could rate their confidence that the event had happened to them. Unlike the practice phase however, solving these anagrams should have been relatively easy to solve because the word was presented in context. Bernstein et al. reasoned that subjects would misinterpret the surprising ease with which they solved the anagram as an indication that they had actually experienced the event in childhood. In fact, that's exactly what happened: Subjects were more confident that they had experienced anagrammed events than intact events. Taken together, this body of research shows that any task that encourages subjects to think about, talk about, or imagine past experiences can lead subjects to become more confident that those experiences really happened.

### Changing Confidence for Bizarre Events

Though no studies have examined whether confidence can be altered for traumatic experiences, studies have examined whether confidence can be altered for bizarre events. Thus, there is every reason to expect that the same results could be expected for traumatic experiences. Thomas and Loftus (2002) adapted Goff and Roediger's (1998) paradigm by asking subjects to either perform or imagine some ordinary actions (flipping a coin), and some bizarre actions (sit on the dice). Later, subjects imagined some of those actions between zero and five times. Thomas and Loftus found that imagining the actions in the second phase increased the likelihood that subjects would say that they had performed actions in the first phase. Moreover, just like Goff and Roediger found, the more times subjects imagined an action the more likely subjects were to say that they had performed the action. However, the most important result was that the pattern of results for bizarre actions was the same as the pattern of results for ordinary actions.

Thomas, Bulevich, and Loftus (2003) took these results a step further. They found that subjects who imagined the event in more detail became more confident that the event happened. Thomas et al. gave subjects either simple imagination instructions (imagine kissing the frog) or elaborate imagination instructions (imagine kissing the frog, imagine the feel of the frog on your lips, imagine the smell). They found that subjects given elaborate instructions were more likely to claim that they had performed the actions. So, what can we conclude from this series of studies? First, clearly our confidence about childhood events can be manipulated fairly easily and in surprisingly innocuous ways. Second, the fact that confidence can be manipulated for bizarre events as well as more everyday events suggests that even when we do not have any script-relevant knowledge to rely on (Pezdek et al. 1997), we are not protected from memory distortion.

## False Beliefs and False Memories

Although believing the false event happened is typically a precursor to remembering the event, it is not always the case. It is possible to have a belief that an event happened without a memory, as in the oft-cited example of being born—we know we were born but few, if any of us, actually remember the event. In addition, it is also possible to construct a memory of an event without holding strong confidence in that memory. For example, in many of the implantation studies, subjects' confidence in their false memories is lower than their confidence for true memories (Garry & Wade, 2005). So what is the link between false beliefs and false memories? Do false beliefs typically turn in to false memories?

In two studies, Loftus's students have shown that manipulating subjects' beliefs about a childhood event can lead those subjects to develop memories of the event. Braun, Ellis, and Loftus's (2002) second experiment followed the imagination inflation paradigm. First, subjects completed an LEI, rating their confidence that a series of events had happened to them during childhood. Embedded on the list was the target event: shaking hands with Bugs Bunny at Disneyland, an impossible event because as a Warner Brothers character, Disneyland would have been off-limits. A week later, Braun et al. gave subjects a copy of a potential advertisement. Some subjects saw an advertisement describing meeting and shaking hands with Bugs Bunny at Disneyland, whereas others saw an adverisement that made no mention of any cartoon characters. To mask the nature of the study, they asked the subjects to rate the advertisement on several attitude dimensions. Later, subjects were asked to complete the LEI a second time.

What happened? Subjects who saw the "Bugs at Disneyland" advertisement became more confident that they had shaken hands with him. Moreover, when these subjects were specifically asked if they *remembered* shaking hands with Bugs 16% said that they did, compared with 7% who did not see the advertisement. In a follow-up study, Grinley (2002) showed that the increase in subjects' confidence translated into vivid memories full of sensory detail. Grinley's subjects reported hugging Bugs, shaking his hand, as well as hearing him utter his famous words "What's up, Doc?" These studies show that advertising can have the same impact on memory as a direct instruction to imagine a childhood event.

Mazzoni and Memon (2003) have also shown that false beliefs can translate into false memories. They asked subjects to remember the time that their school nurse took a skin sample from their little finger to carry out a national health test. Of course, no such test existed. They too found that imagining this unlikely scenario caused subjects to become more confident that it had happened to them. In addition, just like Grinley's (2002) subjects, some subjects described memories of the event filled with sensory detail ("the place smelled horrible, " p. 187).

However, though removing a skin sample certainly qualifies as an unpleasant experience, these studies were criticized as having no bearing on cases of abuse. Take, for example, Jennifer Freyd's critique. She noted on her Web site that it was not as if the subjects in Braun et al.'s (2002) and Grinley's (2002) studies remembered being "slapped or fondled by Mickey Mouse." Instead, she insists that who or what does the hugging at Disneyland is not what is important. What is important, according to Freyd, is her children's experiences and reactions to the "big furry creatures," reactions Freyd monitored to determine whether or not the hugging was appropriate. In essence, Freyd's problem with the Braun et al. and Grinley studies is that they show no evidence that people can come to remember an unpleasant encounter with a big furry creature. Berkowitz, Laney, Morris, Garry, and Loftus (2005) answered this challenge.

Berkowitz et al. (2005) tried to induce subjects to remember a bad experience with Pluto: that he had licked their ear in an unpleasant manner. First, Berkowitz et al. asked subjects to complete a series of computer-based questionnaires. One of those questionnaires asked subjects how confident they were that they had experienced certain events at Disneyland, including "had your ear licked by Pluto."

A week later, subjects were given their "computer profile"—a supposedly unique assessment of experiences they likely had as a child based on their answers to the questionnaires. Subjects assigned to the Bad Pluto group were told they probably experienced a set of childhood fears (such as a fear of public displays of affection) and were given an article about a Disneyland event that might be relevant. The article described how a Pluto character in the 1980s had abused hallucinogenic drugs and "developed a habit of inappropriately licking the ears of many young visitors with his large fabric tongue." By contrast, subjects assigned to the Good Pluto group were told they probably experienced a set of enjoyable childhood experiences (such as playing board games) and were given an article about a lovable Pluto who traditionally licked the ears of children. Control subjects were told what their current likely personality characteristics were and were given an article about Disneyland, but not about Pluto.

Finally, all subjects were asked to complete a second set of questionnaires, one of which asked subjects whether they had had certain childhood experiences—including "had your ear licked by Pluto"—and, if they had, to write a few sentences describing the event. If they had no memory of an event, they were asked whether they believed that the event had in fact happened or were positive that it had not happened.

Berkowitz et al. (YEAR) found that by the end of the study, both Bad and Good Pluto subjects were more confident that they had had their ear licked by Pluto than were control subjects. More interestingly, 29% of Bad Pluto and 39% of Good Pluto subjects reported a memory or a belief that they had been licked by Pluto. Thus, imagining an event (either directly or indirectly) can lead to surprisingly vivid memories, even when the event is unpleasant or inappropriate, contrary to Freyd's (2003) criticism.

## False Beliefs and Behavior

In all of the studies presented so far, the primary goal has been to demonstrate whether or not subjects can develop false memories given some form of suggestion. Though obviously informative in their own right, these studies do not tell us anything about the persistence of those false beliefs or memories, and they do not tell us what the consequences of those false beliefs or memories can be. Do false beliefs have consequences for subjects' behavior? The short answer is "yes."

Collins (2001), Loftus's honors student, was the first to demonstrate that false beliefs can have consequences for subjects' behavior. Collins also followed the standard imagination inflation procedure. First, she asked subjects to rate their confidence that they had experienced a list of childhood events. Of course, embedded on the list was the target event: As a young child you "were unexpectedly attacked by a small dog." Then, in the second phase of the study, some subjects were told that their answers from a series of questionnaires (completed in the first phase) suggested that as a child they had been attacked by a small dog. In the third phase, when subjects were questioned about the list of events a second time, they showed the typical imagination inflation pattern of results. Subjects who had received the false feedback were more confident that as a child they had been attacked by a small dog. More importantly, however, when Collins asked subjects to rate how interested they were in now owning a dog, subjects who received the false feedback were less interested. In other words, the false feedback was enough to reduce subjects' preference ratings.

Bernstein, Laney, Morris, and Loftus (2005) followed up on Collins's (2001) results, demonstrating that false beliefs can affect predicted future behavior as well. Bernstein et al. had subjects first complete a questionnaire on their childhood food preferences, what they called a Food History Inventory (FHI). Again, embedded on the list was a target event. For one group of subjects, this target event was that they had "got sick after eating too many hard-boiled eggs"—the egg group. For the remaining subjects, the target event was that they had "felt ill after eating a dill pickle"—the pickle group. A week later subjects were told that their profile, based on questionnaires they had completed in Phase 1, indicated that as a child they had got sick either from eating too many hard-boiled eggs (egg group) or after eating a dill pickle (pickle group). The subjects then completed the FHI a second time. Not surprisingly, subjects' confidence increased that their target event had happened. More interesting, subjects were also asked to imagine themselves at an afternoon barbeque party and to rate the likelihood of consuming a long list of foods and beverages. Subjects who said they believed the false feedback gave lower "likelihood of eating" ratings for their target event. In fact, the consequences of the false-feedback manipulation were not confined to the specific food mentioned. They had what Bernstein et al. called "ripple effects." For example, subjects in the egg group did not just rate their likelihood of eating hard-boiled eggs lower than control subjects did, their new-found dislike for hard-boiled eggs transferred to their predicted likelihood of eating egg salad as well.

Finally, Laney, Morris, Loftus, and Bernstein (2005) showed that our ability to influence subjects' current food preferences is not limited to avoiding targeted foods. In fact, subjects can also be led to believe that they *loved* certain foods as a child, results that also have consequences for predicted future behavior. Laney et al. followed the same procedure as Bernstein et al. (2005), however their false feedback led some subjects to become more confident that they had loved asparagus the first time they tried it as a child. Those who believed the false feedback were more likely to state that they would pick sautéed asparagus to eat from a restaurant menu. In addition, those who believed the false feedback were also willing to pay more for a pound of asparagus at the grocery store.

Taken together, these studies show that false beliefs, and indeed false memories, are problematic in ways that go well beyond the pure fact that they can happen. They have practical consequences as well.

## WHERE ARE WE NOW?

Thanks to Loftus and to the many researchers who followed her lead, the tide has turned. We have seen the number of court cases die down and changes made to what is acceptable therapeutic practice. The luckier families have even been reunited. But for some the damage will never be undone. And for others the controversy is far from over. In fact, some researchers now claim to have discovered a neurobiological mechanism to account for repression (Anderson et al., 2004).

Anderson and Green (2001) asked subjects to learn a series of 40 word pairs. They told subjects that the first word in each pair was to act as a cue for the second word, the target word. In the second phase of the study, subjects were presented with the cue word and were asked to either remember the target word or suppress the target word. Then, subjects were given a memory test. Anderson and Green found that subjects remembered fewer words from the "suppression" trials, evidence they asserted for a "suppression mechanism that pushes unwanted memories out of awareness, " (p. 368) just like Freud suggested.

In a follow-up study, Anderson et al. (2004) repeated the earlier experiment but with two significant changes. First, during the second stage, where subjects were instructed to remember or suppress the cue words, subjects' brains were scanned using fMRI (functional magnetic resonance imaging). Second, memory for each target word was tested twice: with the original cue and also with a word related to the target. Once again, Anderson et al. found that subjects remembered fewer "suppression" targets than "remember" targets. In addition, they found a different pattern of brain activity when subjects were instructed to suppress the cue. Moreover, they observed more activity in the frontal cortex when subjects were successful in suppressing the target word. This time Anderson et al.'s conclusion was much stronger: They claimed to have found the neurobiological mechanism responsible for banishing memories out of conscious awareness.

However, as Garry and Loftus (2004) pointed out, many psychologists have problems with Anderson et al.'s (2004) conclusions. First, Anderson and colleagues' effects were small. In the suppression condition, subjects still remembered 80% of the target words, and although that is certainly less than the 87% remembered at baseline, it hardly qualifies as the "massive repression" mechanism that Herman and Schatzow (1987, p.12) had in mind. Second, the increase in brain activity in the frontal cortex is potentially due to subjects expending more effort thinking of something other than the target word. Third, the notion that the hippocampus is involved in memory is hardly earth shattering—scientists have known the hippocampus is involved in memory for a long time now (Squire & Schacter, 2000; Zola-Morgan & Squire, 1993). Finally, and perhaps most significantly, Anderson et al.'s (2004) results have not been replicated. Bulevich, Roediger, Balota, and Butler (in press) have been unable to reproduce the same effect: poorer memory performance after suppression instructions. Taken together, these results would suggest that even if Anderson et al.'s effect is real, it is certainly not robust enough to be called massive repression. Of course, it is possible that one day researchers will present incontrovertible evidence that repressing, and later recovering, memories is indeed possible. Until that day, the research in this chapter provides a far more parsimonious explanation.

## CONCLUSION

August 1992 is a landmark month in the intersection of psychology and the law. It was during this month that Elizabeth Loftus told the audience at the American Psychological Association's annual conference that she and her students had led some people to recover memories of long-ago experiences. But the experiences were false.

As details of her research hit the media in the weeks that followed, the phrase "false memories" started to share airtime with the word *repression,* and Elizabeth Loftus's name was spoken alongside Eileen Franklin's. Today, 15 years later, the evidence suggests Loftus was right all along, and that Franklin had never really repressed the details of Susan Nason's murder (MacLean, 1993). "Question with boldness even the existence of God," said Thomas Jefferson, "because, if there be one, he must more approve of the homage of reason than that of blindfolded fear." Elizabeth Loftus has long questioned with boldness, and shown us all the triumph of reason over fear.

# APPENDIX

## Elizabeth Loftus and the Recovered-Memory Controversy: A Timeline

Note: Most of the information here has been culled from the archives of the False Memory Syndrome Foundation (FMSF). We are grateful to Pam Freyd for her tireless assistance in helping us reconstruct this information.

| Date | Event |
|---|---|
| 1988: | Ellen Bass and Laura Davis publish *The Courage to Heal*. "If you are unable to remember any specific instances … but still have a feeling that something abusive happened to you, it probably did. … If you think you were abused and your life shows the symptoms, then you were." The book urges readers to "Get strong by suing." |
| 1990 November: | George Franklin convicted of murdering Susan Nason in 1969. His daughter Eileen suddenly remembered the killing in 1989. Lenore Terr and Loftus testify. |
| 1991: | Lenore Terr publishes "Childhood Traumas: An Outline and Overview" in the *American Journal of Psychiatry, 148,* 10–20. She writes that a single traumatic event is more likely to be remembered than a series of traumatic events, and that a recovered string of events will be more accurate than a recovered single event. |
| 1992 March: | First False Memory Syndrome Foundation (FMSF) newsletter. Members: 243 families |
| 1992 April: | Pope & Hudson claim that "Current evidence does not support the hypothesis that childhood sexual abuse is a risk factor for bulimia nervosa." (Pope & Hudson, 1992). |
| 1992 May: | FMSF membership is 413 families. |
| 1992 July: | Renee Fredrickson publishes *Repressed Memories: A Journey to Recovery from Sexual Abuse.*<br>"If you remember almost nothing or very little of your childhood, or if you cannot remember a period of time, such as between the ages of ten and fourteen, you have repressed memories" (p. 46).<br>"You are not trying to stimulate your recall memories. Instead, you need to let yourself imagine or picture what might have happened to you" (p. 112).<br>"Occasionally you may need a small verbal push to get started. Your guide may suggest some action that seems to arise naturally from the image you are picturing." (p. 112) |

| | |
|---|---|
| 1992 July-August: | (1) Richard Ofshe publishes article on Paul Ingram in *International Journal of Clinical and Experimental Hypnosis, 40,* 125–156.<br>(2) Linda Meyer Williams's "Advisor" newsletter appears, a version of her later 1994 article "these preliminary findings confirm the reports from clinical samples that a large proportion of women do not recall childhood sexual victimization experiences." (p. 20) |
| 1992 August: | Loftus gives talk at APA that formed basis of her 1993 "Reality of Repressed Memories" article |
| 1992 October: | FMSF membership is 1,415 families. |
| 1992 November: | (1) FMSF membership is 2,010 families.<br>(2) The *Los Angeles Times* runs an advertisement showing three adorable young girls and the headline reading "1 in 3 American girls will be sexually molested by age 18." |
| 1992 November-December: | Loftus publishes 250th paper: Berliner & Loftus (1992). Sexual abuse accusations: Desperately seeking reconciliation. *Journal of Interpersonal Violence, 7,* 571. |
| 1993 January: | (1) *New York Times Book Review* publishes "Beware the Incest Survivor Machine" by Carol Tavris.<br>(2) Repressed memory lawsuits peak |
| 1993 February: | APA Board recommends to its Council of Representatives that a working group be established to study memories of childhood abuse. Members: Judith L. Alpert, Laura S. Brown, Stephen J. Ceci, Christine A. Courtois, Elizabeth F. Loftus, Peter A. Ornstein |
| 1993 February-April: | Letters of complaint flood in to the *New York Times* about Tavris's article. Judith Herman says, "The best research data indicate that between 25 and 38 percent of girls are sexually abused." Bass & Davis say Tavris's article is "part of a backlash against survivors, their supporters and the significant social progress they have made." |
| 1993 April: | FMSF membership is 3,119 families. |
| 1993 May: | Loftus publishes "Reality of Repressed Memories" in the *American Psychologist.* |
| 1993 July: | Harry MacLean publishes *Once Upon a Time* about the Eileen Franklin case. In the book, MacLean says that Eileen told her mother "that she had visualized the killing while under hypnosis." After learning that hypnotically enhanced evidence was not admissible, she then said that she had not told the truth, that she had retrieved the memory in a dream. Later she said that she had retrieved the memory in therapy. The final version was that she had retrieved the memory when she had a flashback looking at her own daughter (p. 106). |

| | |
|---|---|
| 1993 August: | (1) The American Medical Association regards the use of "memory enhancement" techniques in eliciting accounts of childhood sexual abuse to be fraught with problems of potential misapplication, according to a resolution adopted during the annual meeting of the organization's House of Delegates. The resolution was adopted without comment—the lack of debate surprised some psychiatrists, who said that the wording of the resolution was "harsh."<br>(2) Christine Courtois claims that "we should be talking about amnesia and traumatic amnesia rather than repression or false memories" (*Psychiatric Times*).<br>(3) APA working group holds its first meeting.<br>(4) FMSF membership is 5,144 families. |
| 1993 November: | (1) McGill University invites Dr. Harold Lief to give a talk about false memories but he is prevented from giving the talk by stink bombs and jeering protestors.<br>(2) Steven Cook, of Philadelphia, accuses Cardinal Bernardin of child abuse. The allegations are based on repressed memories that were recovered in therapy 1 month earlier. Loftus is involved in the case.<br>(3) Dale Akiki acquitted of day-care abuse. Loftus involved in the case. Lenore Terr testifies:<br>Q. And among that debate is there some question about the scientific validity of the theory of repression, yes or no?<br>A. Yes. But I think that they are wrong. They are not clinicians, and they are not entitled to make that decision. |
| 1993 December: | British FMS holds its first advisory meeting |
| 1994 January: | (1) American Psychiatric Association publishes vague but "neutral" position on recovered-memory therapy.<br>(2) FMSF membership is 6,007 families. |
| 1994 February: | Lenore Terr publishes *Unchained Memories: True Stories of Traumatic Memories, Lost and Found. NY*: Basic Books. |
| 1994 May: | Gary Ramona wins $500,000 judgment against the psychiatrist, counselor, and the hospital that encouraged his daughter Holly to recover memories that he raped her. Loftus was involved in his case. |
| 1994 June: | Ofshe & Watters publish *Making Monsters.* |

| | |
|---|---|
| 1994 June-July: | (1) Loftus is accused on a radio talk show of sexually abusing her own children. Loftus does not have any children.<br>(2) A new edition of *The Courage to Heal* is released: "Some therapists working with adult survivors have pushed clients to acknowledge abuse or have attributed problems to abuse that did not occur. False allegations have been made" (p 485).<br>(3) "What We Do and Don't Know About Memory," featuring David Calof. |
| 1994 July: | A retractor sues Bass & Davis over *The Courage to Heal Workbook*. The suit is dismissed. |
| 1994 August: | (1) *Applied Cognitive Psychology* has a special issue "Recovery of Memories of Childhood Sexual Abuse." Included, is Lindsay & Read's landmark paper "Psychotherapy and Memories of Childhood Sexual Abuse."<br>(2) Roediger presents "sleep" list paper at APA.<br>(3) Hays & Stanley present paper showing link between fear of dentists and CSA. |
| 1994 September: | Loftus & Ketcham's *The Myth of Repressed Memory* is released. Amazon reviews from 2000 to 2004:<br>"These two women are geniuses. All I have to say is with the intelligence of these women combined this book will blow you away. Ketcham is a fantastic writer, leaving the reader in a state of awe and utter amazement. Two thumbs way up."<br>"Beware of this book. Loftus is not a trauma expert. If she were, she would acknowledge that normal memory and traumatic memory are different creatures; they work differently and involve different areas of the brain."<br>"Poorly researched and openly manipulative. Dr. Loftus et. al., as a participant in the false memory hysteria, has managed to combine initially poor research on a totally different topic to support her beliefs in memory in trauma. She utilizes adult eyewitness testimony (using poor, non-valid studies) and blithely applies it to childhood memory without any consideration of childhood developmental, dissociative and traumatic issues, and without having any experience in clinical practice (either adult or child)!! Try Lenore Terr, MD, any of her books, but especially 'Too Scared To Cry' and 'Unchained Memories'"<br>"Dismissing repression as invalid, Loftus overlooks concrete evidence of dissociation, repression and later remembrance of traumatic abuse."<br>"This is a courageous book that bends over backwards to be fair, yet is uncompromising in its expression of the truth."<br>"A step backwards in the fight against child abuse." |
| 1994 September-October: | Ceci, Huffman, Smith, & Loftus publish the "mousetrap" study. *Consciousness and Cognition: An International Journal, 3*, 388–407. |
| 1994: | Loftus, Polonsky, & Fullilove (1994). Memories of Childhood Sexual Abuse. *Psychology of Women Quarterly, 18*, 67–84. |

| | |
|---|---|
| 1994 November: | (1) Fred Crews publishes "Revenge of the Repressed" in the *New York Review of Books*.<br>(2) John Kihlstrom slams interim report from APA Working Group on the Investigation of Memories of Childhood Abuse. |
| 1994 December: | Los Angeles Superior Court Judge Burton Bach dismisses a lawsuit against Gary Ramona, brought by his daughter, Holly, for sexual abuse. |
| 1995 February: | (1) Washington State becomes first state to act on third-party complaint (Chuck Noah) against a mental health professional.<br>(2) British Psychological Society begins offering an insurance policy for negligence claims from clients, including allegations of planting false memories of child abuse; 35% of members sign up. |
| 1995 March: | *State v. Joel Hungerford* (New Hampshire). Two women entered therapy and recovered memories of being raped years earlier, one by her father and one by her junior high teacher. Both men were indicted. Hillsborough County Superior Court Judge William J. Groff stated that before either woman can testify at trial, the state must prove that "repressed memories" exist and that remembering them through therapy is generally accepted in psychology. In addition, Judge Groff stated that the state must show that once recovered, those memories are accurate. The hearing for the admissibility of recovered memory evidence was set for March 27, 1995. The experts for the state are Jon Conte, PhD, Bessel van der Kolk, M.D., and Daniel Brown, PhD. The experts for the defense are Elizabeth Loftus, PhD, Paul McHugh, M.D., James Hudson, M.D. |
| 1995 April: | (1) Ofrah Bikel's "Divided Memories" on TV.<br>(2) George Franklin's conviction overturned because jurors had been wrongly told that Franklin's silence in jail was an admission of guilt. In addition, the Judge prevented the defense from introducing media coverage that showed where Eileen's memory account could have come from. |
| 1995 May: | *State v. Joel Hungerford,* New Hampshire Superior Court rules " ...the phenomenon of memory repression, and the process of therapy used in these cases to recover the memories, have not gained general acceptance in the field of psychology; and are not scientifically reliable." |
| 1995 July: | Minnesota District Court jury finds Diane Humenansky negligent and awards more than $2.6 million to a woman who had alleged that Humenansky planted false memories of sexual abuse. Loftus testifies in the case. |
| 1995 August: | Washington State, acting on complaint filed by Chuck Noah, suspends license of therapist Linda MacDonald. |
| 1995 December: | Loftus & Pickrell publish "The Formation of False Memories." |
| 1996 January: | Loftus resigns from APA. In her letter, she describes how APA's committees and members "...have moved away from scientific and scholarly thinking...." |

| | |
|---|---|
| 1996 April: | Loftus presents first outcome data on recovered-memory therapy (RMT) using cases from Washington State Crime Victims Compensation Program: recovered-memory therapy associated with poorer everyday functioning; The average cost of nonrepressed-memory claims was $2,672; the average cost of repressed-memory claims was $12,296 (median $9,296). |
| 1996 June: | Paul Ingram clemency hearing. Loftus testifies. |
| 1996 July: | George Franklin's prosecutors decide against a retrial after learning that Eileen has also accused him of a second murder that he could not have committed, and because Eileen's memories were retrieved with the help of hypnosis. |
| 1997 May: | (1) Loftus elected president of American Psychological Society (APS). (2) Corwin & Olafson publish Jane Doe article in *Child Maltreatment: Journal of the American Professional Society on the Abuse of Children, 2,* 91–112. They claim it is a case study providing clear evidence of a recovered memory of childhood abuse. |
| 1997 July: | (1) Loftus named James McKeen Cattell Fellow for her contributions to applied research by the American Psychological Society, "for outstanding lifetime contributions to the area of applied psychological research." (2) Hungerford case: New Hampshire Supreme Court upholds lower court ruling that repressed-memory testimony is unreliable. |
| 1997 August: | Romona case finally ends. Second District Court of Appeal ordered a lower court to dismiss the "repressed memory" claim brought by Holly Ramona against her father. Ramona's lawyer noted in a brief to the court that Holly did not know if her memories were true or false since all memories are fallible. Loftus submits expert affidavit. |
| 1998 February: | (1) *Toronto Star* publishes piece claiming Loftus resigned from APA because of complaints that she misrepresented their cases. (2) APA Working Group on the Investigation of Memories of Childhood Abuse releases final report. (3) Alpert, Brown, & Courtois publish "Symptomatic Clients and Memories of Childhood Abuse: What the Trauma and Child Sexual Abuse Literature Tells Us." *Psychology, Public Policy and Law, 4,* 941–995. (4) Ornstein, Ceci, & Loftus publish a reply to the Alpert, Brown & Courtois, "The Science of Memory and the Practice of Psychotherapy." (5) The reply is followed by several replies and counterreplies: "The Politics of Memory: A Response to Ornstein, Ceci & Loftus" (Alpert, Brown, & Courtois). "Adult Recollections of Childhood Abuse: Cognitive and Developmental Perspectives" (Ornstein, Ceci, & Loftus). Response to "Adult Recollections of Childhood Abuse: Cognitive and Developmental Perspectives" (Alpert, Brown, & Courtois). "More on the Repressed Memory Debate: A Rejoinder to Alpert, Brown and Courtois" (Ornstein, Ceci, & Loftus). |
| 1998 May: | Loftus assumes presidency of APS. |
| 1998 June: | Wenatchee civil rights suit goes to jury after 10 weeks of testimony. Loftus testifies for plaintiffs. Plaintiffs lose. |
| 1998 October: | Washington State court finds recovered memory evidence inadmissible. Loftus testifies. |
| 1999 April: | Rhode Island trial court rules recovered memory evidence unreliable. Loftus had testified in earlier hearing. |

| | |
|---|---|
| 1999 September: | University of Washington (UW) begins "investigating" a complaint made by Jane Doe against Loftus for invasion of privacy. With only 15 minutes' notice, John Slattery, UW's OSI, seizes Loftus's files. |
| 1999 October: | Jury Awards $862,000 in malpractice suit, *Hess et al. v. Juan Fernandez* (Wisconsin). Loftus testifies. |
| 1999 November: | UW finally tells Loftus what they are investigating her for. However, they only say that the charge was "scholarly misconduct" including, "possible violations of human subjects research." |
| 2000 February: | (1) *Franklin v. Terr, et al.* U.S. App. 9th Cir LEXIS 1280, George Franklin may not sue psychiatrists Kirk Barrett and Lenore Terr for allegedly conspiring to present false testimony at his murder trial in 1990. The 9th U.S. Circuit Court of Appeals said that witness testimony is legally protected from damage suits.<br>(2) Loftus's lawyer finally obtains documents from UW investigation, including a "Confidential Memo" by Stanley Berent on the University of Michigan IRB (Mel Guyer's IRB). Guyer never knew the memo existed, and to this day, even taking FOI action, he hasn't seen it. The memo, Guyer says, "was the harshest document, filled with false innuendo, malicious insinuations, and outright falsities. Keeping it secret from me denied me the opportunity to correct its mischaracterizations." But that didn't stop a University of Michigan lawyer from sending it right to the UW to be used against Loftus. |
| 2000 August: | Loftus invited to be keynote speaker at the New Zealand Psychological Society annual conference. Protests occur after the society refused to revoke its invitation to Loftus. Former Victoria University of Wellington clinical academic Judith McDougall says, "Elizabeth Loftus has shown that memory is fallible, which is useful, but it's gone beyond that. She argues long-term memory is fallible. That's not true. Adult memories of childhood are quite robust." |
| 2001 May: | Loftus receives William James Award from APS, for significant lifetime intellectual contributions to the basic science of psychology. "Elizabeth Loftus is an example of the rare scientist who is instrumental both in advancing a scientific discipline and in using that discipline to make critical contributions to society." This is a part of her acceptance speech:<br>The public thinks this epidemic is over. But many families have never recovered, and many promulgators and victims of the recovered-memory movement remain angry and vengeful.<br>For so many years, I have tried to understand their position, sympathize with the emotionally disturbed young women whom I regard as victims of misguided or misinformed therapists, and find common ground. |
| | Now I realize that for these people, there may be little in the way of common ground. I am their enemy—scientific evidence is their enemy—and I will not be able to persuade them otherwise, not with all the good data and good intentions in the world.<br>This was a terribly difficult realization for me. The research findings for which I am being honoured now generated a level of hostility and opposition I could never have foreseen. |

> People wrote threatening letters, warning me that my reputation and even my safety were in jeopardy if I continued along these lines.
>
> At some universities, armed guards were provided to accompany me during speeches. People misinterpreted my writings and put words in my mouth that I had never spoken. People filed ethical complaints and threatened lawsuits of organizations that invited me to speak. People spread defamatory falsehoods in writings, in newspapers, on the Internet.
>
> As I stand here, the happy recipient of an award that honors me for my research, I continue to be the target of efforts to censor my ideas. I am gagged at the moment and may not give you any details.
>
> But to me, that itself is the problem. Who, after all, benefits from my silence? Who benefits from keeping such investigations in the dark? My inquisitors. The only people who operate in the dark are thieves, assassins, and cowards.
>
> Those of us who value the first amendment and open scientific inquiry must bring these efforts to suppress freedom of speech into the light, and tonight I vow to you that when my own situation is resolved, that is precisely what I'm going to do. I am honored to receive this award.

| | |
|---|---|
| 2001 May: | The UW investigating committee (two clinicians and a sociologist) conclude that Loftus is not guilty of scholarly misconduct. However, the two clinicians recommend to the Dean that she be reprimanded and put on a program of remedial education focusing on professional ethics. |
| 2001 July: | UW Dean writes Loftus a letter of exoneration on all charges, but says she must not contact Jane Doe's mother again nor interview anyone else involved in the case without IRB approval. The investigation lasted 21 months, even though the UW's own rules say all investigations must be concluded within 4 months. |
| 2002 May: | Loftus delivers first annual Henry and Bryna David Article/Lecture, for "application of the best social and behavioral sciences research to public policy issues." The speech is delivered at NAS, and the article is selected for inclusion in: *The Best American Science and Nature Writing* (2003). |
| 2002 May-June: | *Skeptical Inquirer* publishes "Who Abused Jane Doe?" by Loftus & Guyer. Carol Tavris publishes commentary. Shortly afterward, Jane Doe sues all of them for invasion of privacy, emotional distress, fraud, and defamation of character. Only Loftus and Guyer knew Jane Doe's real name but had never used it. In filing the lawsuit, Jane Doe revealed her real name. |
| 2002 August: | Loftus takes up Distinguished Professorship at University of California, Irvine. Sets her homepage to report Seattle weather and Irvine weather for contrast. |
| 2003 January: | Loftus publishes 400th paper: Nourkova, V. V., Bernstein D. M., & Loftus, E. F. (2003). Echo of explosions: Comparative analysis of recollections about the terrorists attacks in 1999 (Moscow) and 2001 (New York City). *Psychological Journal, 24,* 64–72. |

2003 May: At APS Loftus says:

> I got some satisfaction out of thinking that we'd put the case study to rest. But the cost was tremendous. The University's actions left me feeling betrayed. And so a year later I left. I turned down a generous counteroffer that was not accompanied by a real apology. University officials would only say that they were sorry that the process took so long. I left the university where I had worked for 29 years. I left my friends. I left my lovely old house with its view of Lake Washington. And the breakfast place where I had eaten most days for more than a decade. I moved to the University of California, Irvine, where happily I found great colleagues, wonderful new friends, a little house with no view, and a coffee pot that works just fine.
>
> That we can be sued into silence delivers an ominous message for all academic researchers, even those who haven't been sued. Meritless, harassing litigation not only affects the direct defendants, but others who might be discouraged from speaking out on matters of public concern for fear that they are next. We need cures for this problem at the judicial level, ways to educate judges to recognize this class of harassing case and prevent the case and the chill to drag on to a jury. We need judicial sanctions-the awarding of attorney's fees and court costs against people who file such harassing cases. We need legislative safeguards to protect public advocacy. As you can see from my own case, we need our universities to be on our side. As a friend of mine, a biological scientist and member of the National Academy of Sciences phrased it: "universities have lost their nerve to serve as reservoirs of social criticism."
>
> Psychological scientists, teachers, practitioners, scholars & students, embrace both the goals of science and our right to express what the findings might mean. These are goals that we hold dear, and which we must now, more than ever, step up our efforts to defend.

---

2003 August: Loftus receives Distinguished Scientific Award for the Applications of Psychology, American Psychological Association.

---

2004 April: Loftus elected to National Academy of Science, "I was so excited when Duncan Luce called me at 5:58 a.m. that I rolled over onto the phone and hung it up."

---

2005: (1) Loftus receives the Grawemeyer Award for "Outstanding Ideas in the Science of Psychology," a $200,000 prize.
(2) "Bethschrift" held in Wellington, New Zealand

## REFERENCES


Alpert, J., Brown, L., & Courtois, C. (1998). Symptomatic clients and memories of childhood abuse: What the trauma and child sexual abuse literature tells us. *Psychology, Public Policy, and Law, 4,* 941–995.

Anderson, M. C., & Green, C. (2001). Suppressing unwanted memories by executive control. *Nature, 410,* 366–369.

Anderson, M. C., Ochsner, K. N., Kuhl, B., Cooper, J., Robertson, E., Gabrieli, S. W., et al. (2004). Neural systems underlying the suppression of unwanted memories. *Science, 303,* 232–235.

Bass, E., & Davis, L. (1988). *The Courage to heal: A guide for women survivors of child sexual abuse.* New York: Harper & Row.

Berkowitz, S. R., Laney, C., Morris, E. K., Garry, M., & Loftus, E. F. (2005). *Plutos behaving badly: False beliefs and their consequences.* Manuscript under review.

Berliner, L., & Loftus, E. (1992). Sexual abuse accusations: Desperately seeking reconciliation. *Journal of Interpersonal Violence, 7,* 570–578.

Bernstein, D. M., Godfrey, R., Davison, A., & Loftus, E. F. (2004). Conditions affecting the revelation effect for autobiographical memory. *Memory & Cognition, 32,* 455–462.

Bernstein, D. M., Laney, C., Morris, E. K., & Loftus, E. F. (in press). False memories about food can lead to food avoidance. *Social Cognition, 23,* 11–34.

Bernstein, D. M., Whittlesea, B. W. A., & Loftus, E. F. (2002). Increasing confidence in remote autobiographical memory and general knowledge: Extensions of the revelation effect. *Memory & Cognition, 30,* 432–438.

Blume, E. S. (1985). *Secret survivors: Uncovering incest and its aftereffects in women.* New York: Wiley

Braun, K. A., Ellis, R., & Loftus, E. F. (2002). Make my memory: How advertising can change our memories of the past. *Psychology and Marketing, 19,* 1–23.

Brown, D., Scheflin, A. W., & Hammond, D. C. (1998). *Memory, trauma treatment, and the law.* New York: Norton.

Bulevich, J. B., Roediger, H. L., Balota, D. A., & Butler, A. C. (in press). Failures to find suppression of episodic memories in the think/no-think paradigm. *Memory & Cognition.*

Candel, I., Merckelbach, H., & Kuijpers, M. (2003). Dissociative experiences are related to commissions in emotional memory. *Behavior Research and Therapy, 41,* 719–725.

Ceci, S. J., Huffman, M. L., Smith, E., Loftus, E. (1994). Repeatedly thinking about a non-event. *Consciousness & Cognition, 3,* 388–407

Collins, H. R. (2001). *Another reason to dislike Chihuahuas and other small dogs: Behavioral consequences of false memories.* Unpublished honors thesis, University of Washington, Seattle.

Corwin, D. L., & Olafson, E. (1997). Videotaped discovery of reportedly unrecallable memory of child sexual abuse: Comparison with a childhood interview videotaped 11 years before. *Child Maltreatment: Journal of the American Professional Society on the Abouse of Children, 2,* 91–112.

Costa, P. T., & McCrae, R. R. (1992). The five-factor model of personality and its relevance to personality disorders. *Journal of Personality Disorders, 6,* 343–359.

Courtois, C. A. (1992). The memory retrieval process in incest survivor therapy. *Journal of Child Sexual Abuse, 1,* 15–31.

Crews, F. (1994, November 17). Revenged of the repressed. Part One. *The New York Review,* 54–60.

Crews, F. (1995). *The memory wars: Freud's legacy in dispute.* New York: New York Review of Books.

Darnton, N. (1991, October 7). The pain of the last taboo. *Newsweek,* pp. 70–72.

Eisen, M. L., Morgan, D. Y., & Mickes, L. (2002). Individual differences in eyewitness memory and suggestibility: Examining relations between acquiescence, dissociation and resistance to misinformation. *Personality & Individual Differences, 16,* 133–137.

Engel, B. (1990). *The right to innocence: Healing the trauma of childhood sexual abuse.* New York: Ivy Books.

Erdelyi, M. H. (1990). Repression, reconstruction, and defense: History and integration of the psychoanalytic and experimental frameworks. In J. L. Singer (Ed). *Repression and dissociation: Implications for personality theory, psychopathology, and health* (pp. 1–31). Chicago: University of Chicago Press.

Fredrickson, R. (1992). *Repressed memories: A journey to recovery from sexual abuse.* New York: Simon & Schuster.

Freyd, J. (2003). *Commentary: Response to 17 February 2003 Media Reports on Loftus' Bugs Bunny Study.* Retrieved [August 18, 2005] from http://dynamic.uoregon.edu/~jjf/bugs.html

Garry, M., & Loftus, E. F. (2004). I am Freud's brain. *Skeptical Inquirer, 28,* 16–18.

Garry, M., Manning, C. G., Loftus, E. F., & Sherman, S. J. (1996). Imagination inflation: Imagining a childhood event inflates confidence that it occurred. *Psychonomic Bulletin and Review, 3,* 208–214.

Garry, M., & Wade, K. A. (2005). Actually, a picture is worth less than 45 words: Narratives produce more false memories than photographs. *Psychonomic Bulletin & Review, 12,* 359–366.

Gay, P. (1988). *Freud: A life for our time.* New York: Norton.

Gladwell, M. (2000). *The tipping point: How little things can make a big difference.* Boston: Little, Brown.

Goff, L., & Roediger, H. (1998). Imagination inflation for action events: Repeated imaginings lead to illusory recollections. *Memory & Cognition, 26,* 20–33.

Grinley, M. J. (2002). *Effects of advertising on semantic and episodic memory.* Unpublished master's thesis, University of Washington, Seattle.

Gudjonsson, G. H. (1995). Interrogative suggestibility: Does the setting where subjects are tested make a difference to the scores on the GSS 1 and GSS 2? *Personality and Individual Differences, 18,* 789–790.

Heaps, C. M., & Nash, M. (2001). Comparing recollective experience in true and false autobiographical memories. *Journal of Experimental Psychology: Learning, Memory, and Cognition, 27,* 920–930.

Heaps, C., & Nash, M. (1999). Individual differences in imagination inflation. *Psychonomic Bulletin & Review, 6,* 313–318.

Hekkanen, S. T., & McEvoy, C. (2002). False memories and source monitoring problems: Criterion differences. *Applied Cognitive Psychology, 16,* 73–85.

Herman, J. L., & Schatzow, E. (1987). Recovery and verification of memories of childhood sexual trauma. *Psychoanalytic Psychology, 4,* 1–14.

Herman, J. L. (1992). *Trauma and recovery.* New York: Basic Books.

Holmes, D. (1990). The evidence for repression: An examination of sixty years of research. In J. Singer (Ed.), *Repression and dissociation: Implications for personality, theory, psychopathology, and health* (pp. 85–102). Chicago: University of Chicago Press.

Holmes, D. (1995). The evidence for repression: An examination of sixty years of research. In J. Singer (Ed.), *Repression and dissociation: Implications for personality, theory, psychopathology, and health. The John D. and Catherine T. MacArthur Foundation series on mental health and development* (Reprint ed., pp. 85–102.) Chicago: University of Chicago Press.

Horselenberg, R., Merckelbach, H., Muris, P., Rassin, E., Sijsenaar, M., & Spann, V. (2000). Imagining fictitious childhood events: The role of individual differences in imagination inflation. *Clinical Psychology & Psychotherapy, 7,* 128–137.

Hyman, I. E., Jr., & Billings, F. J. (1998). Individual differences and the creation of false childhood memories. *Memory, 6,* 1–20.

Hyman, I. E., Husband, T. H., & Billings, F. J. (1995). False memories of childhood experiences. *Applied Cognitive Psychology, 9,* 181–197.

Hyman, I. E., & Kleinknecht, E. E. (1999). False childhood memories: Research, theory, and applications. In L. M. Williams & V. L. Banyard (Eds.), *Trauma and memory* (pp. 175–188). Thousand Oaks, CA: Sage.

Hyman, I. E., & Loftus, E. F. (1998). Errors in autobiographical memory. *Clinical Psychology Review, 18,* 933–947.

Hyman, I. E., & Pentland, J. (1996). The role of mental imagery in the creation of false childhood memories. *Journal of Memory and Language, 35,* 101–117.

Jenkins, P. (1998). *Moral panic: Changing concepts of the child molester in modern America.* New Haven, CT: Yale University Press.

Johnson, M., Hashtroudi, S., & Lindsay, D. S. (1993). Source monitoring. *Psychological Bulletin, 114,* 3–28.

Kantrowitz, B. (1991, February 11). Forgetting to remember. *Newsweek,* p. 58.

Laney, C., Morris, E. K., Loftus, E. F., & Bernstein, D. M. (2005). *Healthier eating could be just a false belief away.* Manuscript under review.

Lindsay, D. S., Hagen, L., Read, J. D., Wade, K. A., & Garry, M. (2004). True photographs and false memories. *Psychological Science, 15*(3), 149–154.

Loftus, E. F. (1993). The reality of repressed memories. *American Psychologist, 48,* 518–537.

Loftus, E. F., & Ketcham, K. (1994). *The myth of repressed memory.* New York: St. Martin's Griffin.

Loftus, E. F., & Loftus, G. R. (1980). One the permanence of stored information in the human brain. *American Psychologist, 35,* 409–420.

Loftus, E. F., & Pickrell, J. (1995). The formation of false memories. *Psychiatric Annals, 25,* 720–725.

Loftus, E. F., Polonsky, S., & Fullilove, M. T. (1994). Memories of childhood sexual abuse: Remembering and repressing. *Psychology of Women Quarterly, 18,* 67–84.

MacLean, H. N. (1993). *Once upon a time: A true story of memory, murder, and the law.* New York: HarperCollins.

Maltz, W., & Holman, B. (1991). *Incest and sexuality: A guide to understanding and healing.* Lexington, MA: Lexington Books

Mazzoni, G. A. L., Loftus, E. F., & Kirsch, I. (2001). Changing beliefs about implausible autobiographical events: A little plausibility goes a long way. *Journal of Experimental Psychology: Applied, 7,* 51–59.

Mazzoni, G. A. L., & Memon, A. (2003). Imagination can create false autobiographical memories. *Psychological Science, 14,* 186–188.

McNally, R. J. (2003). *Remembering trauma.* Cambridge, MA: Belknap Press.

McNally, R. J., Lasko, N. B., Clancy, S. A., Macklin, M. L., Pitman, R. K., & Orr, S. P. (2004). Psychophysiological responding during script-driven imagery in people reporting abduction by space aliens. *Psychological Science, 15,* 493–497.

Merckelbach, H., Muris, P., & Rassin, E. (1999). Fantasy proneness and cognitive failures as correlates of dissociative experiences. *Personality and Individual Differences, 26,* 961–967.

Miller, A. (1997). *The drama of the gifted child: The search for the true self* (Rev. ed.). New York: Basic Books. (Original work published 1969; R. Ward, Trans.)

Ofshe, R. (1992). Inadvertent hypnosis during interrogation: False confession due to dissociative state; Mis-identified multiple personality and the satanic cult hypothesis. *International Journal of Clinical and Experimental Hypnosis, 40,* 125–156.

Ofshe, R., & Watters, E., (1994). *Making monsters: False memories, psychotherapy, and sexual hysteria.* Berkeley: University of California Press.

Oldenberg, D. (1991, June 20). Dark memories: Adults confront their childhood abuse. *The Washington Post,* p. D1.

Olio, K. A. (1989). Memory retrieval in the treatment of adult survivors of sexual abuse. *Transactional Analysis Journal, 19,* 93–100.

Ost, J., Fellows, B. J., & Bull, R. (1997). Individual differences and the suggestibility of human memory. *Contemporary Hypnosis, 14,* 132–137.

Ost, J., Foster, S., Costall, A., & Bull, R. (2005). False reports in appropriate interviews. *Memory, 13,* 700–710.

Ost, J., Vrij, A., Costall, A., & Bull, R. (2002). Crashing memories and reality monitoring: Distinguishing between perceptions, imaginings and false memories. *Applied Cognitive Psychology, 16,* 125–134.

Paddock, J., Noel, M., Terranova, S., Eber, H., Manning, C., & Loftus, E. F. (1999). Imagination inflation and the perils of guided visualization. *Journal of Psychology, 133,* 581–595

Pezdek, K., Finger, K., & Hodge, D. (1997). Planting false childhood memories: The role of event plausibility. *Psychological Science, 8,* 437–441.

Platt, R. D., Lacey, S. C., Lobst, A. D., & Finkelman, D. (1998). Absorption, dissociation, and fantasy-proneness as predictors of memory distortion in autobiographical and laboratory-generated memories. *Applied Cognitive Psychology, 12,* S77–S89.

Poole, D. A., Lindsay, D. S., Memon, A. & Bull, R. (1995). Psychotherapy and the recovery of memories of childhood sexual abuse: U.S. and British practitioners' opinions, practices, and experiences. *Journal of Consulting and Clinical Psychology, 63,* 426–437.

Pope, H. G., & Hudson, J. I. (1992). Is childhood sexual abuse a risk factor bulimia nervosa: *American Journal of Psychiatry, 149,* 455–463.

Porter, S., Birt, A. R., Yuille, J. C., & Lehman, D. R. (2000). Negotiating false memories: Interviewer and rememberer characteristics relate to memory distortion. *Psychological Science, 11*(6), 507–510.

Porter, S., Yuille, J. C., & Lehman, D. R. (1999). The nature of real, implanted, and fabricated memories for emotional childhood events: Implications for the recovered memory debate. *Law and Human Behavior, 23,* 517–537.

Ritter, M. (1991, June 30). Sudden recall of forgotten crimes is a puzzler for juries, experts say. *The Los Angeles Times*, p. A10.

Russell, D. E. H. (1974). *The politics of rape: The victim's perspective.* New York: Stein & Day.

Sagan, C. (1979). *Broca's brain: Reflections on the romance of science.* New York: Random House.

Scoboria, A., Mazzoni, G., Kirsch, I., & Relyea, M. (2004). Plausibility and belief in autobiographical memory. *Applied Cognitive Psychology, 18,* 791–807.

Sharman, S. J., Garry, M., & Beuke, C. J. (2004). Imagination or exposure causes imagination inflation. *American Journal of Psychology, 117*(2), 157–168.

Snyder, M. (1974). Self-monitoring of expressive behavior. *Journal of Personality and Social Psychology, 30,* 526–537.

Squire, L., & Schacter, D. (2000). *Neuropsychology of memory* (3rd ed.). New York: Guilford.

Tavris, C. (1993, January 3). Beware the incest-survivor machine. *The New York Times Book Review,* pp. 16–17.

Terr, L. (1991). Childhood traumas: An outline and overview. *American Journal of Psychiatry, 148,* 10–20.

Terr, L. (1994). Unchained memories: True stories of traumatic memories, lost and found. New York: Basic Books.

Thomas, A. K., & Loftus, E. F. (2002). Creating bizarre false memories through imagination. *Memory & Cognition, 30,* 423–431.
Thomas, A. K., Bulevich, J. B., & Loftus, E. F. (2003). Exploring the role of repetition and sensory elaboration in the imagination inflation effect. *Memory & Cognition, 31,* 630–640.
Toufexis, A. (1991, October 28). When can memories be trusted? *Time,* pp. 86–88.
Wade, K. A. (2004). *Factors that influence source monitoring do not necessarily influence false childhood memories.* Unpublished doctoral thesis, Victoria University, Wellington, New Zealand.
Wade, K. A., Garry, M., Read, J. D., & Lindsay, D.S. (2002). A picture is worth a thousand lies: Using false photographs to create false childhood memories. *Psychonomic Bulletin and Review, 9,* 597–603.
Weiser, J. (2002). PhotoTherapy techniques: Exploring the secrets of personal snapshots and family albums. *Child & Family, 2,* 16–25.
Wilkinson, C., & Hyman, I. E., Jr. (1998). Individual differences related to two types of memory errors: Word lists may not generalize to autobiographical memory. *Applied Cognitive Psychology, 12,* S29-S46.
Wiliams, L. M. (1992). Adult memories of child sexual abuse: Preliminary findings from a longitudinal study. *American Society for Prevention of Child Abuse Advisor,* 19–20.
Zola-Morgan, S. & Squire, L. R. (1993). Neuroanatomy of memory. Annual Review of Neuroscience, 16, 547-563.

*My first year of grad school, I lived in graduate women's housing. I took up, as a hobby, painting bottles. I met a local artist who painted this incredible bottle, wine bottles and stuff. You take a bottle and you paint it and, you know, I had some bottles, and so I thought well, they just splatter them like famous artists.*

*Well, at the end of the year, what they do is if the place isn't clean enough, they clean it and then they charge you. So, they sent me a bill for cleaning in which they removed—as part of the cleaning—bottles and trash off the balcony.*

*They took all of my painted bottles, including the one by the artist, and all my artwork, and threw it away. Then they charged me for it! I hit the roof and I filed a complaint and I saved the settlement letter. It says 25 dollars settlement for claim of loss of eight decorated bottles occurring on or about 28 November 1967 at Hume House 6H per memo from F E Gallagher Junior, Director of Married Student Housing, Eskenvito Village. And that was my first legal case.*

*But I wasn't always so successful with my early legal endeavors. I also saved a clipping from the Stanford newspaper. The story says, "Psychology backfired Monday night on Geoffrey Loftus, 24, a graduate student in psychology at Stanford University. On Monday night Loftus and his wife were away from their apartment. Due to numerous burglaries in the neighborhood, Loftus had mounted a sign on his $300 multiplex stereo receiver that said 'Beth, don't touch this or you'll be fried—there's a short somewhere, I've gone to find an electrician. Officer Kilpatrick—be right back.' What the story doesn't say is that the burglar came in anyhow and didn't get deterred by our psychological tricks, and stole the stereo anyway.*

CHAPTER

# 9

# Incorporating Elizabeth Loftus's Research on Memory Into Reforms to Protect the Innocent

Jacqueline McMurtrie

> A major reason for my writing this book has been a long-standing concern with cases in which an innocent person has been falsely identified, convicted, and even jailed.
>
> —Elizabeth Loftus (*Eyewitness Testimony,* 1979)

The frequency with which innocent people are convicted of crimes has come to light in a way that most of us could not have imagined at the time Elizabeth Loftus wrote the introduction to her seminal book on eyewitness identification. Recent events make it clear that people are convicted and sentenced, sometimes to death, for crimes that they did not commit. More than 180 people in the United States have been freed after postconviction DNA tests proved they did not commit the crime for which they were imprisoned (Weinstein, 2006). Hundreds more have been exonerated through other means of evidence (Gross, Jacoby, Matheson, Montgomery, & Patil, 2005). High-profile exonerations in child sex abuse cases have exposed miscarriages of justice in cases where individuals were charged and convicted of horrific acts of sexual abuse against children. It is difficult to accurately assess the number of factually innocent people who remain in prison. However, the sizeable number of exonerations should cause grave concern about the criminal justice system's capacity for error and give incentive to reforming the system. To that end, the legal field must draw from the research of other disciplines, particularly the field of psychology, to institute safeguards and procedures that will decrease the number of erroneous convictions.

More than any other scholar in the field of psychology, Elizabeth Loftus has focused her extraordinary career on how various influences on memory can affect the accuracy of the legal system's decision-making process. Although the reasons for wrongful convictions are multifaceted, errors caused by the malleability of human memory play a prominent role in conviction of the innocent. Every study of wrongful convictions has found that mistaken eyewitness identification is the leading cause of conviction of the innocent. Elizabeth Loftus's research has shown how eyewitness memory is susceptible to suggestion, how it can be shaped by postevent information, and how it can include reports of events that were never witnessed. The mind's ability to create memories has also been at issue in sex abuse prosecutions, where memories of abuse were allegedly repressed and then recovered through the use of therapy. Elizabeth Loftus's courageous research challenging the science of repressed memories has placed her at the center of professional and personal controversies. Throughout her prolific career, Elizabeth Loftus has faced these challenges because of her commitment to improving the truth-seeking mission of the legal system, and her compassion for those who are falsely accused and convicted by that system.

In this chapter, I discuss in more detail how the research and scholarship of Elizabeth Loftus and her colleagues has contributed to understanding the causes of wrongful convictions and to the mission of preventing erroneous convictions. First, I provide an overview of the history and research on wrongful convictions. Next, I examine the legal system's current theory of how memory works and discuss problems associated with eyewitness identification and repressed memories within the context of two case histories. I use the cases to highlight the importance of educating participants in the legal system about the malleability of memory and its adverse consequences on innocent defendants. Finally, I outline reforms that focus on changing the methods by which eyewitness evidence is gathered and changing the legal standards for admissibility of memory evidence. The primary challenge will be to take what has been learned from the invaluable contributions of Elizabeth Loftus and her colleagues and apply those findings toward changing the system in an effort to prevent conviction of the innocent.

## WRONGFUL CONVICTIONS

### Studies of Exonerations

The first legal scholar to examine wrongful convictions in depth was Yale Law Professor Edwin Borchard, whose book, *Convicting the Innocent,* was published in 1932. Professor Borchard, an expert in international law, brought a comparative perspective to the field of criminal law. In an early scholarly article, Professor Borchard urged the United States to follow the lead of European countries by recognizing the principle of indemnity for erroneous convictions (Borchard, 1941). In *Convicting the Innocent,* Professor Borchard examined 65 cases of wrongful convictions and found that mistaken identification, circumstantial evidence (from which erroneous inferences are drawn), and perjury were the leading causes of error. Professor Borchard's recommendations for reform are ones that continue to be advocated in today's legislatures and courts. He recommended that state and federal courts grant remuneration, as a matter of right, to innocent people who are released from prison. Professor Borchard also recommended new eyewitness identification procedures, limiting the use of a defendant's prior convictions, interrogating suspects in front of a magistrate or in the presence of "phonographic records," establishing state public defender offices for indigent defendants, allowing appellate courts broader authority to review findings of fact rather than restricting the court to issues of law, having expert witnesses in the employ of the public rather than the parties, and abolishing the death penalty in cases based only on circumstantial evidence.

The flaws in the United States' death penalty system were the focus of Radalet, Bedau, and Putman's book, *In Spite of Innocence,* published in 1992. The authors identified 416 cases, occurring between the years of 1900 and 1990, where the wrong person was convicted of murder or of capital rape. Approximately one third of those individuals were sentenced to death (see also Bedau & Radelet, 1987). The authors identified mistaken eyewitness testimony and perjury by government witnesses as the primary factors that led to the erroneous convictions. In the majority of the cases, the defendants were released due to "fickle good fortune," rather than through the rational workings of the criminal justice system. However, in 23 cases that the authors identified as false convictions, the defendants were executed. They conclude by endorsing the words of the Marquis de Lafayette: "Till the infallibility of human judgment shall have been proved to me, I shall demand the abolition of the death penalty."

In the early 1990s, postconviction DNA testing began to play an influential role in exonerating innocent prisoners. The Innocence Project at the Cardozo School of Law at Yeshiva University, founded by Barry J. Scheck and Peter J. Neufeld in 1992, was the first organization to use postconviction DNA testing to establish the innocence of falsely convicted individuals. Rapidly developing technology in DNA typing led to the ability to do tests on smaller samples of biological evidence as well as on samples that were previously considered too degraded for testing. The advent of mitochondrial DNA testing allowed forensic scientists to extract DNA from the shaft of a hair, whereas under prior methods of testing, the root of the hair was needed. As the Innocence Project achieved success in freeing individuals through postconviction DNA testing, it began to receive thousands of requests for legal assistance from inmates around the country. The first published study of DNA exonerations was a 1996 monograph by the U.S. Department of Justice (U.S.

National Institute of Justice, 1996). It reported on 28 cases of wrongful conviction that were overturned by postconviction DNA analysis. Of the 28 cases, 23 (or 82%) were based on mistaken eyewitness identification. In one case, the wrong man was convicted and sentenced to death on the basis of testimony from five mistaken eyewitnesses. A subsequent study of the first 62 exonerations in the United States found that 52 (or 84%) of the cases were based on mistaken eyewitness identification (Scheck, Neufeld, & Dwyer, 2000). At the time of publication of this article, the number of DNA exonerations in the United States has increased to 180 (Weinstein, 2006).

In 2005, Professor Samuel Gross and colleagues at the University of Michigan published a comprehensive study of exonerations occurring from 1989 to 2003 (Gross et al., 2005). The study identified 340 exonerations in that 15-year period, 144 cases of exonerations based on postconviction DNA testing, and 196 cases where individuals were freed through other types of evidence. The study confirms prior research on what errors lead to conviction of the innocent (see also Brandon & Davies, 1973; Frank & Frank, 1957; Rattner, 1988.). The leading causes of wrongful convictions are mistaken eyewitness identifications (present in almost 90% of the rape exonerations), perjury by government witnesses, and false confessions in cases of juvenile defendants and defendants with mental disabilities. The authors, though noting that the study was the most exhaustive list of exonerations to date, conceded that their final count of exonerations was conservative. Individuals freed in mass exonerations were not included in the study. Thus, the exonerations of at least 135 people who were framed and then cleared in the Tulia, Texas, and Los Angeles Rampart police scandals were not included in the total. In Tulia, Texas, 35 defendants convicted of drug offenses on the uncorroborated word of an undercover narcotics agent were pardoned after it was shown that the officer had lied, and that the drug sales had never occurred. In Los Angeles, at least 100 criminal defendants had their convictions vacated and dismissed upon proof that Los Angeles Rampart officers routinely lied in arrest reports, planted guns on suspects after shooting them, and fabricated evidence. The authors did not include the mass exonerations in the study because the cases' unique circumstances made the exonerations fundamentally different from the individual cases that were the focus of the study. Nor did the authors include more than 70 individuals whose convictions were overturned in child-care sex abuse cases. Although the study concludes that there is no doubt that most of these individuals in the child-care cases were falsely convicted, the complexity of the cases made it difficult for the authors to officially state that the defendants were exonerated.

The problems inherent in interviewing children—and the ability to suggest and shape their memories through questioning—are covered in an accompanying chapter (chap. 5, this volume). Those problems were the basis for overturning the convictions of many individuals who were prosecuted in high-profile cases and convicted of outrageous and incredible acts of sexual abuse against children (see Brito, 2000; Ceci & Bruck, 1993; Gross et al., 2005). One of the most far-reaching sex abuse investigations occurred in Wenatchee, Washington, in 1994 and 1995. The investigators used coercive interviewing techniques, as well as recovered-memory therapy to uncover past acts of alleged abuse. During 2 years, 43 adults were arrested on 29,726 charges of child sex abuse involving more than 60 children. The investigation began with allegations about incest in family homes and evolved into bizarre accounts of group sex rings where parents swapped children with other adults who stood in line to have sex with children, and where children sometimes fell into trances during the orgies. The allegations arose in sessions where interviewers used leading and suggestive questions, called children liars when they denied abuse or said they didn't know anything, promised children their cooperation would keep their parents out of prison, and told children about the accusations made by other children. Many children were sent to Pinecrest Hospital, an out-of-state psychiatric facility, to undergo recovered-memory therapy. Of the 26 people convicted in the sex abuse investigations, 17 were released from prison largely through the efforts of volunteers with the Innocence Project Northwest. The nine other defendants either received suspended sentences or served out their sentences (McMurtrie, 2002).

## How Many Innocent People Remain In Prison?

Although there is no precise figure for the number of inmates who are currently incarcerated for crimes they did not commit, perhaps the most compelling data comes from information collected by the FBI. In 1989, the FBI began doing DNA testing on biological evidence that it received from state and local police agencies investigating sexual assault and sexual assault homicide cases. The tests were generally requested in order to confirm or exclude the suspect(s) who had been arrested or indicted for the crime, usually as a result of eyewitness identification. In June of 1996, the FBI reported that out of the 10,000 cases it examined from 1989 to 1996, the agency had excluded the primary suspect in 25% of the cases in which DNA results could be obtained (U.S. National Institute of Justice, 1996). Even taking into account the possibility that some of the prime suspects excluded could have been guilty and falsely excluded (because the perpetrator wore a condom or did not ejaculate), the exclusion rate is extraordinary.

The logical inference from the FBI data is that thousands of individuals would have been wrongfully convicted in the United States from 1989 to 1996, had it not been for the DNA testing conducted by the agency. The implication for those who were convicted prior to the routine use of DNA tests in criminal investigations is also striking. Thousands of inmates, convicted when DNA testing did not exist, could now prove their innocence if they could obtain tests of critical biological evidence. Another study also concluded that, based on the rate of exonerations between 1989 to 2003, the total number of cases in which innocent people were convicted of crimes in the last 15 years in America has to be in the thousands, perhaps tens of thousands (Gross et al., 2005).

# THE CRIMINAL JUSTICE SYSTEM'S THEORY OF MEMORY: SCIENCE OR SUPPOSITION?

How is it that the criminal justice system has condemned so many innocent people to prison? Why is it that eyewitness evidence continues to be a leading cause of conviction of the innocent? Although the DNA exonerations have confirmed, with scientific certainty, that eyewitness testimony is subject to error and that memory is malleable, DNA testing is not a panacea for preventing wrongful convictions. The number of suspects in the United States who become defendants on the basis of eyewitness identification has been conservatively estimated at 77,000 suspects per year (Wells et al., 1998). In most crimes that involve eyewitness evidence—murders, robberies, burglaries, and thefts—the perpetrator does not leave any biological evidence at the scene of the crime. In many child abuse cases, and in all cases relying on evidence of recovered memories, the evidence consists only of the witnesses's memory for the event. How can the legal system draw from the research of psychology and the findings of the studies on exonerations to enact legal safeguards and procedures that ensure that eyewitness testimony identifying a person or describing an event is accurate?

## Science: Adopting a Theory of Memory as Trace Evidence

Wells and Loftus advocate that the criminal justice system treat memory evidence similarly to the way it treats other types of trace evidence admitted at trial to identify the perpetrator of the crime (Wells & Loftus, 2003; see also Wells, 1995.). Like fingerprints, fiber, or blood, memory evidence can be contaminated, lost, destroyed, or otherwise made to produce results that lead to an incorrect reconstruction of the event in question. Additionally, the method used to gather memory evidence, just as the method by which fingerprints or blood evidence is collected, can affect the accuracy of the results.

Wells and Loftus suggest that one of the reasons the criminal justice system has failed to adopt a scientific model for eyewitness evidence is because eyewitness testimony was commonly used in criminal investigations long before any scientific studies of eyewitnesses had been conducted. When eyewitness identification testimony was first introduced into court as evidence against the accused, there was no scientific protocol in place for gathering the evidence. In contrast, with other types of physical evidence such as DNA typing, testing methods were first developed in scientific laboratories. Protocols for gathering the evidence were then adopted by law enforcement, and the validity of the scientific methodology was litigated in court prior to admitting the evidence and presenting it to the jury. If photo spreads and lineups had been invented by scientists before their use was common, law enforcement agencies might be following a scientific protocol for gathering the evidence, which would include carefully worded instructions, double-blind procedures, and thorough documentation of identification procedures (Wells & Loftus, 2003).

Though eyewitness identification evidence has been part of the criminal justice system for centuries, the use of repressed-memory evidence is a relatively recent phenomenon in the criminal justice system. The first time repressed-memory evidence was used in a criminal trial in the United States was in 1990 (Loftus, 1993). One would expect the legal system to evaluate the scientific worth of this new type of evidence before allowing jurors to consider the evidence. (See chap. 8, this volume, for a discussion of the scientific research on repressed memories.) Instead, courts have taken diametrically opposed positions about whether a scientific basis exists for the concept of memory repression. In some cases, courts have held: "The phenomenon of recovery of repressed memories has not yet reached the point where we may perceive these particular recovered memories as reliable" (*State v. Hungerford,* 1997). And in others, courts have allowed the evidence to serve as the sole basis for a criminal conviction (Loftus & Ketcham, 1994).

One reason for this piecemeal approach to memory evidence is that the criminal justice system lacks a focused theory of memory (Wells & Loftus, 2003). The criminal justice system either does not have any unified theory of how memory works, or it is operating under several different theories of how memory functions, including ones based on supposition rather than science.

## Supposition: Memory Is Retrieved, Not Reconstructed

Wells and Loftus suggest that one of the assumptions the criminal justice system may be operating under is that a memory for an event is stored in an individual's mind where it remains unchanged until it is retrieved and played back, much like videotape, through the telling of the event (Wells & Loftus, 2003). Under this theory, a memory of an event cannot be tainted by information that the individual receives after the event. Instead, the failure of memory comes about only through the act of forgetting, in a method that mimics an erasure of the videotape.

Research has established that the process of retaining and retrieving memories is much different from playing a videotape, and that memories for events can be shaped and influenced by external factors. For example, Elizabeth Loftus has shown through her research how leading questions can influence a person's memories (see Loftus, 1996, for a summary of the research). Memories can also be influenced by information that is received after the event in a process called the "misinformation effect" (Loftus & Hoffman, 1989; see also chap. 4, this volume). Through exposure to misinformation, people have recalled nonexistent broken glass and tape recorders, a clean-shaven man as having a mustache, and a barn in a bucolic scene that contained no buildings at all (Loftus & Ketcham, 1991). Loftus and her colleagues have also been able to plant false childhood memories in subjects including being lost in a shopping mall, meeting Bugs Bunny (a Warner Brothers character) at a Disney resort, and witnessing demonic possession as a child (see Loftus, 2003, for a summary of the research).

What are the consequences of the legal system's failure to adopt a theory of memory that is based on a scientific model? The magnitude of the problem of conviction of the innocent poignantly establishes that they are severe. In order to appreciate the critical need for reform, I would like to describe the cases of Larry Youngblood and the Cunninghams to illustrate problems with eyewitness identification and repressed memories.

## LARRY YOUNGBLOOD: THE POWER OF AN EYEWITNESS

Most criminal law practitioners know *Arizona v. Youngblood* (1988) as the leading U.S. Supreme Court case on police destruction of evidence. However, it is also a tragic example of the powerful impact mistaken eyewitness evidence has on a jury. Mr. Youngblood was convicted of child molestation, sexual assault and kidnapping solely on the basis of the eyewitness testimony of the 10½-year-old victim. The dissent, citing the work of Elizabeth Loftus, warned against the "inherently suspect qualities" of eyewitness testimony, particularly an identification made by a child. In contrast, the majority described the evidence as "overwhelming."

The case arose on October 29, 1983, when a middle-aged African American man abducted a 10 ½-year-old White boy. The boy had been at a church service and left the service to go to a carnival behind the church. He was taken from the carnival by his assailant and over the next hour-and-a-half the assailant molested and sodomized the boy. After threatening to kill the victim if he told anyone about the attack, the assailant dropped the victim off at the carnival. The victim, who was described as a very observant youngster, told law enforcement that his assailant was a Black man named Damian or Carl who had greasy gray hair, facial hair, no facial scars, and whose right eye was almost completely white. He also gave details about the car driven by the assailant, describing it as a white, medium-size, two-door sedan with a passenger door that did not work. The car had a loud muffler, country music was playing on its radio, and the car was started using a key (*State v. Youngblood,* 1986).

Immediately after the assault, the victim's mother took him to a hospital where a physician gathered evidence in a sexual assault kit. The kit was given to the police along with the boy's underwear and T-shirt. The rape kit was secured in a refrigerator at the police station, but the clothing was not refrigerated or frozen. Because the police did not properly store the evidence, it degraded to the point where serology tests could not be performed on the semen stains on the boy's clothing *(Arizona v. Youngblood,* 1988*)*.

The identification procedure took place 9 days after the attack. A police detective came to the victim's school and told him that the police had arrested the man who raped him. The detective asked the boy to pick out his assailant from a photographic lineup, telling him that the perpetrator might not be in the lineup. The photomontage consisted of three photographs where the individual's left eye was whited out, and three with the right eye whited out. After looking at the pictures by holding them very close to his face, the victim identified Mr. Youngblood as his assailant, saying he was "pretty sure." He then put on his glasses and again identified Larry Youngblood as his attacker. At trial, the boy testified that he was able to see his assailant, had a good chance to look at his face, and, based on that experience and the time he had to look at the assailant, he was positive Larry Youngblood was the man who raped him (*Arizona v. Youngblood Brief*, 1986).

At trial, the jurors saw that Larry Youngblood was, at the time of the incident, a 30-year-old Black male with dry black hair, a scar on his forehead, and a bad left eye. They heard from Mr. Youngblood and other witnesses that Mr. Youngblood's car was not operative on the night of the incident, that when it was working it ran quietly, that the radio did not work, and that the car could be started only by using a screwdriver. The jurors saw that Mr. Youngblood walked with a noticeable limp due to a foot injury that he received as a child in an automobile accident. The jurors were told that the police seized Mr. Youngblood's car and that their examination of the car failed to reveal any fingerprints, hair, or clothing fibers from the victim. They learned that the police did not have the victim view the car, nor did they check to see whether the car radio worked or whether the car could be started with a key. Instead, the police turned the car over to a wrecking company where it was dismantled. The jurors were told that the police had mishandled the physical evidence and they learned what could have been shown by tests had the samples been tested shortly after they were gathered or had the clothing been refrigerated. The judge instructed the jury that if they found that the state had lost or destroyed evidence they could infer that the evidence would have been favorable to Mr. Youngblood (*Arizona v. Youngblood Brief*, 1988).

The jury convicted Mr. Youngblood. On appeal, Mr. Youngblood argued that his due process rights were violated when the state failed to preserve semen samples that could have been tested to identify the perpetrator of the crimes. The Arizona Supreme Court agreed and reversed Mr. Youngblood's conviction. However, the Supreme Court reinstated the conviction, ruling that Mr. Youngblood had not shown that the police had acted in bad faith when they destroyed the potentially exculpatory evidence (*Arizona v. Youngblood Brief*, 1988).

Mr. Youngblood served the term of his 8-year sentence and after being paroled was arrested in 2000, for failing to register as a sexual predator. Mr. Youngblood's new attorneys discovered a swab of semen that had been retrieved from the victim's skin at the time the crime occurred (Neufeld, 2001). The sample was too small to have been tested using the inferior technology that existed at the time of trial. Mr. Youngblood's attorneys sought DNA testing and as a precondition to testing, the police forced Mr. Youngblood to sign an agreement giving up his right to sue the police (Simon, 2003). When the swab was tested, Larry Youngblood was exonerated. In 2001, the DNA profile was entered into a national felon database. It inculpated Walter Cruise, a man who had a deformed eye and who was serving time in Texas on a drug offense. Cruise, who also had two prior child sex convictions in Texas, was convicted of the crime and sentenced to 24 years in prison (Teibel, 2002).

## Confidence and Accuracy

Mr. Youngblood's case illustrates that jurors place a great deal of faith in the accuracy of a positive eyewitness identification. As Elizabeth Loftus wrote in *Eyewitness Testimony:*

> "All the evidence points rather strikingly to the conclusion that there is almost nothing more convincing than a live human being who takes the stand, points a finger at the defendant, and says, 'That's the one! '"

In Mr. Youngblood's case, the jurors were willing to disregard differences between the physical features of the assailant and Mr. Youngblood, and differences in the description of the cars driven by the assailant and Mr. Youngblood. They were willing to overlook the shoddy police work in the case and the police destruction of potentially exculpatory evidence. The jury convicted even after being instructed by the judge that if they found that the state had allowed evidence to be destroyed or lost, they could infer that the evidence would have been exculpatory to Mr. Youngblood and unfavorable to the state. In the end, the positive, confident, identification was all that mattered.

In one of her earliest studies on eyewitness identification, Elizabeth Loftus found that jurors give eyewitness testimony a great deal of weight even when the evidence is suspect (Loftus, 1974). In this study, the mock jurors were given a description of a robbery at a grocery store in which two victims were killed. The jurors were then divided into three different groups. One group was told that there were no eyewitnesses to the crime. The second group was told that an eyewitness, the store clerk, testified that he saw the defendant shoot the two victims, although the defense attorney claimed he was mistaken. The third group of jurors heard that the store clerk's eyewitness testimony was discredited by defense evidence that the clerk had not been wearing his glasses on the day of the robbery and that his vision was too poor to allow him to see the face of the robber from where he stood. In the first group of jurors, 18% arrived at a verdict of guilty. In the second group, with the single eyewitness, 72% voted guilty. The third group, which heard testimony discrediting the eyewitness account, still voted by 68% for conviction. The study suggested that jurors give eyewitness testimony a great deal of weight, even when there are legitimate questions about the credibility of the testimony.

Other studies have gone on to examine the effect that a confident eyewitness has on a jury and to test the relationship between confidence and accuracy. In fact, this issue is one of the most researched questions in all of scientific eyewitness literature (see Wells et al., 1998, for a summary of the research). The studies establish that the confidence an eyewitness expresses in his or her identification is uniformly the most powerful determinant of whether or not observers of that testimony will believe the eyewitness has made an accurate identification. Other factors that are known to genuinely influence accuracy—such as disguises worn by the perpetrator and a victim's focus on a weapon during an incident—are not relied on by jurors as much as eyewitness confidence. This phenomenon is particularly troubling because extensive research has established that high confidence on the part of an eyewitness does not necessarily correlate with high accuracy. Instead, such confidence can come from external sources and postevent information.

An early study conducted by Elizabeth Loftus and colleagues found that witnesses become more confident in the accuracy of their selections when they are questioned repeatedly about the event (Hastie, Landsman, & Loftus, 1978). The findings have been replicated in more recent studies (Shaw, 1996; Shaw & McClure, 1996; Turtle & Yuille, 1994). Research has also shown that confidence increases when the eyewitness receives confirming feedback (e.g., "You picked the right one") from the line-up administrator (Wells & Bradfield, 1998). Given that mock jurors believe confident incorrect identification testimony just as frequently as confident correct testimony, their reliance on confidence is a matter of considerable concern and importance (see Wells et al., 1998, for a summary of the research). Jurors are not the only ones who are uneducated about the psychological research regarding the weak relationship between confidence and accuracy. Surveys of public defenders, prosecutors, and private defense attorneys indicate that the substantial majority of lawyers also believe that confident eyewitnesses are more likely to be accurate in their identification (see Wells et al., 1998, for a summary of the research). Nor do judges fare much better in their understanding of the psychological research on eyewitness confidence. A recent survey of judges found that 34% of the judges surveyed believed that eyewitness confidence was a good predictor of accuracy, 33% disagreed with the statement, and 34% neither agreed nor disagreed (Wise & Safer, 2003).

### Cross-Race Identifications

Mr. Youngblood's case also illustrates the problems that exist with cross-racial identifications. Extensive research has established that it is more difficult for people to identify individual members of other races than it is for them to identify members of their own race (Shapiro & Penrod, 1986). The cross-race effect is substantial across races, as studies of eyewitness identifications made by Whites, Blacks and Mexican Americans have established (Platz & Hosch, 1988). However, one study of the collection of research found that the cross-racial effect was stronger for Whites than for Blacks (Anthony, Cooper, & Mullen, 1992).

Errors in cross-racial identifications have played an invidious role in false convictions. Gross and colleagues found that in about 50% of rape exonerations, the defendants were Black men who were misidentified by White victims. That was true despite the fact that fewer than 10% of rapes in the United States involve a Black perpetrator and a White victim. The study confirmed that Black men are greatly overrepresented among defendants and particularly among defendants who are falsely convicted and exonerated for rape (Gross et al., 2005).

## THE CUNNINGHAMS: FLOATING, RECOVERED MEMORIES

One of the families caught up in the Wenatchee, Washington, sex-ring maelstrom was the Cunningham family. In June of 1994, Henry and Connie Cunningham lived in Wenatchee with three of their four daughters, ages 19, 17, and 15. Henry Cunningham worked as a vocational rehabilitation counselor and Connie Cunningham was a homemaker. However, the Cunningham family was not without its problems. Mr. Cunningham was seeing a psychiatrist for treatment of a bipolar/manic depression disorder. And in May of 1994, Jessika (age 15), who had behavioral problems, attempted suicide. Her parents took her against her wishes to Pinecrest Hospital for inpatient treatment and during the course of the treatment, an angry Jessika revealed sexual abuse that had allegedly occurred 12 years earlier (*In re the Personal Restraint of Henry Cunningham, 1998*).

After Jessika's disclosure, Henry Cunningham contacted the police on the advice of his psychiatrist. Mr. Cunningham wanted to straighten out the matter and let the police know he was innocent. Before going to the police station, Mr. Cunningham took several Klonopin, a potent antianxiety medication, to calm himself. The interview did not go as Mr. Cunningham had expected. The detective, rather than accepting Mr. Cunningham's denial of the accusations, began interrogating him in a threatening and coercive manner. After 7½ hours of interrogation, Mr. Cunningham signed a six-page statement, typed by the detective. The statement detailed Mr. Cunningham's daily sexual abuse of his four daughters, as well as his wife's participation in the abuse. Mr. Cunningham was booked into jail on 900 counts of sexual abuse and his wife Connie was later charged with 66 counts of child incest and rape (Schneider & Barber, 1998; *In re the Personal Restraint of Henry Cunningham,* 1998).

The Cunningham's other daughters, Sarah and Jennifer, were then questioned about the abuse. They denied that they had been victims of sexual abuse and asked to see their father's confession. The detective did not allow them to read the confession, but told them that their father had admitted to many acts of abuse against all four of his daughters. The girls eventually gave statements that mirrored the language contained in their father's confession describing daily acts of abuse at home and at their father's place of work (*In re the Personal Restraint of Henry Cunningham,* 1998).

Six days after the interrogation, the detective and a child protective service official interviewed Jessika at Pinecrest Hospital. The interview began with the detective telling Jessika that her father had already confessed to committing various acts involving her and her sisters, and asking what, if anything, had happened to her. Jessika replied that she could only remember some things but thought she might have been hypnotized by her father and made to forget events. She relayed that Henry Cunningham knew how to hypnotize her and her sisters and he would swing a chain back and forth in front of them or move his index finger back and forth to hypnotize them. Jessika also stated that her father had taught her how to do mind control over animals (*In re the Personal Restraint of Henry Cunningham,* 1998).

Rather than question Jessika's stability, the detective continued to press her to disclose abuse. He told her that her father had already given a confession, detailing certain events that involved her and her sisters, and that if she was able to corroborate his statement he would be sent away for a long time. Jessika then disclosed sexual abuse that occurred "probably every day or maybe just sometimes once a week" (*In re the Personal Restraint of Henry Cunningham,* 1998).

At Connie Cunningham's trial, Sarah testified that her father had been molesting the girls since they were about 2. Although she did not initially recall any abuse when first interviewed (including an act of abuse that occurred the night before the interview) she stated: "Well, after I had calmed down from such a tragic event, my memory started coming into play; and I relaxed and started talking. Because this had happened—been going on for so long, I had blocked out so much, you know. So I just relaxed and, you know, let it come to me" (*In re the Personal Restraint of Henry Cunningham,* 1998).

When asked about the "blanking out" technique, Sarah said that she had not come to her own conclusions about blocking or blanking out memories, but instead had been told about the technique by several different counselors. She testified: "It's a defense mechanism, to where you use it to kind of protect yourself. You dissociate yourself with the situation. Kind of just—kind of drift off, blank it out. I don't—I'm not sure how else to explain it. You just try to dissociate yourself with the situation, to make it easier" (*In re the Personal Restraint of Henry Cunningham,* 1998).

The girls testified that they had "fragments" and "fractions" of memories, and that their memories were also "floating," and "disjointed." They testified that they chose when to bring the memory into play and that the police had "triggered" memories of sexual abuse by reading from their father's confession. One of the girls testified that she did not remember incidents that had taken place 1 year prior, when she was 18 and 19, from start to finish because she did not "wish to remember them" (*In re the Personal Restraint of Henry Cunningham,* 1998).

The girls also testified that they were able to repress certain memories. The ability to repress memories came and went and on some days they were able to "repress them more than others." Jennifer testified: "Sometimes my memory comes back at odd times. I don't try and control when they come back." When asked if on some days she recalled things and other days she didn't, Jennifer replied: "That is a good possibility, yes" (*In re the Personal Restraint of Henry Cunningham,* 1998).

On the basis of the floating, fragmented, disjointed memories that were triggered by their father's confession, the jury convicted Connie Cunningham. She was sentenced to 46 ½ years in prison. Henry Cunningham had pled guilty the morning he and his wife were scheduled for trial, after his defense attorney advised him that it was the only way he could save his wife from being convicted. His defense attorney gave this advice without having secured any type of plea offer from the prosecutor; much less any promise that the prosecutor would offer leniency to his wife based on his guilty plea. Henry Cunningham was sentenced to 47 years in prison (*In re the Personal Restraint of Henry Cunningham,* 1998).

During postconviction proceedings in Henry Cunningham's case, his attorneys called upon the expertise of Elizabeth Loftus. Dr. Loftus provided expert evidence on a pro bono basis. After reviewing the girls' testimony and the police reports in this case, Dr. Loftus noted that initially the daughters denied being victims of sexual abuse or said that they did not recall any abuse. Their father's confession was then relayed to the daughters to "trigger" their memory and they were told that they merely had to "corroborate" things that had already been established in the confession. Both Sarah and Jennifer testified that they had blanked-out or repressed memories and that they had recalled events of sexual abuse only after therapy sessions with counselors where they were told about the concept of repressing memories. Dr. Loftus discussed the problems associated with the use of recovered memories of child sexual abuse and concluded that there were serious reliability problems with the memories that were repressed and later recovered by the daughters (*In re the Personal Restraint of Henry Cunningham,* 1998).

The volunteer lawyers and law students working with the Innocence Project Northwest also uncovered other exculpatory evidence during the course of the postconviction proceedings. The janitors who cleaned the building where Henry Cunningham worked (and who lived adjacent to the building) never saw any evidence to support the claims that he sexually abused his daughters at work on a daily basis. The psychiatrist treating Mr. Cunningham informed the court that Mr. Cunningham's psychiatric problems made him particularly susceptible to the detective's coercive interrogation techniques. Jessika Cunningham also provided information that her sister had been pressured into making allegations of abuse and had lied about the abuse. Jessika herself could not trust her own memory, which had been muddled by psychoanalysis and long interrogations, enough to say what truly happened to her (*In re the Personal Restraint of Henry Cunningham,* 1998).

Henry Cunningham's conviction was overturned on the basis of the newly discovered evidence and because his attorney's deficient representation—including his failure to consult an expert on false memories—violated Mr. Cunningham's constitutional right to effective assistance of counsel. The state elected not to retry him. However, Henry Cunningham had already served 5 years of a 47-year sentence (New suit in Wenatchee Cases, 2000). Connie Cunningham's conviction was also overturned on appeal and she was freed after serving 3 years in prison (Schneider & Barber, 1998). The investigation that shook the community of Wenatchee took a devastating toll on the Cunningham family. They lost their home and all of their savings; the two younger daughters were placed in foster care and did not finish high school; Connie Cunningham struggles with physical disabilities resulting from improper treatment of a stroke she suffered in prison; and the Cunninghams divorced (Schneider & Barber, 1998).

## THE NEED FOR EDUCATION

Each case of wrongful conviction has a narrative similar to the tragedy experienced by Mr. Youngblood and the Cunninghams. The compelling power of the stories of the exonerated has served to educate the public about the societal problem of conviction of the innocent (see Blank & Jensen, 2004; Scheck, Neufeld, & Dwyer, 2000; Simon, 2003). They show that false convictions have repercussions beyond those experienced by the individual who is accused and convicted. In cases of misidentification, such as Mr. Youngblood's, an innocent person is convicted and the real perpetrator remains free. During the misidentified person's incarceration, the real perpetrator will often commit more crimes, resulting in additional suffering for victims and families. In cases involving false memories, such as the Cunninghams, families are torn apart by the accusations and do not reconcile even after the convicted are exonerated.

Elizabeth Loftus's influential books on eyewitness identification and repressed memories have also been of critical importance in educating members of the legal community about the incalculable suffering caused to individuals who are accused and convicted on false and mistaken memory evidence. The scholarship of *Eyewitness Testimony* has been cited in several U.S. Supreme Court opinions and *The Myth of Repressed Memory* has been discussed in most of the state and federal court cases considering recovered memory evidence. In *Eyewitness Testimony, Civil and Criminal,* Elizabeth Loftus and James M. Doyle (1997) offer the criminal defense practitioner an overview of the research on mistaken eyewitness identification and a step-by-step analysis of how to challenge eyewitness testimony during each part of the trial.

Elizabeth Loftus has also increased awareness of issues regarding memory evidence by consulting as an expert on memory in hundreds of cases (Loftus, 2003). Research has shown that expert testimony on memory and eyewitness identification is the only legal safeguard that is effective in sensitizing jurors to eyewitness errors (Penrod & Cutler, 1999). Cross-examination, usually a powerful tool for exposing lies, is not particularly effective when used against eyewitnesses who believe they are telling the truth (Wells, Lindsay, & Ferguson, 1979). Nor do jury instructions provide much assistance in educating jurors about the accuracy of eyewitness identification (Greene, 1988; Ramirez, Zemba, & Geiselman, 1996). Despite evidence that expert witness testimony can serve as a valuable educational tool, the majority of courts have excluded expert testimony on eyewitness evidence and appellate courts have sustained the exclusions (Giannelli & Imwinkelried, 1999). Many judges exclude eyewitness expert testimony because they are not informed about how eyewitness factors and procedures affect the accuracy of an eyewitness identification (Wise & Safer, 2003).

Other difficulties also counter the effectiveness and value of expert eyewitness testimony. There are a limited number of experts who work in the field and there are considerable expenses involved in expert witness testimony (Kassin et al., 2001; Wells et al., 1998). Additionally, when a criminal defense attorney offers expert testimony within the context of an adversarial trial, prosecutors will contest the admissibility and the validity of the defense expert testimony. A recent article in *Prosecutor* noted that the "growing momentum of the innocence project has drawn national attention to the occasional errors that eyewitnesses make" and offered strategies for challenging the expert testimony, rigorously cross-examining the expert, and introducing opposing expert testimony (Cutler, 2003).

However, expert eyewitness testimony is not the only means by which to educate the legal community about how memory works. Increasingly, efforts have turned toward expanding educational efforts beyond the confines of the adversarial process. The focus has shifted toward bringing together members from across the spectrum of the criminal justice system to work on issues of education and reform. The American Judicature Society (AJS) recently convened a national conference to examine the problem of wrongful convictions, in recognition of the fact that false convictions have damaged trust and faith in the justice system. The

AJS assembled teams of defense attorneys, police chiefs, prosecuting attorneys, victim advocacy groups, innocence project directors, and academics to create strategic plans for reform within their region (Sobel, 2002). These efforts recognize the importance of educating participants in the legal system about the malleability of memory and the need to integrate the psychological sciences into law and courtroom practice (Loftus, 2002).

## THE NEED FOR REFORM

### Changing Methods by Which Eyewitness Evidence Is Gathered

Part of the educational process is to promote the need to adopt a scientific model of gathering eyewitness evidence. A number of studies have made specific recommendations about procedural safeguards that could significantly reduce the number of erroneous eyewitness identifications without affecting the number of accurate identifications (e.g., Turtle, Lindsay, & Wells, 2003; U.S. National Institute of Justice, 1999; Wells et al., 1998). The recommendations have focused primarily on five guidelines:

1. The person who conducts the lineup or photospread should not be aware of which member of the lineup or photospread is the suspect.
2. Eyewitnesses should be explicitly told that the person in question might not be in the lineup or photospread and therefore should not feel that they must make an identification. They should also be told that the person administering the lineup does not know which person is the suspect in the case.
3. The suspect should not stand out in the lineup or photospread as being different from the distracters based on the eyewitnesses' previous description of the culprit or based on other factors that would draw extra attention to the suspect.
4. A clear statement should be taken from the eyewitness at the time of the identification and prior to any feedback as to his or her confidence that the identified person is the actual culprit.
5. Sequential lineups and photospreads are preferred over simultaneous lineups and photospreads (Turtle, Lindsay, & Wells, 2003; Wells et al., 1998).

For example, the simple procedures of having the lineup administrated by an officer who is unaware of which lineup member is the suspect and using sequential, rather than simultaneous lineups, could greatly reduce the number of erroneous eyewitness identifications without significantly affecting the number of accurate identifications (Wells et al., 1998, summarizing research). Many law enforcement agencies in Canada and the United States (Ottawa-Carlton, New Jersey, Boston, Minneapolis) have adopted these recommendations in a commitment toward reducing the number of erroneous convictions (Ehlers, 2005).

## Changing the Standard for Admissibility of Eyewitness Identification

The powerful impact of eyewitness confidence on an observer's assessment of accuracy, as well as the research that challenges the correlation between confidence and accuracy, was discussed earlier. One reason the legal system places such emphasis on confidence is that it is one of the factors that the U.S. Supreme Court ruled must be considered in judging the reliability of an identification. In *Neil v. Biggers* (1972), the Court enunciated a two-prong test for determining the admissibility of eyewitness identification. The first prong asks whether or not the eyewitness identification procedure was unduly suggestive. If it was suggestive, the court must determine under the second prong of the test whether or not the identification is nonetheless reliable. In assessing reliability, the judge should consider: (a) the opportunity of the witness to view the criminal at the time of the crime, (b) the witness's degree of attention, (c) the accuracy of the witness's prior description of the criminal, (d) *the level of certainty demonstrated at the confrontation,* and (e) the time between the crime and the confrontation. In the 30 years since *Neil v. Biggers* was decided, there has been a considerable expansion in understanding how memory works. The judiciary should reevaluate the reliability factors and base the standard of reliability and admissibility on criteria that integrate the findings of psychological and social research.

## Adopting a Scientific Model for Admissibility of Repressed Memory Evidence

The 1990s saw an increase in the number of reports of cases of previously repressed memories of childhood abuse (see chap. 8, this volume; Loftus, 1993, 2002; Loftus & Ketcham, 1994). Whether or not the allegations lead to criminal charges depends partly on whether the statute of limitations for filing a criminal charge has passed. For some crimes, such as murder or manslaughter, there is no statute of limitations. Many states have enacted legislation that significantly augments the time period under which criminal charges can be brought in child sex abuse prosecutions (Loftus, Paddock, & Guernsey, 1996; Pudelski, 2004).

Because of the questions that exist regarding the accuracy of repressed and recovered memories, courts should engage in a careful analysis of the underlying science of repressed memories. The New Hampshire Supreme Court has offered a model by which the admissibility of this type of evidence should be judged. In *State v. Hungerford* (1997), the court conducted a 2-week admissibility hearing to determine whether repressed memory evidence should be admitted in a sexual assault prosecution. Elizabeth Loftus testified at the hearing and her research on repressed memories was cited extensively in the court's opinion. The New Hampshire court lists eight factors that trial courts should consider in order to assess the reliability of recovered memories:

(a) the level of peer review and publication of the phenomenon of repression and recovery of memories, (b) whether the phenomenon has been generally accepted in the psychological community, (c) whether the phenomenon may be and has been empirically tested, (d) the potential or known rate of recovered memories that are false, (e) the age of the witness at the time the event or events occurred, (f) the length of time between the event and the recovery of the memory, (g) the presence or absence of objective, verifiable, corroborative evidence of the event, and (h) the circumstances attendant to the witness's recovery of the memory, that is, whether the witness was engaged in therapy or some other process seeking to recover memories or likely to result in recovered memories.

Although the *Hungerford* court noted that someday research might develop sufficiently to support the conclusion that repressed and recovered memories were reliable, it found: "That day is not here." Trial courts considering repressed or recovered memory evidence should follow the standards set forth by *Hungerford* to assess whether or not the evidence should be admitted.

## CONCLUSION

The magnitude of the problem of conviction of the innocent has been likened to a train wreck or a plane crash within the criminal justice system. When such an accident occurs in the United States, the National Transportation Safety Board convenes an immediate inquiry to examine what went wrong and, most important, what can be done to correct the problem and prevent future problems. Scheck and Neufeld have proposed that the National Traffic Safety Board model be used to form Innocence Commissions that will conduct investigations into erroneous convictions and propose reforms (Scheck & Neufeld, 2002). Interestingly, Elizabeth Loftus's early research in the field of memory also had a traffic theme. The U.S. Department of Transportation funded some of her studies on the observations of eyewitnesses to automobile accidents (Loftus, 1979). In keeping with the traffic theme and metaphor, Elizabeth Loftus has suggested the formation of a National Memory Safety Board to study why the failing of memory has led to conviction of the innocent. In her words, "It has a nice ring" (Loftus, 2002). I propose, in tribute to the remarkable and generous contributions that Elizabeth Loftus has made on behalf of those falsely accused and convicted of crimes, the formation of a "Loftus National Memory Safety Board." Now that truly has a nice ring.

## REFERENCES

*Arizona v. Youngblood,* 488 U.S. 51 (1988).

*Arizona v. Youngblood,* Appellate Brief for Petitioners, 1986 WL 727352 (1986).

*Arizona v. Youngblood,* Appellate Brief for Respondent, 1988 WL 1025800 (1988).

Anthony, T., Cooper, C., & Mullen, B. (1992). Cross-racial facial identification: A social cognitive integration. *Personality and Social Psychology Bulletin, 18,* 296–301.

Bedeau H. A., & Radelet, M. L. (1987). Miscarriages of justice in potentially capital cases. *Stanford Law Review, 40,* 21–179.

Blank, J., & Jensen, E. (2004). *The exonerated: A play.* New York: Faber & Faber.

Borchard, E. M. (1932). *Convicting the innocent: Errors of criminal justice.* New Haven, CT: Yale University Press.

Borchard, E. M. (1941). State indemnity for errors of criminal justice. *Boston University Law Review, 21,* 201–11.

Brandon, R., & Davies, C. (1973). *Wrongful imprisonment: Mistaken convictions and their consequences.* Hamden, CT: Archeon Books.

Brito, T. L. (2000). Paranoid parents, phantom menaces, and the culture of fear. *Wisconsin Law Review, 2000,* 519–520.

Ceci, S. J., & Bruck, M. (1993). The suggestibility of children's recollections: An historical review and synthesis. *Psychological Bulletin, 113,* 403–439.

Cutler, B. L. (2003). Strategies for mitigating the impact of eyewitness experts. *Prosecutor, 37,* 19–20.

Ehlers, S. (2005, April). Eyewitness identification: State law reform. The Champion, p. 34–36.

Frank, J., & Frank, B. (1957). *Not guilty.* Garden City, NY: Doubleday.

Giannelli, P. C. & Imwinkelried, E. J. (1999, with updated supplements). *Scientific evidence* (3rd ed.). Charlottesville, VA: Lexis Law.

Greene, E. (1988). Judge's instructions on eyewitness testimony: Evaluation and revision. *Journal of Applied Psychology, 18,* 252–276.

Gross, S. R., Jacoby, J., Matheson, D. J., Montgomery, N., & Patil, S. (2005). Exonerations in the United States: 1989 through 2003. *Journal of Criminal Law and Criminology, 95,* 523–560.

Hastie, R., Landsman, R., & Loftus, E. F. (1978). Eyewitness testimony: The dangers of guessing. *Jurimetrics Journal, 18,* 1–8.

*In re the Personal Restraint of Henry Cunningham* (1998). Petitioner's brief (on file with author).

Kassin, S. M., Tubb, V. A., & Hosch, H. M., & Memon, A. (2001). On the "general acceptance" of eyewitness testimony research: A new survey of the experts. *American Psychologist, 56,* 405–416.

Loftus, E. F. (1974). Reconstructing memory: The incredible eyewitness. *Psychology Today, 8,* 116–119.

Loftus, E. F. (1993). The reality of repressed memories. *American Psychologist,* 48, 518-537.

Loftus, E. F. (1996). *Eyewitness testimony* (Reprinted). Cambridge, MA: Harvard University Press. (Original work published 1979).

Loftus, E. F. (2002). Memory faults and fixes. *Issues in Science and Technology, 18*(4), 41–50.

Loftus, E. F. (1993). The reality of repressed memories. *American Psychologist, 48,* 518–537.

Loftus, E. F. (2003). Make-believe memories. *American Psychologist, 58,* 864–873.

Loftus, E. F., & Doyle, J. M. (1997). *Eyewitness testimony: Civil & criminal* (3rd ed.). Charlottesville, VA: Lexis Law.

Loftus, E. F., & Hoffman, H. G. (1989). Misinformation and memory: The creation of memory. *Journal of Experimental Psychology: General, 118,* 100–104.

Loftus, E. F., & Ketcham, K. (1991). *Witness for the defense: The accused, the eyewitness, and the expert who puts memory on trial.* New York: St. Martin's Press.

Loftus, E. F., & Ketcham, K. (1994). *The myth of repressed memory.* New York: St. Martin's Press.

Loftus, E. F., Paddock, J. R., & Guernsey, T. F. (1996). Patient–psychotherapist privilege: Access to clinical records in the tangled web of repressed memory litigation. *University of Richmond Law Review, 30,* 109–154.

McMurtrie, J. (2002). Justice —a cautionary tale—the Wenatchee cases. *Butterworths Family Law Journal, 4,* 15–23.
*Neil v. Biggers,* 409 U.S. 188 (1972).
Neufeld, P. (2001). Legal and ethical implications of post-conviction DNA exonerations. *New England Law Review, 35,* 639–647.
New Suit in Wenatchee cases. *The Seattle Times*, p. A11. (2000, October 7).
Penrod, S. D., & Cutler, B. L. (1999). Preventing mistaken identification in eyewitness identification trials. In R. Roesch, S. D. Hart, & J. R. P. Ogloff (Eds.), *Psychology and law: The state of the discipline* (pp. 89–118). New York: Kluwer Academic/Plenum Publishers.
Platz, S. J., & Hosch, H. M. (1988). Cross racial/ethnic eyewitness identification: A field study. *Journal of Applied Social Psychology, 18,* 972–984.
Pudelski, C. R. (2004). The constitutional fate of mandatory reporting statutes and the clergy–communicant privilege in a post-Smith world. *Northwestern University Law Review, 98,* 703–738.
Radalet M. L., Bedeau, H. A., & Putman C. E. (1992). *In spite of innocence: Erroneous convictions in capital cases.* Boston: Northeastern University Press.
Ramirez, G., Zemba, D., & Geiselman, R. E. (1996). Judge's cautionary instructions on eyewitness testimony. *American Journal of Forensic Psychology, 14,* 31–66.
Rattner, A. (1988). Convicted but innocent: Wrongful conviction and the criminal justice system. *Law and Human Behavior, 12,* 283–293.
Scheck, B. C., & Neufeld, P. J. (2002). Toward the formation of "Innocence Commissions" in America. *Judicature, 86*(2), 98–105.
Scheck, B., Neufeld, P., & Dwyer, J. (2000). *Actual innocence: Five days to execution and other dispatches from the wrongly convicted.* New York: Doubleday.
Schneider, A., & Barber, M. (1998, February 23–27). The power to harm [Article series]. *Seattle Post-Intellgencer.*
Shapiro, P. N., & Penrod, S. D. (1986). Meta-analysis of facial identification studies. *Psychological Bulletin, 100,* 139–156.
Shaw, J. S., III. (1996). Increases in eyewitness confidence resulting from postevent questioning. *Journal of Experimental Psychology: Applied, 12,* 136–146.
Shaw, J. S., III, & McClure, K. A. (1996). Repeated postevent questioning can lead to elevated levels of eyewitness confidence. *Law and Human Behavior, 20,* 629–654.
Simon, T. (2003). *The innocents.* New York: Umbrage Editions.
Sobel, A. D. (2002). At the very core of why AJS exists. *Judicature, 86,* 65.
*State v. Hungerford,* 697 A.2d 916 (N.H. 1997).
*State v. Youngblood,* 734 P.2d 592 (Ariz. 1986).
Teibel, D. L. (2002, August 2). Man gets 24 years in '83 child-sex case. *The Tucson Citizen,* p. 5C.
Turtle, J. W., Lindsay, R. C. L., & Wells, G. L. (2003). Best practice recommendations for eyewitness evidence procedures: New ideas for the oldest way to solve a case. *The Canadian Journal of Police and Security Services, 1,* 5–18.
Turtle, J. W., & Yuille, J. C. (1994). Lost but not forgotten details: Repeated eyewitness recall leads to reminiscence but not hypermnesia. *Journal of Applied Psychology, 79,* 260–271.
U.S. National Institute of Justice. (1996). *Convicted by juries, exonerated by science; Case studies in the use of DNA evidence to establish innocence after trial* (Report No. NCJ 161258). Washington, DC: U.S. Department of Justice.
U.S. National Institute of Justice. (1999). *Eyewitness evidence: A guide for law enforcement* (Report No. NCJ 178240). Washington, DC: U.S. Department of Justice.
Weinstein, H. (2006, June 27). Execution imminent, DNA tests urged. *The Los Angeles Times*, p. 12.

Wells, G. L. (1995). Scientific study of witness memory: Implications for public and legal policy. *Psychology, Public Policy and Law, 1,* 726–731.

Wells, G. L., & Bradfield, A. L. (1998). "Good, you identified the suspect:" Feedback to eyewitnesses distorts the perception of the witnessing experience. *Journal of Applied Psychology, 83*, 360–376.

Wells, G. L., Lindsay, R. C. L., & Ferguson, T. J. (1979). Accuracy, confidence, and juror perceptions in eyewitness identification. *Journal of Applied Psychology, 64,* 440–448.

Wells, G. L., & Loftus, E. F. (2003). Eyewitness memory for people and events. In A. M. Goldstein (Ed.), *Handbook of psychology: Vol. 11. Forensic psychology* (pp. 149–160). New York: Wiley.

Wells, G. L., Small, M., Penrod, S., Malpass, R. S., Fulero, S. M. & Brimacombe, C. A. E. (1998). Eyewitness identification procedures: Recommendations for lineups and photospreads. *Law and Human Behavior, 22,* 603–647.

Wise, R. A., & Safer, M. A. (2003). A survey of judges' knowledge and beliefs about eyewitness testimony. *Court Review, 40,* 6–16.

CHAPTER

# 10

# Elizabeth F. Loftus: Warrior Scientist

Mahzarin R. Banaji

Beth Loftus, you are many things to me. Warrior scientist. Intellectual adventurer. Cotraveler extraordinaire. Socratic mentor. Happiness maker. Big sister. You taught me to take my earliest steps into the universe we call the mind. You gave me confidence in myself at a time when I was deeply doubtful. How fast were you going when I smashed into you? Very fast. You whisked me away on your concert tours (to Annenberg, to Wales, to Washington) where I saw a rock star in action. You shoved me into the limelight wherever there was even a crack of it. "This is Marzu Banaji" you would say, "and you should hire her."

You taught me to put my thoughts on paper without fear, and what a gift that has been. You revealed to me that naming things matters—retroactive interference is the principle at work but the misinformation effect—now that's what the funding public will understand and remember, and that's important, beyond the science. You made me realize just what William James meant when he said that thinking is for doing—that the deepest abstract questions about the nature of the mind are exactly the ones that also contain the deepest solutions to the troubles of our day. You never pulled punches. You showed me the blunt choices that confront every intellectual, should she choose to accept the mission. To a 20-something-year-old, you exuded a confidence that firmly said: We don't have to tow the line. We do have to change the world. Remarkably, you did this without an iota of arrogance. Instead, you told your stories, you giggled, you always had fun, and you made me want to be like you. But most important, you produced a body of work that shines like a beacon for those who seek what is right and true and scares the hell out of those who don't. For this, generations of scientists will offer you their gratitude as yours will be a shoulder to stand on to gaze past the next horizon.

To my amazement, you also became my friend. You gave me your old sweaters, and you cared that I was healthy and well. You tried to introduce me to men and when I reminded you that I was married, you said: "But he's in New York!" You taught me to enjoy white wine. I thought it was your sophisticated taste that led you to white instead of red until I realized that you wouldn't allow red wine into your house because of that damn white rug. You once asked me to cook at your home and too late did I realize that the only spices you owned were salt, pepper, and paprika. Thank god for the paprika, I thought, but alas prematurely, as I discovered that it had grown rock solid in the jar. "I guess I've had that since I was in graduate school at Stanford," you said. We laughed and ordered Chinese food. From this, you taught me that girls who are scientists are just like boys who are scientists. They don't cook and they don't clean.

I call you a warrior scientist. The war you wage is a good war. Raised as a Zoroastrian, I was taught that my daily task was to identify what was right and wrong and to fight on the side of the good. The trouble is that most often one doesn't know which side is the good side, and the more one learns and understands, the more blurry that line can get. That's why you were so important. You represented the obvious, unadulterated good. My ancestors, the kings of ancient Persia—Darius, Cyrus, Jamshed—all smile when I hang out with you.

I do wonder how you did it. Did you always know that what you were unearthing was so fundamental that you would lead a movement, that you would make enemies? You know, Martin Luther King Jr. said to an audience of psychologists, only weeks before his assassination, that the job of us scientists was quite simple: It was to "tell it like it is." That's all. But more than anybody else, he knew that there was more to it. The truth could be told, but the truth need not be accepted. You have, in my broad experience "told it like it is" as no other. Whether they listened or not, whether they liked what they heard or not. You just told it and told it and told it.

Nothing delights me more than to see you be recognized as you have been. The cowardly national organization that did not lend its support when you needed it eventually gave you its highest honor. The National Academy of Science bestowed on you and your career the highest recognition a scientist can receive. I puff up with pride when news of these honors travels to me because it is not always that good is rewarded. And I know that you will put each of these recognitions to good use—you will ratchet it up another step, and push on with even greater force.

For everything you have done and who you are, dear Beth, I'd go to the ends of the earth for you. So here I am, in fact, in New Zealand! I've likened you to Zena the warrior, said you taught like Socrates, showed that you put MLK Jr.'s words into practice, and that you are blessed by the kings of ancient worlds. But these comparisons don't do you justice. For you are unique, more unique than all the other unique and amazing ones. For this and more, you have my love and admiration, Elizabeth Fishman Loftus, warrior scientist, changer of the world.

*Beth:* When I was getting into the repressed memory stuff, I was learning all about it, and I discovered *The Courage to Heal* and I was devouring these books. I remember I had a big layover—I think I was visiting Don [Read] in Lethbridge or something. I went into a bookstore and I bought up a bunch of these books on sex abuse and I just showed up and I said, "Look at this stuff they're saying." You know, I mean I was just so focused, and I got angry. Even then I was still not as angry as I would get later on.

I was still being open-minded that maybe, possibly, maybe there really is repression. But when people fight so dirty and get so nasty and they didn't care about anybody except supporting the abuse story, no matter who gets hurt. That was, and still is, so upsetting.

*Q:* So how did you deal with people getting so mad at you?

*Beth:* It must be a lifetime challenge. When friends became enemies, and people betray you. Like Bessel van der Kolk. I met him at a conference. We even sat in a bar and we even thought, maybe we'll collaborate, you know. And then later, after I had seen all these tragic families—I mean I'd seen a lot of them—he wrote this scathing review of *The Myth of Repressed Memory*. In the review he accused me of deliberately hiding my own evidence in favor of repression. That was quite personal, you know. And other people saying Elizabeth Loftus knows there's evidence for repressed memory but she just decides to ignore it.

*Q:* What did you do?

*Beth:* Just kept going. The letters from the accused parents saying, "Thank God you are there," that helped. And with somebody like Pam Freyd around too, you know, she expresses her gratitude all the time, and she is incredible. And then when the UW exonerated me in 2001 and the Irvine offer came 9 months later in 2002—well, I was still bitter. I hadn't been able to shake it. I didn't hate the Space Needle every time I looked at it anymore, but I hated the administration building and I still resented the place. So I took the Irvine job.

And it feels pretty good here; it's a neat environment. I moved to a good place.

CHAPTER

# 11

# The Cost of Courage

Carol Tavris

When we think of scientific courage, we tend to think of people like Ignac Semmelweiss, ranting at his fellow physicians to wash their hands and thereby prevent the deaths of their female patients in labor from what he thought was a "morbid poison." (He had the right idea, if not the exact mechanism.) In 1847, Semmelweiss ordered his medical students to wash their hands in a chlorine antiseptic solution; death rates from childbed fever dropped rapidly thereafter. Did his colleagues say, "Good work, Ignac! Thank God you found the reason for all those horrifying and untimely fatalities"? On the contrary, many were outraged at Semmelweiss's claim that they were the cause of their patients' deaths, and refused to take his advice.

Beth Loftus is no Ignac Semmelweiss. For one thing, as one historian wrote, Semmelweiss "had a temper like a rattlesnake and was outrageously rude to anyone who questioned his ideas." This is definitely not Beth. And, to the best of my knowledge, she is at little risk of having a psychotic breakdown, as Semmelweiss did. But they share one powerful bond: Both of them produced empirical evidence demonstrating that a widespread practice—doctors who failed to wash their hands, psychotherapists who promoted "recovered memories of sexual abuse"—was not only wrong but harmful. Accordingly, both of them found themselves confronting the wrath of professionals faced with evidence of their mistakes or outright malfeasance. The practitioners of recovered memory therapy did not say, "Good work, Beth! Thank God you found the reason that my client remembers having been molested in a previous life, a previous decade, or a previous personality!"

Elizabeth Loftus is a superb scientist, as the essays in this volume amply demonstrate. But how could she have ever known, when she was starting out doing those elegant hit-versus-smashed studies of memory, that she would also be called upon to be a courageous one? Where is "courage" in the academic job description? By *courage* I don't mean the one-time kind that is difficult enough, such as jumping into a freezing lake to rescue a drowning child, but the day-in, day-out kind that it takes to remain committed to a principle and a purpose when others are trying to shut you up.

Courage is easy if you are daft and delusional, like Don Quixote, or if you are a psychopath, like Don Corleone. For all the rest of us, it takes a tougher kind of courage to keep fighting for academic freedom, fighting for the freedom of individuals who you are sure have been falsely convicted, fighting against the irrational forces of hysteria and moral panic. That kind of courage means never giving up even when you are too weary and depressed to move, never giving up in spite of persistent efforts by your enemies to harass you, never giving up even though you are weeping into your teacup with waves of hopelessness and anger. Most academics will never face the kind of challenge to their ethics, science, and public service that Elizabeth Loftus has, and many who are so challenged will back down rather than keep going. Courage is a special grace given to few.

So, in Beth Loftus's honor for this volume, let the record note another of her enduring contributions to the science of psychology: her determination to tell the truth as she sees it, to continue doing the research that she feels is socially and ethically imperative, and to follow her passion for inquiry and justice wherever it takes her, knowing that it will take her into realms of controversy and rage. I cannot chronicle here the many harassments, big and small, that Elizabeth Loftus has endured for more than 20 years, as her research came to challenge so many of the core assumptions of recovered-memory therapy. But because this volume pays tribute to her contributions to *applied* problems in human memory as well as to basic research, I can tell one story that illustrates this side of her work better than any other: the case of Jane Doe.[1]

The "memory wars" have been and are one of the most bitter and divisive quarrels in modern psychology, and a big part of that quarrel reflects the growing divide between clinicians who rely on the case study as evidence of their point of view and scientists who rely on empirical evidence. All psychological scientists understand the appeal and the limitations of case studies. Case studies can be dramatic and illuminating, but they are inherently limited by what their reporter sees, and what their reporter leaves out. This is especially true if the writer is untrained in the scientific method and is thus unaware of the confirmation bias, the importance of considering competing explanations before making a diagnosis, and other

---

[1]Parts of this article originally appeared in *The Skeptical Inquirer* (2002, July/August), pp. 41–44.

sources of his or her misperceptions—as is increasingly the case among many clinical psychologists and psychotherapists (Lilienfeld, Lynn, & Lohr, 2003; Tavris, 2003).

The most common and serious misuse of the case study occurs when the observer has a theory and forces the subject's experience to conform to it. As Richard McNally (2003) writes in *Remembering Trauma,* the real sources of Freud's notions of unconscious infantile fantasies were not data from his patients. They were, says McNally, "his suggestive techniques and his own extravagant imagination" (p. 168). This combination of suggestive techniques and an extravagant imagination is the greatest inherent danger in the case study, because few clinicians are aware of the confirmation bias or the suggestive techniques they often use to influence their clients.

In 1997, psychiatrist David Corwin and his collaborator Erna Olafson published a paper, a case study that they believed provided clear evidence of a recovered memory of childhood sexual abuse (Corwin & Olafson, 1997). They told the story of a young woman they called Jane Doe, whom Corwin had first interviewed in 1984, when Jane was 6 years old. At the time, her parents were going through a custody dispute, and Jane was living with her mother. Jane's father and stepmother claimed that Jane's mother was sexually and physically abusing the child, and Corwin was brought in to evaluate these allegations. Corwin concluded that Jane's mother *was* abusing her daughter. He was persuaded by the child's statements, and by the fact that the father seemed a more reliable informant than the mother, whom he thought unstable. Corwin was also persuaded by the report of a social worker who said Jane reported that her mother "puts her finger up my vagina in the bathtub. I don't like that. She says she can do anything she wants to me. She puts cream on my vagina. It hurts."

After Corwin's consultation, the court ruled in the father's favor, and Jane's father and stepmother assumed custody of 6-year-old Jane. The mother was even denied visitation.

Eleven years went by, during which time Corwin continued to discuss Jane's case at conferences on memory and child abuse. In 1995, wondering what, if anything, Jane herself remembered about her experiences, he contacted Jane, now age 17, and she agreed to be reinterviewed on videotape. Would she have repressed the memories of her mother's abuse?

According to Corwin, she had. When asked about the past, Jane recalled: "I told the court that my mom abused me, that she burned my feet on a stove, I don't, that's really the most serious accusation against her that I remember." When Corwin asked Jane whether she remembered anything about possible sexual abuse, she said, "No. I mean, I remember that was part of the accusation, but I don't remember anything—wait a minute, yeah, I do." Corwin then showed Jane the videotapes of his interviews with her when she was 6. Jane said, "The little girl that I see in those videotapes I don't see as [having] made up those things, and it doesn't make sense to me that knowing the truth I would out-and-out lie like that. I have to believe that to some extent my mom did hurt me."

Watching the videotapes, Jane Doe wept, and before long was remembering how her mother had sexually abused her, physically abused her, and even taken pornographic photos of her and her brother. According to Corwin, she had repressed these memories for 11 years—a clear example, he thought, of "traumatic amnesia."

Corwin, a member of the editorial board of the journal *Child Maltreatment,* then invited several researchers and clinicians to comment on Jane's case, in print, following the article he and Olafson were preparing to publish in the journal. Most of the professionals who read this case were persuaded that it was a full and accurate account of the story. They were deeply affected by the videotapes. Paul Ekman (1997), who of course is famous for his work on detecting true and false facial expression of emotions, said, "Jane's emotions are genuine and expressed poignantly. Those who see the videotape are moved emotionally. I have yet to see anyone who does not have a tear in his or her eye when Jane first remembers part of what happened to her and begins to cry" (p. 115). Jonathan Schooler (1997), an experimental psychologist, agreed that this case supported Corwin's conclusion that "Jane's mother did in fact engage in inappropriate sexual behavior that was both invasive and painful" (p. 126). He said he was persuaded by the "strikingly consistent characterization of Jane's allegations across interviews with two psychological evaluators, one police investigator, her therapist, and in the three interviews with Corwin" (p. 127). Schooler was also influenced by the "persuasive manner" in which Jane described the abuse, and "the sincerity with which she gave the Brownie Oath that she was telling the truth" (p. 127).

Stephen Lindsay (1997) acknowledged that Jane might have been remembering the *prior allegations* rather than *actual events,* and reminded readers to maintain some uncertainty about the accuracy of her memory. Nonetheless, he too said he was inclined to believe that Jane's mother did "push her finger up Jane's vagina in a sexually abusive way" (p. 189). The foundation for his belief in the bathtub molestation was "somewhat shaky," he said, but he just got "the feeling that Jane experienced a powerful and essentially accurate recovered memory" (p. 190).

Only one psychologist, Ulrich Neisser (1997), was skeptical. He observed that Jane's recovered memories—one of her mother taking pornographic photos of her and her brother, and one of her mother's molesting her in the bathtub—were in fact *not* accurate. The memory of the photos was "entirely false," he said, and the second had changed dramatically (p. 125). That is, the 6-year-old Jane claimed that her mother molested her while bathing her, putting her fingers into Jane's vagina and asking, "That feel good?" many times. But the 17-year-old Jane remembered a quite different event; the picture now in her mind "is of a single, deep vaginal intrusion, several seconds in duration and extremely painful" (p. 124). Neisser wrote that perhaps the single dramatic event in Jane's age 17 memory misrepresents a long series of "unpleasant but relatively pedestrian childhood experiences"—being bathed by her mother (p. 124).

Now, it is interesting, in the clear glare of hindsight, that none of the commentators asked: What, if anything, was Corwin leaving out of his version of events? Do we have the whole story here? Didn't Corwin have a vested interest in confirming his initial clinical decision to side with the father's claim that Jane really had been sexually molested by her mother? Corwin and Olafson wrote a compelling story, and the commentaries show that *few of us, even scientists trained to be skeptical, can suspend disbelief when faced with a compelling story.* Once in the literature, Corwin's case history was embraced by many clinicians, and expert witnesses began presenting the case in court as proof of the validity of repressed memories.

After reading the case of Jane Doe in 1997, Loftus and her colleague Melvin Guyer, at the University of Michigan, decided to examine this alleged evidence of a repressed-and-recovered memory more closely. The stakes were high for their work as scholars, teachers, and expert witnesses, because the case was already being used in court as evidence that recovered memories of sexual abuse in childhood are reliable. Because David Corwin had long been active on the repressed-memory side of the memory wars, they were skeptical about his account of the evidence. The story of what they learned—what Corwin reported and what he omitted—and of what happened to them in the course of their inquiry, is a case study of the hazards today of doing controversial investigations that threaten or question one person's version of events.

Corwin disguised his story of Jane Doe, with anonymous names and places. But he showed the videotapes of her, at ages 6 and 17, at a number of professional meetings, and the tapes mention Jane's real first name and the city where some of her childhood activities took place. Loftus and Guyer searched legal databases with a few key words, and found an important, indeed a landmark appellate court case involving Jane. (This was, by the way, something any journalist or other individual could do on LexisNexis in 5 minutes.) They eventually met Jane Doe's mother, and became convinced that she had been falsely accused so many years before, leading to the loss of custody of her daughter.

From the appellate case, they learned that Jane's parents had spent years in a protracted and venomous fight for the child's custody in which Jane was tossed between them, until the father finally won. The court, based on the father's accusations that the mother had physically abused Jane by burning her feet on a stove, ordered joint custody to the parents and physical custody to the father. The custody war escalated, eventually involving allegations by Jane's father that the mother abused Jane not only physically, but also sexually.

When Child Protection Services (CPS) in the mother's home county investigated these allegations, however, they turned up nothing, and recommended that no action be taken. (This was in 1984, the height of national panic about childhood sexual abuse, when mandatory reporting of even *suspicions* of abuse went into effect.) The father then went to another county court, 80 miles away, to repeat his allegations that the mother was sexually abusing Jane and had burned her feet "months and years before." This involvement of a second court, one that challenged the jurisdiction of the first court, led to the appellate case that resolved the jurisdictional dispute. One appellate judge explicitly criticized the father for this "blatant forum shopping for the sole purpose of avoiding what he anticipated would be adverse rulings by the...court on the various custody and visitation motions then pending in that court." This information does not appear in Corwin's article, nor does the fact that the mother's county CPS had thoroughly investigated the father's charges and recommended that no action be taken.

Corwin does inform readers of the report of the social worker who believed Jane's claims against her mother. But he omitted a letter from a clinical psychologist, Dr. S., who had interviewed Jane, her father, her stepmother, and her mother. Dr. S. had spoken with the mother's therapist and attorney, Jane's psychologist, a CPS worker, and Jane's brother and grandmother. He read police reports, court orders, medical reports, and court transcripts. In short, it appears that he did as thorough and unbiased an assessment of the case as he could, obtaining information from many possible sources. Dr. S. wrote to the judge that although some documents supported the premise that some type of abuse had occurred, "what has not been made clear is the source or nature of the abuse—whether these are actual physical and sexual abuses perpetrated by [the mother] or whether they exist only in the mind and fantasy of [the father] and are communicated to [Jane] as [the mother] contends." Dr. S. noted that Jane's narration of her story was not spontaneous: "She has told her story numerous times to a number of different people and she now sounds mechanical." (Note that this very consistency, which sounded rehearsed to Dr. S., was what persuaded some of the commentators on Corwin and Olafson's article that Jane was telling the truth.) As for the burned feet, Dr. S. said: "It was never determined if her feet and hand were indeed burned, since Jane has a fungus condition that causes her skin to blister and peel." Corwin makes no mention of Dr. S.'s opinion or this letter—let alone that there was another explanation of the "burned feet."

Loftus and Guyer interviewed Jane's biological mother and hired an investigator to interview the mother's closest female friend and Jane's brother "John," now in his 30s. John said that his mother never abused Jane. On the contrary, he said, the father was the abusive one. John had memories of his father beating him with a belt that had metal circles on it, leaving imprints on his skin. John said that Corwin never interviewed him regarding this matter.

The mother briefly got custody of Jane, but within a year the father filed sex abuse charges, Corwin sided with him, and the mother was denied custody again. This time, she gave up. When Jane was 9 years old, her father and stepmother divorced. When Jane was about 15, her father became ill and entered a convalescent hospital. Jane went into foster care; her father died a year later.

Loftus interviewed Jane's stepmother, who told her that the way they got Jane away from her mother was with "the sexual angle." "We proved it," the stepmother said. "We saw abuse on her body. We started documenting it." The stepmother accused the mother of being a prostitute, of locking Jane in her bedroom, of binding the child and placing her feet on the stove, and of taking and peddling soft-porn photos of John and Jane. "The police found it out," she told Loftus, "and also Jane told us she was posing with John and that her mother was taking pictures." But she said she wasn't sure whether the police ever found the photos.

Loftus interviewed Jane's foster mother, who said that she and Jane had tried to put the "puzzle pieces" of her past together. Eventually, the foster mother contacted Jane's mother and invited her to visit. The first meeting, said the foster mother, was "beautiful." During this period of visitations with her mother, Jane began rethinking the subject of sex abuse. According to the foster mother, Jane began to have doubts, wondering whether she could have made up her memories of her mother's abuse. "What if I just said it? What if Dad put me up to it? I said it but did it really happen?" followed by: "I wouldn't have said it if it didn't happen."

And then, according to Jane's foster mother, just as Jane was struggling to find out the truth and beginning to question whether the abuse had even occurred, Corwin reentered the picture. He called the foster mother, saying he was doing research and wanted to interview Jane again. Jane wanted to do it to learn more, so the foster mother took her to the interview. When Corwin showed her the tape of herself at age 6, Jane screamed, "Oh God! She did it! She did it. I can see it. I can see it!" According to the foster mother, Jane became depressed after this interview with Corwin, and not long thereafter she left this woman's home and care.

Every family quarrels over its members' Rashomonic memories of shared experiences. When memories are distorted in the service of a bitter custody dispute, their reliability sinks even lower than usual, and that is pretty low. That is why it is incumbent upon any scientific investigator to look for corroborating and disconfirming evidence for people's memories and to think critically about their claims. Loftus and Guyer assembled considerable evidence that casts doubt on Corwin's claim that Jane Doe's story is reliable evidence of a repressed memory of childhood sexual abuse. For example, Jane's reports at ages 6 and 17 were not consistent. At least one expert, Dr. S., who did a thorough investigation, believed that no abuse had occurred. More over, both Jane's stepmother and foster mother revealed that Jane had not "repressed" a memory; she talked about the abuse *allegations* on innumerable occasions with them, questioning her memories and wondering what had really happened.

One of Jane's "recovered memories" is almost certainly untrue: the pornographic photos. At age 17, Jane told Corwin that she remembered accusing her mother of taking pictures of her and her brother, and selling them. Both Jane's brother and mother deny this claim. No reports or documentation exist to substantiate the claim that such photos exist. They almost certainly would have been noted in police reports, therapists' notes, or other documents had anyone mentioned them. As Neisser observed: "Jane has clearly 'remembered'—and been very upset by—something that never took place." But why didn't Corwin acknowledge that even if he thought Jane's other recovered memories were accurate, this one probably wasn't?

Ultimately, Corwin rested his corroboration of Janes memory on his *clinical opinion* that the alleged abuse occurred when Jane was a child. Corwin indeed behaved like a proper clinician—not like a journalist, a scientist, or a detective. Many clinicians are not trained to question the veracity of a client's story or to investigate other people in the client's world who might see things differently. Nor are they typically trained to speak in the scientist's language of probability and doubt; instead, they tend to speak in the language of certainty: "I know this is so based on my clinical experience and intuition."

Yet a large body of scientific research, much of it done after Corwin's 1984 custody evaluation, has revealed the limitations of forensic assessment based on clinical opinion (Horner, Guyer, & Kalter, 1993a, 1993b). False allegations of child sexual abuse increase in highly contested child custody/visitation cases, and Jane Doe's parents' divorce was as prolonged and bitter as they come. Children can be influenced to recall events that have not occurred, especially if they are questioned about them in suggestive and leading ways (Bruck & Poole, 2002; Dickinson, Poole, & Laimon, 2005). The one factor that most strongly predicts whether children will make false allegations is the bias of the interviewer: When the interviewer is convinced that the child has been sexually molested, he or she will rarely take the child's "no" for a true answer, and keep pressuring the child to give the "right" one (Bruck & Ceci, 2004). Eventually, the child yields. Over time, most children then come to believe these pseudomemories as strongly as they do real ones.

Now, one might assume that Corwin and Olafson's case study, and Loftus and Guyer's reinterpretation, would have simply entered the scholarly debate about memory in general and the method of the case study in particular. In recent years, many scholars have reanalyzed famous case studies—of Genie, Sybil, the Wolf Man, and countless others—and it is thanks to their efforts that we have learned how limited and biased case studies can be (as well as what truly unusual stories can contribute to the clinical or neuropsychological literature). In the olden days, lively scientific disagreements took place at meetings and in print, as investigators found elegant ways of claiming that their critics were terminally mistaken, misguided, or drunk.

That was then. Just as noise trumps silence and rage trumps courtesy, the cudgel of lawsuits to silence or cower the opposition trumps free debate. In universities across the country, lawsuits, even spurious and unsuccessful ones, have weakened the once-sacrosanct guarantees to scholars of free speech and association. Institutional Review Boards (IRBs) and Human Subjects Committees have proliferated, supposedly to protect human subjects from harm caused by unethical scientists—but also to protect universities from lawsuits. The growing power of IRBs in academia, along with the increasing number of restrictions on free speech in the politically correct name of "speech codes" and "conduct codes," has put independent scientific inquiry in jeopardy.

When Jane learned that Loftus had met with her biological mother and was pursuing an inquiry into her life, her first reaction was to try to contact Loftus to ask her help in contacting her mother. She didn't follow up on this request, however. More than a year later, completely "out of the blue" as far as Loftus was concerned,

Jane sent an e-mail to the University of Washington complaining that her privacy was being invaded. (Neither Loftus nor I know why she did this after such a long delay; we both find it unlikely that a young woman with no experience in academia, on her own, would know how and where to complain about an alleged ethics violation.) Considering that David Corwin had *published* his account of her life and was traveling around the country showing videotapes of Jane at 6 and 17, and considering that no one was making her story public and hence violating her "privacy" except Jane herself and Corwin, this complaint should surely have been set aside. Instead, it set in motion a series of endlessly shifting charges against Loftus, a scientist of international stature who had brought luster and prestige to her university for more than 25 years.

The university's "investigation" began on September 30, 1999, when, having given Loftus 15 minutes' advance notice by phone, John Slattery of the University of Washington's "Office of Scientific Integrity" arrived in Loftus's office, along with the Chair of the Psychology Department, and seized her files. Loftus asked Slattery what the charges against her were. It took him 5 weeks to respond, and when he did he had transformed Jane Doe's invasion-of-privacy complaint into an investigation of "possible violations of human subjects research." Loftus later learned that lawyers in another state, who had retained Corwin as their defense expert, were trying to subpoena her personnel file in hopes of finding something there to discredit her as an expert witness for the plaintiffs. Because the university, in the face of her objection, was going forward in complying with this improper subpoena, she was forced to retain her own lawyer to stop them. (Because it was from out of state, the subpoena had no force of law or validity in Washington.)

In February 2000, Loftus and her lawyer dislodged some documents from the University's investigation, and found among them a "Confidential Memo" written by Stanley Berent, a neuropsychologist who was on the IRB at the University of Michigan—*Guyer's* IRB.[2] This memo had played a crucial role in the decision to reprimand Guyer and deny him the right to continue his work on the Jane Doe investigation—a decision that was eventually overturned—yet Guyer was never even told it existed. To this day Guyer has been unable to get his own university to provide him with a copy of this memo, even after repeated requests under the Freedom of Information Act. Yet a University of Michigan lawyer was happy to send it directly to the investigating committee at the University of Washington, to be used against Loftus. This was the modus operandi at both universities: Keep the charges secret, keep changing the charges, keep the meetings secret, keep the accused in the dark.[2]

In the spring of 2001, the three-member investigating committee, consisting of two clinicians and one sociologist, concluded that Loftus was not guilty of the charge of "scholarly misconduct." But the two clinicians recommended to the Dean, David Hodge, that she nonetheless be reprimanded and subjected to a program of remedial education on professional ethics. They instructed Loftus not to

[2]For the story of Mel Guyer's harassment by the IRB at the University of Michigan, as he sought permission to investigate the case of Jane Doe. see Tavris, 2002.

publish data obtained by methods they regarded as inconsistent with the "ethical principals [*sic*]" of psychologists—in this case, methods of any competent journalistic investigation.

On July 3, 2001, 1 year and 9 months after the University of Washington seized her files, and 1 month after Loftus won the prestigious William James Award from the American Psychological Society (now the Association for Psychological Science) for her decades of scientific research, Dean Hodge wrote Loftus a letter of exoneration. Her work, he said, "does not constitute research involving human subjects." She did not commit ethical violations or deviate from accepted research practices. She was not guilty of any misconduct. She would not have to undergo remedial education on how to conduct research. But, oh, one more thing: She was not to contact Jane Doe's mother again or interview anyone else involved in the case without advance approval. Such meetings, he said, would constitute "human subjects research requiring Human Subjects Committee approval." The investigation had lasted more than 21 months, in spite of the university's own statute of limitations—30 days for the selection of a committee and 90 days for its deliberations—for bringing all such investigations to a conclusion.

Of course, Loftus and Guyer's investigation of Corwin's claims was bound to inflame passions: those of Jane Doe herself, a young woman whose life has been filled with conflict and loss; those of David Corwin, who has publicly promoted his case study as a personal vindication and a prototype of how recovered memories should be studied; and those of the many clinicians who still cling to the discredited concept of repressed memories. Loftus and Guyer knew they had enemies. They hadn't known that some of them were at their own universities, and that the shields of tenure and the First Amendment would not be sufficient protection.

Loftus and Guyer's account of the Jane Doe case was published in *The Skeptical Inquirer* in the summer of 2002 (Loftus & Guyer, 2002a, 2002b). Not long thereafter, Nicole Taus ("Jane Doe") filed a lawsuit claiming invasion of privacy, emotional distress, fraud, and defamation of character by Loftus, Guyer, me, the *Skeptical Inquirer,* its publisher The Committee for the Scientific Investigation of Claims of the Paranormal, the Center for Inquiry West, a private investigator, and, in a stroke of irony, the University of Washington. Although Taus accused us of having invaded her privacy, neither the *Skeptical Inquirer* nor I even knew her real name until she filed the lawsuit against us. In 2004, the California Appellate Court dismissed most of the charges against the defendants (and those against me specifically), but left a few accusations unresolved. The case was accepted in 2005 by the California Supreme Court, with amicus briefs filed on the defendants' behalf by many of the top memory scientists in the world. A group of clinicians who still support recovered-memory therapy filed their own amicus brief on behalf of Nicole Taus. The court will issue its decision sometime in 2006.

The story of Jane Doe offers a challenge: How do we, as scientists and citizens, weigh Jane Doe's personal feelings against the uses to which her story is being put? Once David Corwin published his version of her story, a case study now used in courts as legitimate evidence of a repressed and then recovered memory of sexual abuse, is it not the *obligation* of other scientists to submit his argument to close scrutiny? And if so, must other scholars be bound by the version of the story that Corwin provides, as the six commentators were, or may they try to discover evidence he might have intentionally or inadvertently omitted, as any good literary critic, historian, or journalist would do? No one would question a reporter's right to do investigative journalism, or a historian's right to produce an "unauthorized" biography: that is, *to find out things that the subject of the investigation would prefer to keep hidden, or to tell the subject's life story in a way that he or she disputes.* But the rules are apparently different for scientists today: A journalist may do science, but a scientist may not do journalism.

Corwin's position is that no one has the right to reanalyze Jane Doe's story without her permission. On June 6, 2003, in a published letter to the *Seattle Times* (which had published an article about Elizabeth Loftus and the Jane Doe investigation), Corwin wrote that:

> The most important and far-reaching issue about the situation is the breach of an individual's right to privacy after she had agreed to the publication of a scientific article about her case …
>
> because [v]iolations of privacy like this threaten all those who agree to share confidential information about their health or other personal facts for the advancement of science with the promise that their identity will not be disclosed.

Of course, Loftus and Guyer had not disclosed anything more about Jane Doe's identity than Corwin had—less, in fact, because they were not showing videotapes of her anywhere.

I disagree with Corwin. "The advancement of science" rests on *disclosure:* making your data open to peer review and to the scrutiny of your methods and findings by other scientists. This can be done, and is done all the time, without violating anyone's privacy. The scientific literature in medicine and psychology is full of case studies that *must* be open to reassessment, or anyone could claim anything. If someone claims he cured John Doe of cancer with a steady diet of kumquats, other scientists *must* be free to investigate this claim; they must have the full record of Doe's previous medical history and other pertinent information. And if the full data are suspiciously lacking in the case report, they must have access to it elsewhere. The world doesn't care and needn't know who John Doe really is, unless of course he is the CEO of Kumquat King of California and has a vested interest in the study.

What Corwin really wants, I imagine, is what Freud wanted, what all of us want to say about our work: "I want my interpretation to be the only one." But we don't get to do that, not if we are interested in science rather than in perpetuating our own version of events. Actually, Corwin said in his letter to the *Seattle Times* that he *is* only interested in his own version of events: "If the focus of my article had been to explore evidence for and against the validity of Jane's allegations, then including more facts, both pro and con, would have been warranted." Well, precisely!

Loftus and Guyer called their article in the *Skeptical Inquirer* "Who Abused Jane Doe?" I think that this article, and that question, should be on every psychology student's list; it forms the central question in the memory wars between scientists and clinicians. *Was* Jane Doe abused, and, if so, in what way, and by whom? Was it her mother after all? Her father? Both of them? Neither? Was she simply a victim of a nasty custody dispute? Was she harmed by Corwin's reappearance in her life, just as she was trying to sort out her memories and reconnect with her mother? Or, as she now claims in her lawsuit, was she more greatly harmed by Loftus and Guyer for disputing her memories of her father and her latest account of her life? Whose work has had the *greatest actual influence* on the course of her life: the clinical judgments of David Corwin or the empirically based research of memory scientists like Loftus? Who, if anyone, committed an ethical violation here? Loftus, for not getting Jane Doe's permission, which Jane likely would have withheld? Corwin makes much of the fact that *he* got Jane's informed consent to report her story and show videotapes of her. But is it likely that he informed Jane that once her case study appeared in print, it would be the legitimate target of interpretation and investigation by others who disputed his version of events (and hers) and his methods?

Psychology students who read Corwin and Olafson's original paper and Loftus and Guyer's rebuttal in the *Skeptical Inquirer* will be in a position to understand one of the most important and passionate disputes in psychology. And to understand why the difference between clinical and scientific methods has such crucial contemporary relevance to the law and to our lives. They will understand better the reasons that Elizabeth Loftus has been the center of so much controversy, and why her research matters profoundly to people's lives.

"I don't see how you can write anything of value," the great anthropologist Marvin Harris told me years ago in an interview, "if you don't offend someone." Skeptical inquiry is endangered when those who are offended or threatened by knowledge are able to silence those who have something valuable to say. The lawsuit path is crowded because those who take it usually face no negative consequences: The worst that can happen to them is nothing at all—their target doesn't budge. But often the targets of these threats, weary of being harassed, unable to pay the costs of self-defense, frightened at the prospect of losing their reputations, and unsupported by their publisher or university, do back down. The offending passage is deleted, funny but sarcastic remarks toned down, safer topics chosen, documented evidence of the target's malfeasance removed.

That is why we must be all the more grateful for the courage, persistence, and integrity of scientists who are still willing to "offend" in the pursuit of truth and justice, scientists like Elizabeth Loftus.

## REFERENCES

Bruck, M., & Ceci, S. (2004). Forensic developmental psychology: Unveiling four common misconceptions. *Current Directions in Psychological Science, 13,* 229–232.

Bruck, M., & Poole, D. A. (2002). Introduction to the special issue on forensic developmental psychology. *Developmental Review, 22,* 331–333.

Corwin, D. L., & Olafson, E. (1997). Videotaped discovery of a reportedly unrecallable memory of child sexual abuse: Comparison with a childhood interview videotaped 11 years before. *Child Maltreatment, 2,* 91–112.

Dickinson, J. J., Poole, D. A., & Laimon, R. L. (2005). Children's recall and testimony. In N. Brewer & K. Williams (Eds.), *Psychology & law: An empirical perspective* (pp. 151–176). New York: Guilford.

Ekman, P. (1997). Expressive behavior and the recovery of a traumatic memory: Comments on the videotapes of Jane Doe. *Child Maltreatment, 2,* 113–116.

Horner, T. M., Guyer, M. J., & Kalter, N. M. (1993a). The biases of child sexual abuse experts: Believing is seeing. *Bulletin of the American Academy of Psychiatry and the Law, 21,* 281–292.

Horner, T. M., Guyer, M. J., & Kalter, N. M. (1993b). Clinical expertise and the assessment of child sexual abuse: An empirical study of mental health experts. *Journal of the American Academy of Child and Adolescent Psychiatry, 32,* 925–933.

Lilienfeld, S. O., Lynn, S. J., & Lohr, J. M. (Eds.). (2003). *Science and pseudoscience in contemporary clinical psychology.* New York: Guilford.

Lindsay, D. S. (1997). Jane Doe in context: Sex abuse, lives, and videotape. *Child Maltreatment, 2,* 187–192.

Loftus, E., & Guyer, M. J. (2002a, May/June). Who abused Jane Doe? [Part 1]. *Skeptical Inquirer,* pp. 24–32. Part 2: July/August, 37-40.

Loftus, E., & Guyer, M. J. (2002b, July/August). Who abused Jane Doe? [Part 2]. *Skeptical Inquirer,* pp. 37–40.

McNally, R. J. (2003). *Remembering trauma.* Cambridge, MA: Harvard University Press.

Neisser, U. (1997). Jane Doe's memories: Changing the past to serve the present. *Child Maltreatment, 2,* 123–125.

Schooler, J. W. (1997). Reflections on a memory discovery. *Child Maltreatment, 2,* 126–133.

Tavris, C. (2002, July/August). The high cost of skepticism. *Skeptical Inquirer,* pp. 41–44.

Tavris, C. (2003). The widening scientist–practitioner gap: A view from the bridge. In S. O. Lilienfeld, J. M. Lohr, & S. J. Lynn (Eds.), *Science and pseudoscience in contemporary clinical psychology* (pp. ix–xviii). New York: Guilford.

*Q:* So, you can imagine that some students who read this book will think "I don't want to go through any of the grief that Loftus has been through, so I'm just going to do my research on something that won't upset anyone, like upside-down text processing."

*Beth:* Right, something that won't incur the wrath of whoever.

*Q:* Yes.

*Beth:* Well, it's a bit like a roller-coaster ride. If you want to be low and flat all the time, that's fine. If you want to be up and down, then you can do that too. But I wanted to do this, and I'm happy with this. I mean, I wish some of the stuff hadn't happened, but mostly, it's a good life.

*Q:* And what about people who really want to do controversial research, but who are afraid of the consequences, of incurring the wrath of whoever? What would you tell them?

*Beth:* Do it anyway.

# Author Index

## A


Aaron, F., 84, *100*
Ablin, D. S., 96, *102*
Ackerman, E., 98, *101*
Ackil, J. K., 43, 55, *57, 62, 63*
Adams, D., 110, 111, 119, *132*
Allan, K., 22, 123, *133*
Allen, B. P., 54, *57, 60*
Alpert, J., 93, *102,* 160, *164*
Amador, M., 117, *133*
Aman, C., 72, *76*
Ames, E. W., 98, *100*
Anand, K. J. S., 83, *102*
Anastasi, J. S., 40, *61*
Andersen, S. L., 98, *102*
Anderson, M. C., 153, 154, *164*
Anthony, T., 181, *188*
Arizona, 178, *188*
Atkinson, R. C., 16, *24*
Ayers, M. S., 40, *57*


## B


Bahrick, L., 96, *100*
Balota, D. A., 105, 107, 110, 111, 119, *132,* 154, *164*
Banaji, M. R., 35, *57*
Barber, M., 182, 184, *190*
Barclay, J. R., 106, *132*
Barnes, J. M., 21, *24*
Barr, R., 72, *75*, 83, *102*
Barron, K. L., 90, *100*
Bartlett, F. C., 123, *132*
Bartlett, J., 106, *134*, *136*
Bass, E., 139, 148, 158, *164*
Bauer, P. J., 90, 91, *100*
Bayen, U. J., 114, *136*
Beck, M., 55, *63*
Bedeau, H. A., *188*, *190*
Bekerian, D. A., 38, *57*
Bell, M., 96, *102*
Belli, R. F., 36, 40, 41, 43, 45, *57*, *58, 62*
Berger, A. A., 20, *24*
Bergman, E., 53, *61*, 123, *132*
Berkowitz, S. R., 151, *164*
Berliner, L., 156, *164*
Bernstein, A. E. H., 93, 96, *100*
Bernstein, D. M., 10, *13*, 148, 149, 152, 153, 163, *164*, *166*
Beuke, C. J., 148, *167*
Bhatt, R. S., 84, 85, *100*
Bidrose, S., 96, *102*
Billings, F. J., 8, *13*, 47, *59*, 141, 145, *166*
Birt, A. R., 145, *167*
Bishara, A., 121, *133*

Blacher, R. S., 93, 96, *100*
Blanchard, L., 110, *136*
Blank, J., 184, *188*
Blume, E. S., 139, *164*
Borchard, E. M., *188*, *189*
Bousfield, W. A., 117, *132*
Bower, G. H., 16, *24*
Bowers, J. M., 38, *57*
Bowman, L. L., 40, *58*
Boyer, M. E., 90, *100*
Bradfield, A. L., 55, *62*, 181, *191*
Bradshaw, J. M., 38, *58*
Brandon, R., 174, *189*
Bransford, J., 106, 123, *132*
Braun, K. A., 150, 151, *164*
Brimacombe, C. A. E., 176, 180, 181, 185, 186, *191*
Brito, T. L., 174, *189*
Brown, D., 139, *164*, *165*
Brown, L., 160, *164*
Bruck, M., 47, 54, *58*, 66, 68, 72, 73, 74, *75*, *76*, 95, *100*, 106, *132*, 174, *189*, 206, *210*
Bulevich, J. B., 49, 51, *62*, 127, *136*, 149, 154, *164*, *168*
Bull, R., 144, 145, *166*, *167*
Burch, M. M., 90, *100*
Burns, H., 37, *60*, 66, *76*, 107, 122, *134*
Butler, A. C., 154, *164*
Butler, K. M., 110, 112, 114, 116, 122, 124, 127, 129, 130, *132*, *134*

## C

Campbell, B. A., 87, *100*
Campos-De-Carvalo, M., 84, 85, *117*
Candel, I., 145, *164*
Cary, S. S., 90, *100*
Ceci, S. J., 38, 41, 47, 54, *58*, 66, 68, 71, 72, 73, 74, *75*, *76*, 95, *100*, 106, *132*, 158, *164*, 174, *189*, 206, *210*
Cendan, D., 115, *134*
Chambers, K. L., 43, *58*, *62*
Chan, F. M., 49, *61*
Chan, J. C. K., 53, *60*
Chandler, C. C., 41, *58*
Chatoor, I., 94, *100*
Chisholm, K., 98, *100*
Christiaansen, R. E., 38, *58*
Clancy, S. A., 147, *166*
Clarke-Stewart, K. A., 72, *77*
Clarkson, M. G., 89, *102*
Clifton, R., 89, 90, *102*
Coan, J. A., 8, *13*, 57, *60*
Cohen, G., 123, 124, *132*
Cohen, R. L., 126, *132*
Cole, W., 17, *25*
Collins, A. M., 2, *13*, 22, *24*,
Collins, H. R., 152, *164*
Colombo, M., 83, *102*
Cooper, C., 181, *188*
Cooper, J., 153, 154, *164*
Costa, P. T., 145, *164*
Costall, A., 145, *167*
Cortese, M. J., 107, 110, 111, 119, *132*
Corwin, D. L., 160, *164*, 201, *211*
Courage, M. L., 82, 96, *101*
Courtois, C. A., 138, 160, *164*
Coxon, P., 123, *132*
Craik, F. I. M., *59*, 106, 107, 115, 119, 123, 130, *132*, *134*, *135*
Craw, S., 96, *102*
Crews, F., 138, 159, *164*
Crothers, E. J., 16, *24*
Crowder, R. G., 35, *57*, *58*
Cutler, B. L., 185, *189*, *190*

## D

Dahl, L. C., 53, *60*
Dahlgren, D., 41, *62*
Darley, J. M., 122, *132*
Darnton, N., 139, *164*
Davidson, P. S. R., 112, *133*
Davies, C., 174, *189*
Davis, L., 139, 148, 158, *164*
Davison, A., 148, *164*
DeCasper, A. J., 82, *100*
Deese, J., 107, 108, *132*
Dehon, H., 115, *132*
De Leonardis, D., 107, *133*, *134*
Dickinson, J. J., 206, *211*
Dijkstra, J. P., 20, *25*
Dobson, M., 49, *58*
Dodd, D. H., 37, *58*

Dolan, P. O., 105, 107, *132*
Donders, K., 40, *60*
Dornburg, C. C., 110, 112, 117, 127, 129, *132*, *134*
Doyle, J. M., 185, *189*
Drell, M., 94, *100*
Drivdahl, S. B., 43, 51, 52, 55, *58*, *62*, 63, *77*
Dropik, P. L., 90, *100*
Duchek, J. M., 105, 107, 111, 119, *132*
Dumont, N. L., 98, *102*
Dwyer, J., 174, 184, *190*
Dywan, J., 44, *59*

## E

Eakin, D. K., 40, 41, *59*
Eber, H., 148, *167*
Eisen, M. L., 145, *165*
Ekman, P., 202, *211*
Ellis, R., 150, *164*
Ellsworth, P. C., 38, *61*
Engel, B., 139, *164*
Engelkamp, J., 126, 130, *132*, *133*
Enright, M., 86, *102*
Erdelyi, M. H., 138, *165*
Esplin, P. W., 69, *76*

## F

Fagen, J. W., 86, *102*
Farrar, M. J., 90, *100*
Faulkner, D., 123, 124, *132*
Feinberg, S. E., 18, *24*
Fellows, B. J., 145, *166*
Ferguson, T. J., 185, *190*
Fifer, W. P., 82, *100*
Finger, K., 141, *167*
Finkelman, D., 145, *167*
Finnila, K., 71, 72, *76*
Fisher, L., 98, *100*
Fisher, R. P., 117, *133*
Fishman, (Loftus), 16, *24*
Fivush, R., 82, 93, 96, *100*, *101*
Foley, M. A., 44, 45, 49, *59*, *133*
Foster, R. A., 40, *61*, 119, *136*,
Foster, S., 145, *167*
Francoeur, E., 72, *75*, 95, *100*
Frank, B., 174, *189*
Frank, J., 174, *189*
Franklin, 12, *13*, 161
Franks, J., 106, 123, *132*
Freedman, J. L., 2, *13*, 17, *24*, *25*
Fredrickson, R., 139, 155, *165*
Freud, S., 81, *100*
Freyd, J., 151, *165*
Frost, P., 43, 44, 45, *59*
Fulero, S. M., 176, 180, 181, 185, 186, *191*
Fullilove, M. T., 158, 159, *166*

## G

Gabbert, F., 123, *133*
Gabrieli, S. W., 153, 154, *164*
Gaensbauer, T. J., 93, 94, *100*
Gales, M. S., 41, 43, *58*
Gallo, D., 112, 114, *133*, *135*
Gardiner, J. M., 43, *59*, 118, 119, *133*, *136*
Gargano, G. J., 41, *58*
Garry, M., 38, 49, 50, 52, *59*, *60*, *62*, 126, *133*, 142, 143, 144, 145, 148, 150, 151, 154, *164*, *165*, *166*, *167*, *168*
Garven, S., 70, 71, 72, *76*
Gay, P., 138, *165*
Geiselman, R. E., 117, *133*, 185, *190*
Geraci, L., 114, 121, 122, 123, 124, *133*, *135*
Gerhard, D., 43, *61*
Gerhardstein, P. C., 84, 85, *100*, *101*
Giannelli, P. C., 185, *189*
Giedd, J. N., 98, *102*
Gilch, J., 84, 85, *101*
Gladwell, M., 137, *165*
Glaser, D., 98, *100*
Glisky, E. L., 107, 110, 112, 113, 117, 121, 124, 130, *133*, *134*
Glod, C. A., 98, *101*
Godfrey, R., 148, *164*
Goff, L., 49, *59*, 107, 126, 127, 128, *133*, 148, 149, *165*
Gold, A., 98, *101*
Goldberg, A., 96, *100*
Goldberg, S., 98, *101*
Goldsmith, M., 120, *134*
Goldstein, A. M., *191*

Goodman, G., 71, *76*, *77*, 96, *102*
Goodman, J., 72, *75*
Green, C., 153, *164*
Greene, E., 185, *189*
Grinley, M. J., 150, 151, *165*
Gross, S. R., 171, 174, 175, 181, *189*
Grunau, R. E., 83, *102*
Gruneberg, M. M., 18, *24*, *25*
Gudjonsson, G. H., *54*, *59*, 145, *165*
Guernsey, T. F., 187, *189*
Guyer, M. J., 10, *13*, 95, *101*, 206, 208, *211*
Guynn, M. J., 112, 130, *133*, *134*

## H

Hagen, L., 52, *60*, 144, *166*
Haggbloom, S. J., 23, *24*
Hall, D., 38, *62*
Hammond, D. C., 139, *164*
Handley-Derry, M., 98, *101*
Hartshorn, K., 84, 85, 86, 88, 98, *100*, *101*
Hashtroudi, S., 44, *59*, *166*
Hastie, R., 181, *189*
Hayes, K. H., 112, *133*
Hayne, H., 81, 82, 83, 86, 91, 92, 93, 98, *101*, *102*
Heaps, C., 8, *13*, 126, *133*, 141, 148, *165*
Hekkanen, S. T., 43, *59*, 145, *165*
Hembrooke, H., 54, *58*, 73, *75*
Henkel, L., 106, *133*
Herman, J. L., 138, 139, 154, *165*
Hessels, S., 121, *133*
Hewitt, S. K., 94, 96, *101*
Highfield, R., 11, *13*
Hinrichs, E. L., 112, *133*
Hodge, D., 141, *166*
Hollingshead, A., 112, *133*
Holman, B., 139, *166*
Holmes, D., 138, 139, *165*
Holt, B. C., 41, *58*
Hoffman, H. G., 4, *13*, 40, 41, *60*, 177, *189*
Horner, T. M., 206, *211*
Horselenberg, R., 145, *165*
Hosch, H. M., 181, 185, *189*, *190*
Howe, M. L., 82, 96, *101*
Hudson, J. I., 155, *167*
Huffman, M. L., 47, *58*, 74, *76*, 158, *164*
Hungerford., 177, 187, *190*
Hunt, M., 1, *13*
Hunt, R., 114, *136*
Husband, T. H., 8, *13*, *59*, 141, *166*
Hyman, I., 8, *13*, 47, 49, 50, *59*, 126, 133, 141, 145, 146, 147, *166*, *168*

## I

Imwinkelried, E. J., 185, *189*
Ingraham, M., 43, *59*
Ito, Y., 98, *101*, *102*
Iyer, G., 20, *26*

## J

Jackson, E., 115, *134*
Jacoby, D., 43, 48, *61*
Jacoby, J., 123, *135*, 171, *189*
Jacoby, L. L., 44, 46, *59*, 112, 119, 121, *133*
James, W., 2, *13*
Jamis, M., 41, *63*
Java, R. I., 43, *59*
Jaynes, J., 87, *100*
Jerman, M., 16, *25*
Jenkins, P., 138, *166*
Jenkins, J. J., 108, *135*
Jensen, E., 184, *188*
Johnson, M. K., 43, 44, 45, 46, 48, 49, 51, *59*, *60*, *62*, 106, 107, 123, 126, *133*, *134*, *135*, 148, *166*
Johnston, M., 9, *13*
Jones, V. K., 23, *24*
Jordan, J., 123, *134*
Joseph, A. L., 49, *61*
Jusczyk, P. W., 82, *101*

## K

Kalter, N. M., 206, *211*
Kantrowitz, B., 139, *166*
Kassin, S. M., 56, *59*, 185, *189*
Kausler, D., 106, *135*
Keating, J. P., 18, *24*
Keller, L., 16, *24*
Kelley, C. M., 44, 46, 48, *59*, *60*, 120, *134*
Kellog, R. T., 114, *134*
Ketcham, K., 5, 6, 7, *13*, 17, 22, *25*, 47, *60*, 140, *166*, 177, 187, *189*

Kichler, J., 72, *77*
Kiechel, K. L., 56, *59*
Kintsch, W., 20, *24*, *25*
Kirsch, I., 141, 142, *166*, *167*
Klein, P., 84, 85, *100*
Kleinknecht, E. E., 147, *166*
Koriat, A., 120, *134*
Koshmider, J. W. III, 42, 62
Kounios, J., 46, *59*
Kouststaal, W., 115, *134*
Krekewich, K., 98, *101*
Kroupina, M. G., 90, *100*
Krumnacker, H., 126, *133*
Kuhl, B., 153, 154, *164*
Kuijpers, M., 145, *164*

## L

Labelle, L., 49, *60*
Lacey, S. C., 145, *167*
Laimon, R. L., 206, *211*
Lamb, M. E., 69, *76*
Lampinen, J. M., 38, *60*
Landa, R., 72, *75*
Landsman, R., 181, *189*
Lane, S. M., 43, 46, *60*, *62*
Laney, C., 10, *13*, 151, 152, 153, *164*, *166*
Lasko, N. B., 147, *166*
Latane, B., 122, *132*
Laurence, J., 49, *60*
Leach, K., 45, 49, *59*
Lee, S., 128, *134*
Lehman, D. R., 8, *14*, 47, *61*, 141, 145, *167*
Leichtman, M. D., 47, *58*, 66, 72, 73, *76*
Leo, R. A., 54, *59*
Lepore, S., 72, *77*
Lilienfeld, S. O., 201, *211*
Lindauer, B., 123, *135*
Lindsay, D. S., 39, 41, 43, 44, 45, 46, 52, 53, *54*, *58*, *59*, *60*, *76*, 123, *134*, 142, 144, 146, 148, *166*, *168*, *211*
Lindsay, R. C. L., 185, 186, *190*, *191*
Lindsay, S. D., 48, 51, *59*, 202
Lobst, A. D., 145, *167*
Loftus, E. F., 2, 3, 4, 5, 6, 7, 8, 10, *13*, *14*, 16, 17, 18, 19, 20, 21, 22, *24*, *25*, 36, 37, 38, 39, 40, 42, 43, 45, 47, 48, 49, 51, *57*, *58*, *59*, *60*, *61*, *62*, 66, 71, 73, 74, *76*, 79, 80, 95, 99, *101*, 106, 107, 119, 122, 123, 124, 126, 127, *133*, *134*, *136*, 138, 139, 140, 141, 143, 145, 146, 147, 148, 149, 150, 151, 152, 153, 154, 156, 158, 159, *164*, *165*, *166*, *167*, *168*, 171, 176, 177, 180, 181, 185, 186, 187, 188, *189*, *191*, 208, *211*
Loftus, G. R., 38, 41, *60*, 99, *101*, 138, 139, *166*
Lohr, J. M., 201, *211*
London, K., 68, 72, *75*, *76*
Lozito, J. P., 114, *136*
Lucas, D., 86, *102*
Lynn, S. J., 201, *211*

## M

MacDonald, S., 81, 99, *101*
Macklin, M. L., 147, *166*
MacLean, H. N., 137, 154, 156, *166*
Magliano, J. P., 20, *25*
Mahlberga, N., 72, *76*
Malpass, R. S., 70, *76*, 176, 180, 181, 185, 186, *191*
Maltz, W., 139, *166*
Manber, M., 18, *24*
Manning, C., 49, *59*, *61*, 126, *133*, 148, *165*, *167*
Marburger, W., 19, *25*
Marche, T., 73, *76*, 123, *134*
Marcovitch, S., 98, *101*
Markham, R., 49, *58*
Mason, M. A., 67, *76*
Mather, M., 43, *60*, 107, 123, *134*
Matheson, D. J., 171, *189*
Mazzoni, G., 141, 142, 147, 150, *166*, *167*
McCabe, D. P., 110, 113, 115, *134*
McCarthy, T. T., 41, 43, *58*
McCloskey, M., 38, 39, 40, 41, *60*, *61*, *62*, *63*
McClure, K. A., 181, *190*
McCrae, R. R., 145, *164*

McDaniel, M. A., 110, 112, 114, 116, 117, 126, 127, 128, 129, 130, *132*, *133*, *134*, *136*
McDermott, K. B., 44, 48, *61*, 105, 107, 108, 109, 110, 111, 112, 113, 114, 119, 123, *132*, *133*, *134*, *135*, *136*
McEvoy, C., 43, *59*, 145, *165*
McIntyre, J. S., 106, 123, *134*
McMurtrie, J., 175, *190*
McNally, R. J., 138, 139, 147, *166*, 201, *211*
Meade, M. L., 53, 54, *61*, 107, 118, 119, 120, 121, 122, *134*, *135*
Melnyk, L., 73, 74, *76*
Memon, A., 106, 123, *133*, *134*, *136*, 144, 150, *166*, *167*, 185, *189*
Merckelbach, H., 145, *164*, *165*
Meyer, B. J. F., 20, *25*
Mickes, L., 145, *165*
Milgram, S., 122, *134*
Miller, A., 138, 139, *166*
Miller, D., 37, 40, *60*, 66, *76*, 107, 122, *134*
Miller, J., 20, *25*
Mitchell, K. J., 43, 44, 46, 48, *61*, *62*, 123, *134*
Mitchell, S., 69, *76*
Montgomery, N., 171, *189*
Moores, L., 96, *102*
Morgan, D. Y., 145, *165*
Morita, S. K., 43, *60*
Morris, E. K., 10, *13*, 151, 152, 153, *164*, *166*
Morris, L. W., 107, *132*
Morris, P. E., 18, *24*
Morris, R. G., 107, *132*
Moscovitch, M., 107, *135*
Muench, J., 41, *62*
Mullen, B., 181, *188*
Mullen, M. K., 81, 99, *101*
Muris, P., 145, *165*, *166*
Murachver, T., 93, *100*
Murphy, M., 117, *134*
Myers, N. A., 89, 90, *101*, *102*

## N

Nadon, R., 49, *60*
Nash, M., 8, *13*, 126, *133*, 141, 148, *165*
Naveh-Benjamin, M., 115, 130, *135*
Neisser, U., 18, *25*, 81, 99, *103*, 202, *211*
Nelson, K., 82, 88, *101*
Neufeld, P., 174, 184, 188, *190*
Niemib, P., 72, *76*
Noel, M., 148, *167*
Norman, K. A., 106, 110, 118, *135*

## O

Ochalek, K., 38, *58*
Ochsner, K. N., 153, 154, *164*
Ofshe, R., 141, *166*, *167*
Olafson, E., 201, *211*
Oldenberg, D., 139, *167*
Olio, K. A., 139, *167*
Olafson, E., 160, *164*
Orbach, Y., 69, *76*
Orr, S. P., 147, *166*
Ost, J., 145, *167*
Owre, K., 123, *134*

## P

Paddock, J., 49, *61*, 148, *167*, 187, *189*
Paivio, A., 126, *135*
Paley, J., 93, *102*
Palmer, J. C., 3, *13*, 19, *25*, 36, *61*, 66, *76*, 106, 122, 123, *134*
Paris, S., 123, *135*
Parker, J., 96, *100*
Patel, S., 171, *189*
Payment K., 51, 55, *62*, *63*, 72, *77*
Payne, D. G., 40, 41, *61*
Pearlstone, Z., 117, *136*
Pentland, J., 47, 49, 50, *59*, 126, *133*, 145, 146, *166*
Penrod, S. D., 176, 180, 181, 185, 186, *189*, *190*, *191*
Percer, J. M., 114, *133*
Perlmutter, M., 88, 89, *103*
Perris, E. E., 90, *101*, *102*
Perry, B. D., 98, *102*
Perry, C., 49, *60*
Peterson, C., 96, 97, 98, 99, *101*, *102*
Pezdek, K., 38, *62*, 141, 142, 145, 150, *167*
Phil, C., 90, *100*

Picariello, M., 96, *102*
Pickrell, J. E., 8, 13, *14*, 57, *60*, 140, 141, 143, 145, 146, *166*
Pillemer, D., 96, *102*
Pipe, M. E., 93, *100*, 96, *102*
Pitman, R. K., 147, *166*
Platt, R. D., 145, *167*
Platz, S. J., 181, 190
Polonsky, S., 159, *166*
Polster, M. R., 107, 110, 112, 113, 117, 121, 124, 130, *133*
Poole, D. A., 144, *167*, 206, *211*
Pope, H. G., 155, *167*
Porter, F. L., 83, *102*
Porter, S., 8, *14*, *61*, 141, 145, *167*
Postman, L., 21, *25*
Pradere, D., 106, 109, *136*
Price, A. L., 110, *132*
Prince, S., 115, *134*
Presmanes A. G., 113, *134*
Pressley, M., 126, *134*
Pruett, J. C., 96, *102*
Pudelski, C. R., 187, *190*
Puff, R., 117, *134*

Q

Quas, J. A., 96, *102*

R

Radalet, M. L., 173, *190*
Radelet, M. L., 173, *188*
Rajaram, S., 43, *61*, 119, *135*
Ramirez, G., 185, *190*
Ramirez, J. M., 112, *133*
Rankin, J., 106, *135*
Rassin, E., 145, *165*, *166*
Rattner, A., 174, *190*
Raye, C., 44, 49, *59*, 126, *135*
Read, J. D., 52, *60*, 142, 144, *166*, *167*
Reeder, J. A., 46, *59*
Reese, E., 93, *100*
Reddy, C., 115, *134*
Reder, L. M., 40, *57*
Relyea, M., 142, 167
Rideout, R., 82, 96, 97, 98, 99, *102*
Ritter M., 139, *167*
Robertson, C. L., 113, *134*
Robertson, E., 153, 154, *164*
Robinson, K., 110, *135*
Roediger, H. L. III, 44, 48, 49, 53, 54, *59*, *61*, 105, 107, 108, 109, 110, 112, 113, 114, 118, 119, 120, 121, 122, 123, 124, 125, 126, 127, 128, *132*, *133*, *134*, *135*, *136*, 148, 149, 154, *164*, *165*
Rosen, M. J., 110, *136*
Ross, D. F., 38, 41, *58*, 66, *76*
Ross, G., 88, *102*
Routhieaux, B. C., 107, 110, 112, 113, 117, 121, 124, 130, *133*, *134*
Rovee, C. K., 83, *102*
Rovee, D. T., 83, *102*
Rovee-Collier, C., 82, 83, 84, 85, 86, *100*, *101*, *102*
Rubin, S. R., 112, 130, *133*, *134*
Russel, D. E. H., 138, *167*
Russel, W. A., 108, *135*
Russel, T. M., 23, *24*

S

Safer, A., 181, 185, *191*
Sagan, C., 139, *167*
Sahakyan, L., 120, *134*
Sales, J. M., 96, *100*
Sandnabbaa, K., 72, *76*
Sandoval, V. A., 12, *14*
Santtilaa, P., 72, *76*
Savoie, L., 98, *100*
Schacter, D., 106, 109, 110, 115, 118, *134*, *135*, *136*, 154, *167*
Schatzow, E., 138, 139, 154, *165*
Scheck, B. C., 174, 184, 188, *190*
Scheflin, A. W., 139, *164*
Schneider, A., 182, 184, *190*
Schooler, J. W., 40, 43, *60*, *61*, 119, *136*, 202, *211*
Schreiber, T. A., 40, *59*, *61*
Schwade, J. A., 90, *100*
Scoboria, A., 142, *167*
Scullin, M. H., 72, *76*
Searcy, J., 106, *136*
Sergent, S. D., 40, *61*
Sergent-Marshall, S., 40, *59*

Shapiro, P. N., 181, *190*
Sharman, S. J., 38, *62*, 148, *167*
Shaw, J. S. III, 181, *190*
Sherman, S., 49, *59*, 126, *133*, 148, *165*
Shiffrin, R. M., 16, *24*
Shuman, D., 68, *76*
Siegel, D., 94, *100*
Sifonis, C. M., 107, 118, *136*
Sijsenaar, M., 145, *165*
Simcock, G., 82, 91, 92, 93, 98, *102*
Simon, T., 184, *190*
Small, M., 176, 180, 181, 185, 186, *191*
Smith, A., 110, 113, *134*
Smith, E., 47, *58*, 66, 74, *76*, 158, *164*
Smith, V. L., 38, *61*
Smith, R., 114, *136*
Smith, R. D., 69, 70, *76*
Smith, S. M., 107, 118, *136*
Snyder, M., 145, *167*
Sommers, M., 116, *136*
Spann, V., 145, *165*
Speaker, C. J., 90, *101*
Squire, L., 154, *167*
Stadler, M. A., 113, 114, *136*
State, 159, 177, 187, *190*
Sternberg, K. J., 69, *76*
Stewart, H., 69, *76*
Stines, L., 72, *76*
Strosser, G. L., 112, *133*
Suengas, A. G., 44, 48, *59*, *62*
Sugar, M., 95, *102*
Sukel, H., 56, *59*
Sullivan, M., 86, *102*
Summit, R., 67, *76*
Suppes, P., 2, *14*, 16, *25*
Sykes, R. N., 18, *24, 25*

## T

Tanur, J. M., 18, *24*, *25*
Tavris, C., 22, *25*, 139, *167*, 201, 207, *211*
Taylor, T., 126, *135*
Teibel, D. L., 179, *190*
Teicher, M. H., 98, *101*, *102*
Terr, L., 95, *102*, 155, *167*
Terranova, S., 49, *61*, 148, *167*
Thomas, A., 49, 50, *51, 62*, 116, 127, *136*, 149, *168*
Thompson, W. C., 72, *77*
Thomson, D. M., 81, *103*
Tindell, D. R., 118, *136*
Todd, C. M., 88, 89, *103*
Toglia, M. P., 38, 41, *58,* 60*,* *61*, 66, *76*
Toth, J., 121, *133*
Toufexis, A., 139, *168*
Tousignant, J. P., 38, *62*
Tubb, V. A., 185, *189*
Tuchin, M., 40, 41, *62*
Tulving, E., 43, *62*, 81, *103*, 108, 117, 119, *132*, *136*
Tun, P. A., 110, *136*
Turtle, J. W., 181, 186, *190*
Tversky, B., 20, *26*, 40, 41, *62*

## U

Uesiliana, K., 81, *101*
Underwood, J., 38, *62*
Underwood, N. J., 21, *24*
Usher, J. N., 81, 99, *103*
US National Institute of Justice, 174, 175, 186, *190*

## V

Vaituzis, C., 98, *102*
Valentine, T., 123, *132*
Van Abbema, D. L., 90, *100*
Van Dijk, T. A., 20, *25*
Verfaellie, M., 106, 109, *136*
Villa, D., 43, *60*
Vornik, L. A., 38, *62*
Vrij, A., 145, *167*

## W

Wade, K. A., 52, *60*, 142, 143, 144, 145, 146, 150, *165*, *166*, *168*
Wagenaar, W., 40, *60*
Ward, T. B., 107, 118, *136*
Warnick, J. E., 23, *24*
Warnick, R., 23, *24*
Washington, J., 98, *101*
Wasson, C., 98, *101*
Watters, E., 141, 157, *167*
Watkins, M. J., 118, *136*

Watson, J., 112, *135*
Weiser, J., 144, *168*
Wells, G. L., 55, *62*, 176, 177, 180, 181, 185, 186, *189*, *190*, *191*
Wewerka, S. S., 90, *100*
Whalen, N., 96, *102*
Wheeler, M. A., 119, *135*
White, G., 96, *102*
Whittlesea, B. W. A., 148, *164*
Wiebe, S. A., 90, *100*
Wilkenfeld, M. J., 107, 118, *136*
Wilkinson, C., 145, *168*
Williams, L. M., 156, 166, *168*
Wilson, B., 43, *59*
Windschitl, P. D., 41, *58*, *62*
Winfrey, S. E., 41, *58*
Wingfield, A., 110, *136*
Winocur, G., 107, *135*
Wise, R. A., 181, 185, *191*
Woloshyn, B., 46, *59*
Wondoloski, T. L., 84, 85, *101*
Wood, J. M., 70, *76*
Wurtzel, N., 84, 85, *100*

## Y

Yarbrough, G. L., 23, *24*
Youngblood, 178, *188*, *190*
Yuille, J. C., 8, *14*, 47, *61*, 141, 145, *167*, 181, *190*

## Z

Zacks, J. M., 20, *25*
Zanni, G., 66, *76*
Zaragoza, M. S., 38, 39, 40, 41, 44, 45, 46, 47, 48, 50, 51, 55, *57*, *58*, *60*, *61*, *62*, *63*, 72, *77*
Zeanah, C. H., 94, *100*
Zemba, D., 185, *190*
Zola-Morgan, S., 154, *168*
Zwaan, R. A., 20, *25*

# Subject Index


## A

Alien abduction, 146–147
Alzheimer's disease, 110–111
American Academy of Arts and Sciences, 23
American Judicature Society, 185
American Psychological Association, 156–160, 163
American Psychological Society, 23, 160–163, 208
Amnesia
  childhood, *see* Childhood amnesia
  drugs and, 12
  source amnesia, 47
  traumatic, 157, 202
Associative word paradigm, *see* Deese-Roediger-McDermott paradigm
Attention, 46–47
  witnesses and, 187
Attribution *see* Misattribution
Autobiographical memory, x, *see also* False memory
  belief and, 142, 148

## B

Belief,
  autobiographical belief, 142, 148
  false belief, 8, 10, 41–43, 56
    and behavior, 152–153
    in children, 67
    and false memories, 150
  and source monitoring, 43–44

## C

Child sexual abuse, 67, 80, 94, 96, 106, 138, 171, 174–176, 184
  and mental disorder, 139
  and repression, 99, 138, 201, 205
Child Sexual Abuse Accommodation Syndrome, 67–68
Childhood amnesia, 81–82, 98–99
Children *see also* Infants
  children's disclosure of trauma, 67
  memories of trauma, 93
  questioning children, 68–71
    repeated questioning, 72–73
    structured interviews, 69, 96
  sexually abused children, 67
  suggestibility, 38, 65–67, 206
    individual differences, 73–75
  verbal memory, 82–83, 91–92
Confabulation, 54–56
Confessions, *see* False confessions
Confidence, 121, 141
  for bizarre events, 149–150

confidence-accuracy relationship, 179–181, 187
eyewitness identification, 186
in false memories, 42, 48, 55, 146
imagination and, *see also* imagination inflation, 148–149
in older adults, 120
Convictions, *see* Wrongful convictions
Corwin, David, 202–203
Criminal justice system, 172, 176–177, 185, 188
Cross-examination, 185
Cross-race identification, *see* Eyewitness identification
Cued recall *see* Recall

## D

Death penalty, 173
Deese-Roediger-McDermott paradigm, 107–108, 113, 118, 121, 124, 129
and elaborative detail, 116
individual differences, 109–110
older adult subjects, 110
DES-C, *see* Dissociative Experiences Scale
Dementia, 110
Discrepancy detection, *see* Misinformation effect
Dissociative Experiences Scale, 145
Distinctive feature encoding, *see* Encoding
Doe, Jane, 9–10, 160–162, 200–210
DRM, *see* Deese-Rodiger-McDermott paradigm

## E

Eileen Franklin, *see* Repression
Elicited imitation paradigm, *see* Infants
Encoding,
distinctive feature encoding, 114–115, 129
encoding specificity in Infants, *see* infants
in infants, 80
and misinformation, *see* Misinformation effect
and source monitoring, 44, 46, 112–113
supportive encoding, 116
Expert testimony, 21, 30, 75, 173, 185, 207
and children, 67–70
Expert witness (*see* Expert testimony)
Eyewitness,
identification, 172, 175–177, 185
confidence, 179
cross-race identification, 33, 181
mistaken identification, 174, 186
testimony, 5, 37–38, 173, 176, 178, 185
and confirmatory feedback, 55
and jurors, 180
*Eyewitness Testimony*, 122, 171
*Eyewitness Testimony: Civil and Criminal*, 185

## F

False confessions, 54–56, 182–183
False feedback, 8, 152–153
False memory, 2, 10, 41–42, 137–159, *see also* Illusory memories; Memory impairment; Misinformation effect; Memory illusion; Recognition, false
autobiographical *see* Autobiographical memory
confabulation, 54–56
development of, 45–48, 147–153
elaboration and, 48–51
in elderly,
low-frontal adults, 112–117
false beliefs and, 150–151
implanting of, 9, 11, see also Implantation paradigms
individual differences, 109–110
personality factors and, 145–146
plausibility and, 141–142
rich false memories, 8
vs. false belief, 42–43
vs. true memories, 146–147
False Memory Syndrome Foundation, 155
False recall, *see* recall, false
False Photo paradigm, *see* Implantation paradigms
Familiarity, 45, 46, 49
Feminism, 138
Fluency, 48, 119, 144
fMRI, *see* Functional magnetic resonance imaging
Forgetting, 36

due to sedation, 12,
in infants, *see* infants
in older adults, 105
and source monitoring, 46
traumatic forgetting, 79, 83, *see also* Repression
Franklin, Eileen, *see* Repression
Functional magnetic resonance imaging, 153

G

Grawemeyer Award, 23, 163
Guyer, Mel, 161, 203–204, 207
Guided imagery, 8, 67, 144, 148, *see also* Imagination

H

Hypnosis, 22, 139, 156, 160

I

Illusory memory, 106–108, 125, 129, 131, *see also* False memory
associative illusory memories, *see* Deese-Roediger-McDermott paradigm
of category members, 117–122
Imagination, 141, 201
guided imagery, *see* Guided imagery
inflation, 21, 126–129
for actions, 107, 126–127
for bizarre events, 149
for childhood events, 126, 148, 150
consequences for behavior, 152
in older adults, 127–128
and reality monitoring, 49
Implantation studies, 54, 66, 141–142, 145–146, 150
false photograph paradigm, 142–143
photographs vs. narratives, 143–144
true photographs, 144–145
Lost in the Mall paradigm, 7–8, 140–141, 177
false narrative studies, 47, 143–145
plausibility, 141
Infants *see also* Children
elicited imitation paradigm, 90–91
encoding in, 89, 91
encoding specificity, 81–82
forgetting, 86–88, 90
mobile conjugate reinforcement paradigm, 83–84, 86–87
memory retention in, 86–88
mnemonic, 83, 90, 117
train paradigm, 84–86
preverbal memory, 83
language and, 80, 82, 89–92, 96
verbal reports of,, 87, 92, 99
Innocence Project, 173, 175, 184, 185
Institute for Mathematical Studies in the Social Sciences, 28
Interference, 121
retroactive, 21, 40, 119, 193
source monitoring and, 115
Interview,
clinical, 94–95
cognitive, 117
forensic, 35
postevent, 44, 52, *see also* misinformation
repeated, 47, 72, 98
structured, 96
suggestive, 7, 35, 46, 67, 70–71, 73–75

J

Jane Doe, *see* Doe, Jane

K

Know judgments, *see* Recognition

L

Legal system, 65, 172, 176–177, 186–187, *see also* criminal justice system
Lost-in-the mall paradigm, *see* Implantation paradigms

M

Mel Guyer, *see* Guyer, Mel
Memory enhancement, 117
Memory impairment, 39–41
"Memory wars," 9, 200, 203, 210, *see also* Repressed memories
Misattribution, 44, 46, 50, *see also* Source monitoring
Misinformation, 4, 21, 56

effect, x, 4–5, 36–39, 106, 122–126, 177
coexistence vs. impairment, 38–41
discrepancy detection, 38
encoding, 46
extensions of, 53
modified test vs. standard test, 39
older adults vs. younger adults, 123
repetition, 48, 73
retroactive interference, 21, 193
source monitoring test, 42–43, 45, 54, 124
theoretical framework of, 43–45
warnings and, 43
Misleading suggestion, *see* Suggestion
Mobile conjugate reinforcement paradigm, *see* Infants
Modified test, *see* Misinformation effect
MRI, *see* Functional magnetic resonance imaging
*Myth of Repressed Memory*, 7, 140, 185, 197

**N**

National Academy of Sciences, 23, 163, 194
NEO Five Factor Inventory, 145
New School for Social Research, 17, 29
Nicole Taus, *see* Doe, Jane

**O**

Oprah Winfrey Show, 6

**P**

Photographs, *see* Implantation paradigms
Posttraumatic stress disorder, 147
Preverbal memory, *see* Infants
Psychoanalysis, 79, 138

**R**

*Reality of Repressed Memories*, 80, 156
Recall
cued, 119, 120, 122
false, *see also* false memory
in Deese-Roediger-McDermott paradigm, 108–114
in older adults, 121
reduction of, 115
forced, 118, 119
free, 16, 108, 110
Recognition, 41, 43
children's, 91–92
false, 108–109, 113, 116, 124–125
forced-choice, 39
old-new, 47
remember/know judgments, 44, 47, 94, 108, 119, 120
source monitoring, 124
yes–no, 45, 124
Recovered memory, *see also* Repression
as evidence, 159–161, 185, 188
"memory wars," 9
repressed and, xi, 80, 203, 208
Reinforcement,
Mobile conjugate reinforcement, *see* Infants
selective, 71
Remember/know judgments, *see* Recognition
Reminiscence,
childhood, 144
Repression, 79–80, 183, *see also* Recovered memory
evidence of, xi
admissibility, 187–188
as evidence, 177
Franklin, Eileen, 6, 12, 137, 154, 156
Freud, Sigmund, 79
history of, 137–140
in infancy, 99
neurobiological mechanisms, 153–154
recovery of, 22
repressed memories, 8–11, 155, 157, 172, 177–178, 203, 208
and false memory, 31, 154
repressing trauma, x
Retrieval,
of associations, 21
cues, 82, 87, 119, 126
encoding, storage and, 80
failure, 41
repeated, 86
semantic, 3, 17
source monitoring and, 44, 46
Retroactive interference, *see* Interference

**S**

Satanic ritual, 80
Self-help books, 139–140, 148
Semantic,

details, 49–50
elaboration, 51
information, 112, 115
memory, 2, 17, 29
retrieval, *see* Retrieval
Sensory,
-perceptual detail, 50, 140, 150
-perceptual elaboration, 49–51
Sigmund Freud, *see* Repression
SMF, *see* Source monitoring
Social-contagion, 53–54
Social factors,
in misinformation studies, 37
Source monitoring,
attribution, 44–46, 123, 148
and familiarity, 45
framework, 44–45
older adults, 106
source amnesia, 46
source specifying information, 45, 46
test, *see* Misinformation
Stanford University, 16, 27–29
Suggestion, 8
false, 144–145
misleading, 36, 39, 41, 42, 45, 50, 71
repeated, 47–49, 72
resistance to, 37
unintentional, 12

## T

Taus, Nicole, 208, *see also* Doe, Jane
Traumatic events, *see also* Posttraumatic stress disorder
children's disclosures of, 67–68
experience of, 66
memory for, x, 69, 147, 155
forgetting of, 83, 93–98, 157, 202
repression of, 79, 138, *see also* Repression
sexual abuse, 6–7, 9, 12–13, 69

## U

University of Washington, 4, 7, 19, 29–31, 161, 207–208
U.S. Department of Justice, 138, 173

## W

Wrongful conviction, xi, 172–174, 176, 184–185